Gaining Ground

Gaining Ground

A Story of Farmers' Markets, Local Food, and Saving the Family Farm

WITHDRAWN

Forrest Pritchard

LYONS PRESS
Guilford, Connecticut
An imprint of Globe Pequot Press

Copyright © 2013 by Forrest Pritchard

ALL RIGHTS RESERVED. No part of this book may be reproduced or transmitted in any form by any means, electronic or mechanical, including photocopying and recording, or by any information storage and retrieval system, except as may be expressly permitted in writing from the publisher. Requests for permission should be addressed to Globe Pequot Press, Attn: Rights and Permissions Department, PO Box 480, Guilford, CT 06437.

Lyons Press is an imprint of Globe Pequot Press.

All photos by the author.

Project editor: Meredith Dias
Text design: Lisa Reneson, twosistersdesign.com
Layout: Justin Marciano

Library of Congress Cataloging-in-Publication Data is available on file.

ISBN 978-0-7627-8725-8

Printed in the United States of America

10 9 8 7 6 5 4 3 2

To my teachers, especially Laura Robb,
who read poetry to their students. I listened.

"Career opportunities are
the ones that never knock."

— *The Clash, 1977* —

FOREWORD

Why do we read adventure and travel books about places we've never visited and can't possibly imagine having the wherewithal to visit? Answer: All of us fantasize about the other world in which people live.

In today's profound disconnect with our ecological dependency generally, and with food production (also known as farming) specifically, a book about profitable farming from an agricultural adventurer could be classified in this travel genre. I remember the day Forrest and his dad came to Polyface for a visit. Of course, I had no idea of the angst behind the trip that Forrest describes with impeccable clarity and gut-wrenching transparency in this wonderful book.

But in only a few minutes, as they stood on the threshold of my front door, I could tell that here was a young man who truly believed he could do what reasonable men—like his father—considered madness: make a living on a farm. No outside paycheck. No off-farm-derived nest egg to provide life support. Just straight-up farming as a credible business. We walked the farm that day like I do with thousands of bright-eyed farmer wannabes, discussing how-to, looking at portable infrastructure, and frequently delving into big-picture ideology and politics. Over the years I've followed Forrest's progress from afar, met a few of his customers, and enjoyed his success as a vicarious extension of my own. Too many don't follow through. Forrest has. And is.

Forrest has done all of us a great service in eloquently articulating the emotional turmoil, familial prejudices, and personal doubts that accompany the announcement from smart, well-educated young people: "I want to farm for a living." I don't know any full-time farmer under fifty years old who has not encountered, to some degree, this well-meaning prejudice from family and friends: "But why would you want to throw your life away doing the drudgery and work for little pay?"

Those of us who have survived in this business for a few decades know both the brutality and brilliance of farming. We're pounded by weather, government regulations, societal marginalization, pests, and sickness. But more often, we step into the brilliance of dew-diamonds dripping off orchard grass in the early morning sun.

Since Forrest and I live not too far apart, we share similar surroundings and similar rural beauty. Daily, we enjoy nature's balm for the soul . . . if we can stop from mending fences, cutting wood, and repairing the hay mower long enough to behold the decor of our office.

This tension between getting it done and enjoying it is what makes the life of a real farmer such a difficult adventure to comprehend. Forrest's stories and descriptions touch me deeply because they are mine. I've lived them too. A few years ahead, but incredibly similarly. I remember looking out on our farm as a young man, inheriting it from my parents, yearning to do what they did not do: make it and it alone a full-time living. The first year, I started selling firewood—just like you'll see Forrest describe. The first several years were touch and go. But gradually it progressed.

Too many people see only one end of the farming spectrum. They either see all the long hours, work, and sweat, or they romanticize it into some idyllic pastoral fantasy of nature-communing and luxury. The truth, as Forrest so perfectly captures, is in the middle. It's a middle incomprehensible to most people in our culture, who are far removed from a true farming lifestyle and ethic.

While farmers—both the dabblers and the full-timers—will thoroughly enjoy this book, I think its best audience is the seeker, the adventurer who will never farm. Why? Because those of us out here doing the real work of farming desperately need the rest of the world to come on this journey with us. Not everyone can farm. Not everyone should. Assuredly, no one would want me to design and fly an airliner. By the same token, most folks are not cut out to be farmers.

But farming determines the landscape our grandchildren will inherit. Farming determines the quality of our food, the humane handling of our animals. Every time we eat, we participate in farming. This is why everyone needs to take this journey with Forrest, to vicariously enjoy this adventure with him. We cannot escape our responsibilities to, nor our interactions with, soil, air, and water— the basic ingredients in the farmer's alchemy.

Acquainting ourselves with the ecstasy and the heartache of farming creates integrity in our food decisions, common sense in our land-use policies, and appreciation of the effort required to correctly massage our ecological womb.

Unlike other vocations that are arguably more or less necessary, farming is basic to human existence. Because it is at the root of civilization, it has perhaps the greatest capacity to either heal or hurt humankind's planetary nest. As co-stewards of this great creation, we all owe future generations the benefit of knowing something about farming, food production, and land care. Few intellectual journeys could be this necessary and far-reaching. For this reason, I think adding adventurous farming books to the mix—along with novels, business books, biographies, and other genres—is a must for well-rounded people.

Forrest has blessed us with a delightful peek into this farming life, and I invite you to travel with him during the metamorphosis: from dreamer to doer. Not that any of us ever stops dreaming. But when we actually do turn some dreams into doing, well, I agree with Forrest: That's gaining ground.

—Joel Salatin, September 2012

INTRODUCTION

A lot can be learned from baking a cake.

As a child, I helped my grandmother sift flour and crack eggs for her famous pound cakes, regional treasures she sold each Sunday morning in the parking lot after church. Having spent her formative years struggling through the Great Depression, she let nothing go to waste in her kitchen. With a practiced index finger, she wiped the eggshells clean before composting them. The previous week's newspaper was spread out to capture sifted flour, ensuring that every speck was accounted for. She even saved old butter wrappers, using them to grease the cake pans.

Fresh from the oven, her cakes emerged as golden, encrusted halos, moist and fragrant, dense and delicious. Served as a thick wedge, with a glass of fresh milk provided by our next-door neighbor's dairy, they were the epitome of freshness, wholesomeness, wonderfulness.

But it was this very glass of milk that let me know, even as a preschooler tied to my grandmother's apron strings, that something was amiss. My grandmother drove me once a week to the neighboring dairy and parked her car in front of the milking parlor. Each time, before we entered, she cautioned me.

"Don't tell anyone we get our milk here, or the farmer will get in trouble. If anyone asks, just tell them it's for our cats."

Don't tell who? I wondered. I was only four years old. And besides, what kind of trouble could a grown man get into?

I held my grandmother's hand as we entered the parlor. The cattle stood in line, contentedly belching and chewing their cud, waiting to be milked. Through a side door, several large, stainless-steel refrigerated tanks held the day's fresh milk. The farmer filled the glass jars we had brought from a spigot near the tank's base. The milk was pleasantly cool, brilliantly white, and when allowed to rest motionless for a few moments, it would separate itself into two layers, with a thick stratum of cream rising to the top.

Back home, from the front porch, I would see stainless-steel tanker trucks leaving his farm each day, bound for distant locations beyond the realm of my limited geography. I was full of questions. Why were they taking the milk away? Didn't other people stop by the farm to pick up their own freshly filled bottles?

"The milk has to go to a processor," my grandmother explained, wrapping the jars in newspaper to keep them cool, cushioning their clink, "where it gets mixed with lots of other farmers' milk. Then they heat it up to kill off any bacteria that might be in there, and quickly cool it back down again. It's called pasteurization.

"Next, they mix it in such a way that it blends the cream and milk together. This is called being homogenized."

Whoa, grandmother. This was *way* over my head. But she wasn't done.

"Sometimes they take out the cream entirely, and that's what they call 'skim' milk. They skim the cream off the top, you see. There's all sorts of ways to do it—2 percent fat, or left whole, with the cream still in it. Then they bottle it into plastic jugs and ship it to the supermarkets for people to buy."

"But why would the farmer get in trouble for giving it to us?"

"That's just the way the rules are. The laws. The farmer has to follow the laws, and we do, too." She studied me in the rearview mirror. "Except," she added, adjusting the mirror so she could see me more clearly, "except, every once in a while, when we bend the rules. Just a little."

Later that afternoon, helping out in the family strawberry patch, I wished there was some rule I could bend to escape the hot June sun. I compromised, settling for a warm, sweet strawberry instead.

People often stopped by the farm for our berries, and customers were always coming by for my grandmother's fresh eggs. Her pound cakes rarely had time to cool before they found a new and appreciative home. Yet our neighbor, transparent to the point of having cows on one side of his parlor and cooling tanks on the other, risked being fined for selling fresh milk to us. As much as I enjoyed the pound cake, and especially the cool milk, something didn't make sense.

Each year, my grandparents' farm raised hundreds of cattle, grew tractor-trailer loads of apples, and cultivated enough corn to fill several freight cars. Their land produced abundant, fresh, nourishing food. It's difficult to say for sure, but the farm of my childhood must have been responsible for feeding thousands of people each year.

Ironically, in spite of all the care and attention my grandparents devoted to their land, all the food they grew each year ultimately became anonymous, and it ended up being eaten by complete strangers. Young calves were sent to feedlots in the Midwest to be fattened on grain. Apples, their skins never perfect enough to be sold as "fresh fruit," were transformed into juice, or sauce, or apple pies. The corn, like most grain raised in America, was destined for animal feed. It was, perhaps, fed to the very calves that they had sold, now a thousand miles away.

Once the food left their farm, the entire system was turned on its head. The freshness they had worked so hard to attain, picking the fruit at the peak of harvest, was replaced with shelf life. Their food's identity, soon to be advertised for its freshness and flavor by the purchasing company, became murky almost as soon as it left the farm.

Their harvest was trucked all across America. It was processed, boxed, frozen, and then shipped again. Their food was trucked down the interstate in eighteen-wheelers, and hauled away by trains while they slept. Their apples might end up in the filling of a doughnut in Chicago, or their beef in a taco in Alabama. They had no way of ever really knowing.

It was 1978. Although we maintained a large garden, it wasn't enough to support the entire family. Like everyone in our small community, we shopped at the A&P grocery store in Charles Town, West Virginia.

Nestled into the corner of a tiny strip mall, the A&P had the drowsy, casual feel of a local town square. Neighbors bumped into one another there. The butcher and produce manager knew my family's particular tastes and dislikes, and they pointed out new arrivals or certain items that were on special as our shopping cart swiveled through their department.

Out in the parking lot, families met to drop their children off at the school bus or rendezvous for soccer games. On Saturday nights, high school kids met there to hang out, and on Sunday mornings, people dropped in early to buy provisions for church picnics. Farmers leaned from pickup truck windows or started impromptu get-togethers from the seat of a lowered tailgate. It was, for several decades, our de facto community hub.

And yet, despite serving a community of farmers, and despite the open, verdant land that physically bordered the grocery, little, if any, of the food in the store actually came from anywhere nearby.

Who would have been able to tell, even if it had? Shrink-wrapped, cartoned, frozen and freeze-dried, it had been trundled and bundled, bagged and tagged into anonymity. The aisles and shelves were filled not so much with food as they were with packaging, brightly colored brand names, cartoon mascots, designer labels perched next to generic knockoffs.

It was a store devoted to creating an identity for food that had been stripped of its identity. Where, exactly, did rainbow-colored, sugar-frosted, air-puffed, marshmallow-infused cereal come from? Was it raised by cartoon rabbits and harvested by mischievous leprechauns? These products were so distantly removed from the local farms, so thoroughly metamorphosed, that we couldn't even be sure what the raw ingredients had been.

Did any of this stuff—the bleached and re-enriched flour, the high-fructose corn syrup, the partially hydrogenated soybean oil—even look like actual food anymore? Reading the ingredients on the back of a frozen pizza conjured images of vats and vials instead of gardens and fields.

Looking back on these farming families standing in line with their shopping carts, I wonder if the money they received for growing the raw ingredients even covered the costs of their shopping bills. Could a farmer who planted fields of wheat and oats now afford a box of cereal made from his own grain? Our neighbor, the dairy farmer, certainly kept some of his own milk for his personal use, and was courageous enough to provide his neighbors with a little as well, thumbing his nose at the law. But what did it say about my grandparents' cattle farm, selling calves for seventy cents a pound live weight, but buying back the steaks for ten dollars?

I didn't have any special insight as a child, any opinion about these matters, but these were the concerns discussed around our dinner table, at the livestock auction, at the feed store. Everyone felt helpless to control any of it, much less enact change. The system had effectively handcuffed them to the fluctuating whimsy of the commodity market.

Somewhere along the way, however, my family began noticing farmers who opted out of this system. These were the trailblazing types, pioneers who carved a path through the purgatory of conventional production. We couldn't articulate it at the time, but we held a quiet admiration for these people, praising them from afar. As fellow farmers, we felt an undeniable kinship with them as well.

Each year, as another FOR SALE sign appeared on the edge of another neighboring farm, we watched with veiled interest whenever someone went slightly against the grain, starting a pick-your-own pumpkin patch, or raising free-range turkeys for Thanksgiving. These were farms that wouldn't go down without a fight. Whenever this happened, my family privately discussed ideas of our own. Talking. Dreaming.

It was now the mid-1980s, and John Mellencamp and Willie Nelson launched Farm Aid as families across America defaulted on their agricultural loans. As a young man, I was told over and over again by experienced farmers that there was no future in agriculture. Faced with bank loans and low prices, many local farmers retired, changed careers, or simply gave up. After my grandfather passed away, our own farm slipped into debt practically overnight.

All along, we only wanted to save our family farm. Like countless families before us, we sought a life of simple but meaningful work, a connection to the land and the seasons. We were either too stubborn or too stupid to quit without trying first; perhaps we were both. But we knew we had to fight a system destined for its own self-destruction.

As the years passed, we made friends. It's funny how sometimes people get together, cultivating a landscape all their own. Before we knew it, what had once been empty, barren soil gradually took root. It required only a sprinkling of tiny seeds, some rain and sun, and a little patience. Years passed, and we stood our ground.

The fields of swaying grass now look like they have been there all along.

Chapter One

The farmer climbed our front porch steps, his worn-out blue jeans frayed at the knees, a red seed cap pulled tightly over his head. Tractor grease stained the fabric of his T-shirt in dark, finger-wide streaks, and several days of neglected stubble shadowed his deeply suntanned face. He held a jumbled sheaf of receipts in his hands, the bills and invoices of the season. Somewhere in that pile, he had promised, was a large check that would save our family farm. He rang our doorbell with a calloused, blunted finger.

It was the mid 1990s, and we were suffering the worst drought in decades. All summer, the Shenandoah Valley had been scorched by the sun, baked week after week into listless tones of sepia. Heat shimmered in opalescent waves above the brown hills. Our cattle wandered from field to field, mouthing tufts of dry, sparse grass.

My mother and I met him at the door. Dust coated his work boots, the same dust that covered the farm. Beads of sweat lay on his forehead, and he absently wiped them away with a handkerchief as he greeted us.

The farmer, Albert, had managed our land that year, and was here to give us an accounting of the season. He had planted our rolling hills with corn and soybeans earlier that spring, and had recently harvested the crop. It was the first time in a generation that grain was grown on our land, and my family was relying on him to make sure that everything went just right.

The previous week, combines had augured the corn and soybeans into large, cumbersome trucks, hauling it away to waiting railcars. As on most farms, the harvest had to carry us through the frozen winter, paying for our electricity, fuel, and food. Rolling the dice, we sacrificed reliable cow pastures for fields of crops, hoping the reward would be worth the risk. Once the unending drought arrived, we knew this year we would be cutting it desperately close.

I had graduated from college only five months earlier, wild-haired and bearded, my Birkenstocks worn to rags and a copy of Walt Whitman's *Leaves of Grass* tucked under one arm. Growing up on the farm, I had spent summers baling hay and tending to our small flock of chickens, but college was to be my passport away from the hard and grueling life of agriculture. I returned home penniless, an unreliable truck and a pair of wire-rimmed spectacles my only assets. Degrees in Literature and Geology, I was convinced, left me positioned for some wonderful career opportunity. I just didn't know what it would be yet.

On commencement day, my grandfather on my father's side, a retired chemist of forty years, summarily looked me up and down and loudly asked my gathered family, "How does he expect to get a job with all that *hair?*" I didn't know the answer myself. For the time being, helping out on the farm would be a useful diversion until I figured out my next move.

After a week back at the farm, his question still echoing in my ears, I acknowledged that he had a point. My education had prepared me for something more challenging than frying and holstering french fries but had otherwise done little to bolster a résumé of marketable skills. My college roommate, who wrote his thesis on the Mexican peso crisis, had already turned down several job offers before securing a plump salary at a bank in Manhattan. I remained confident that the right job would eventually fall into my lap.

Strangely, as I sat near the phone stuffing envelopes with poems addressed to obscure literary magazines, no Manhattan banks called to inquire about my services. In fact, no one at all called, not even my skeptical chemist grandfather. I spent the hot summer days doing odd jobs around the farm, nailing sagging fence boards, tacking down the sheet metal on the barn roof, and watching Albert working in the distance.

The farm had been passed down on my mother's side of the family. Although she believed that agriculture was a noble pursuit, she never became a farmer herself. After marrying my father, his job in the USDA Forest Service took them to Seattle, almost as far away from the Shenandoah Valley as they could go. It wasn't until her own father, the farmer, fell ill that she returned East; when he passed away, she was unexpectedly thrust into the role of ownership. She hired managers to run the farm, while she and my father commuted to jobs in nearby cities.

This was 1984, and I was ten. My sister Betsy and I eavesdropped as my parents farmed by phone each evening, arriving home exhausted and microwaving a round of TV dinners before calling the manager to check on daily operations. The news was rarely positive. Cattle and apple prices, our two main crops, were at historical lows. Our tractors, dated from the 1950s, were in sore need of an overhaul. My parents bickered as their city paychecks began to subsidize bills that our farm's modest production couldn't cover.

The operation became a revolving door for managers. Despite their best intentions, my parents had enlisted drunkards, thieves, liars, desperadoes, and dimwits. With no daily supervision, and no greater bond than a handshake, these men were usually gone in less than six months.

Albert was their first attempt to tweak the pattern. They had finally given up on the system of managers and farmhands, and recruited him in hopes of collaborating on a crop of corn and soybeans. He owned his own equipment and possessed arcane knowledge of fertilizer applications, harvesting protocols, and strategies to sell at the proper time to ensure the highest returns. Most important, he was honest and had sterling references. We supplied the land rent-free and Albert provided his experience, splitting the profit fifty-fifty. The partnership was a perfect fit.

This new arrangement with Albert left us cautiously optimistic, but my sister and I couldn't help but be influenced by decades of desultory results. Six years older than I, she had studied horticulture during her first year of college, but family and teachers talked her out of the farming life. She pursued nursing school instead. In my sophomore year of college, I walked a wooded campus path with my future wife, Nancy, trying to explain my own conflicted emotions.

"More and more, I'm thinking of becoming a farmer," I told her, kicking absently at the autumn leaves that swirled around our feet. My mind was back at the farm, hours away. "If I don't . . ." The words trailed into the evening air. Farming had been little more than an afterthought my entire childhood, yet suddenly I couldn't get it off my mind. For reasons I didn't understand, I felt a burgeoning responsibility for our farm's future.

"If you don't?" she asked, gently prompting. She had visited the farm several times, and, though she had been raised in the city herself, Nancy had immediately fallen in love with the sweeping views, the rustic buildings, and the open spaces. "If you don't, what do you think will happen?"

I shook my head. "It's just a feeling I've had lately. My grandfather's gone, and no matter who we've hired, we just can't turn the place around. My parents are barely hanging on. The only thing keeping the farm going right now is inertia."

She was thoughtful for a long time. "I've never worked on a farm," she said at last, "but doesn't it make sense that a farm would need a farmer?" She slipped her hand into mine. "Maybe that's what you've been feeling. Maybe the farm needs *you*."

Two years later, as the hot, dry summer after graduation wore on, I revisited this conversation over and over again. With the rest of my family away at their day jobs, and Nancy now in graduate school, I had the farm mostly to myself that season. I stretched lengths of barbed wire along distant fencerows, enjoying the peaceful solitude. I had never minded getting dirty, accumulating calluses on my rough palms. July slipped into August, and I awoke each morning to the simmering heat of the endless drought. I sweated, strained my muscles, and worked outside through all types of weather. Daily farm life required these tolerances, and I conditioned myself to accept them without complaint.

I watched Albert working the distant hillsides, his equipment gleaming in the unrelenting sun. The thought of my own fleet of tractors and shiny equipment seemed like a worthwhile dream, and it was easy to visualize myself perched atop one of these powerful machines, a roaring, mobile throne atop my agricultural kingdom. I daydreamed about how wonderful our old barn would look with several new tractors waiting behind the bay doors, an army of machinery ready to plow, plant, and harvest.

Even so, a voice in the back of my mind constantly urged me to look for a career with an actual paycheck. Albert was managing the fields without my help, and in spite of the dry weather, he remained convinced that the diminished harvest would cover our bills. Besides, no one in my family considered farming to be economically viable; we had witnessed too many small farms in our community go out of business to think otherwise. Perhaps Albert was the farmer our land had been waiting for. I bought a copy of the local newspaper and began circling want ads.

Age 20, home from college for the summer.

The weeks passed and, for any array of reasons, I was turned down as a sports reporter for my local newspaper, as a waiter for two different restaurants, as a full-time whitewater raft guide, and finally, as a custodian at the animal shelter, cleaning up dog poop. I honestly didn't know whether to be insulted or grateful.

Worried that autumn would arrive without the nourishing milk of the teat of academia, I signed up at the last possible moment to get my teaching certification. Perhaps, I speculated, I could be a teacher *and* a farmer. It didn't seem like a far-fetched idea.

This last-minute decision was greeted with a sigh of relief from my father. A lifelong government employee who worked in Washington, D.C., my father had spent years devoted to weekend agricultural projects of his own, hoping to discover a modern, profitable direction for the farm. Over the years, our salaried managers had politely tolerated his hastily conceived side projects, offering polite encouragement but rolling their eyes at him behind his back. Time and again, as my father's small enterprises fell by the wayside, he grew entrenched in the belief that farming could never be a "real job." These days, he spoke to me encouragingly of teaching tenure, summer vacations, and guaranteed benefits. To his dismay, by the end of October, I had fully withdrawn from classes.

"You did *what?*" my father boomed. Normally easygoing, he stood before me with his mouth agape, his eyes disbelieving.

"I dropped out. I don't want to be a teacher. I've decided to make a real go at farming."

"Oh, no. No, no, no." He shook his head emphatically back and forth. "Big mistake. This is just a . . . this is just *such* a big mistake." He paused. "Are you sure you're unenrolled? Maybe you can still show up at class tomorrow and they won't mind."

"Dad, I'm telling you, I'm done. I'm done with school. Farming is something that I just have to do. If I don't try, I'm going to regret it for the rest of my life."

He looked at me as though I had just told him I wanted to push helpless old ladies down long flights of stairs.

"Oh, you'll end up regretting it, I can guarantee that. What a mistake!" At a loss for additional words, he turned on his heel and strode away from me. At nearly six-foot-six, he could cover ground quickly. But he didn't get far.

Turning back to me, he said, "Farming? Are you *kidding* me? You don't even know how to grow a turnip!" Rueful with skepticism, he turned away again.

I wanted to call after him, to somehow convince him I was making the right choice, but I couldn't get the words out. I can *learn* to be a farmer, I wanted to say. I'm strong, and I'll stick with it. But he was right about one thing: Even though I had grown up on the farm, my agricultural experience was very limited. If I could only cultivate some small success, a minor triumph or two, I felt, he might be persuaded the farm could still work.

My mother had her own doubts about my decision but was vastly more encouraging. It had been, after all, her side of the family through which the farm had passed hands. On my father's side, steady, predictable jobs had been the norm: shopkeeper, chemist, government contractor. In contrast, on my mother's side, it had been six straight generations of farmers. If I were somehow able to follow in their footsteps, I would be the seventh farmer in the family to work the land, dating from just after the American Revolution.

Later that evening, the taste of my father's reprimand still bitter on my tongue, I told her about my dream of working on the family farm.

"If that's what you really want to do," my mother began before correcting herself. "If that's what you *need* to do, then we'll stand behind you. Your father's upset, but that's because he wasn't raised this way, on a farm. He's a city person at heart. He's just trying to protect you in his own way."

She paused. "It's going to be hard, you know. I've always told you, 'We're land rich and cash poor.' It's as true today as it's ever been."

I knew that better than anyone. For more than fifteen years, since my grandfather had died, my parents had paid nearly all of the farm bills through their off-farm salaries. If they had ever quit their well-paying jobs, the farm would have failed within a matter of months. This fact was a considerable source of family stress, and slowly, insidiously, matters of money had become an emotional flashpoint in our family. My parents did their best to avoid the subject entirely, mechanically waking each morning, getting in their cars, and driving into the city before dawn.

"Your father's discouraged because the farm hasn't turned a profit for years, not since your grandfather ran the place."

"Discouraged's an understatement," I agreed.

"Well, he's got a right to be. He's put years of his own paychecks into this place and never gotten a dollar of it back. That would discourage anybody."

"But I know," she continued, with increasing conviction, "that there's a way we can do this. It might not be the same way your grandfather did it, and letting Albert run the farm might be only a temporary solution. Whatever the answer is, we'll help you the best we can."

My father, who had silently entered the room as we were talking, leaned against the doorjamb, arms crossed, equal parts sullen and resigned. I smiled at him, the most beaming, bearded smile I could conjure. He shook his head wordlessly, in disbelief that he was being outvoted.

"And your father will help, too," she added on his behalf, as he continued to shake his head. "Just as soon as he gets over his shock."

———————

In spite of the drought, the fall harvest began. We observed as truck after truck lumbered slowly away, brimming with glittering kernels of corn, cascades of resplendent soybeans. I didn't know what a tractor-trailer load of grain was worth, but imagined it must be more money than I had ever seen in my life. We had done the math and knew we'd need a little more than ten thousand dollars to pay our bills through the winter. Although it would barely keep our heads above water, we took comfort in the idea that we had finally done it—our little farm had made a real profit.

Albert stood on our front porch, a crumpled bouquet of pink and yellow invoices in his hand. The receipts looked as though they had been salvaged from the chaos of his dashboard, smudged and corrugated with a season's worth of hard living.

"Well," he began. "It was *dry*."

Yes, yes, I said to myself, impatient despite my polite upbringing. Everyone was tired of the drought, entirely worn out by it. How did we *do*, I wanted to know.

He paused, as though awaiting confirmation that the only green to be found in the entire county was the paint on the John Deere combine.

"So," my mother was forced to ask, after a few more moments of awkward silence, "how did the numbers turn out?"

Albert nodded at the papers. "Right. That's what those are for. That's the fertilizer bill, spray bill, seed bill. I got my fuel figured up on that other sheet." He pointed to a notation written in pencil. "We broke a chain on the auger sprocket, but that was only five dollars to fix, so that's what that is there."

He fell silent again, giving us time to look over the receipts. Was it just me, or was he stalling? It seemed like a long-winded way to get around to the bottom line.

This time, I prompted him. "Well, once all that's hashed out, how much did we make? Seemed like a lot of trucks rolled out of here."

He took off his hat, roughly scrubbing his hair with his worn-down fingers. "Yeah, I'm getting around to that. See, the thing is, even though there was no corn or beans to be had around here, the Midwest's had themselves the bumper crop of a decade. Turns out the price this year is the worst it's been in ten years." He replaced and adjusted his hat. I glanced sidelong at my mother. Her face revealed the concern I was trying to mask.

"Albert," my mother said firmly. "What kind of numbers are we talking about here?"

"Bottom line?" he asked.

"Bottom line," she replied.

He exhaled slowly. "Eighteen sixteen."

I couldn't believe it. Eighteen hundred dollars? We had been hoping for ten thousand, and were nervous about anything less than eight. How could anyone's farm expect to survive on less than two thousand dollars?

My mother was the first to find her voice. "My goodness. I . . . I don't know what to say. Albert, when we talked about it this spring, we all agreed that ten thousand apiece was a reasonable expectation."

"Yes ma'am, but, like you already know, it was dry as a bone. We were darn lucky to get the crop that we did." He nodded at the receipts. "And most of them costs is fixed. Of course, the profits jump when the harvest goes up, but if it don't . . ." he said and shrugged helplessly, "well, the costs came back to bite us."

Albert genuinely looked as if he'd rather be anywhere else on the planet right now. "I'd be the last person to lead you on, Mrs. Pritchard. I just never expected nothing like this."

"Yes, but . . . " She shook her head in disbelief. "I mean, Albert, eighteen hundred and sixteen dollars is a *long* way from ten thousand. I just don't understand how it happened."

Albert's eyes widened.

"Eighteen hundred?" He shook his head. Without a trace of irony or humor, he corrected her. "Mrs. Pritchard . . . it was eighteen *dollars* and sixteen *cents*."

I was fairly certain that, just for a moment, the earth listed sideways.

She looked at him in disbelief. "Eighteen dollars," she repeated. "How . . . how is that *possible?*"

Albert, red with embarrassment, gestured at the accounts. "It's all right there, ma'am." He searched for words. "Believe me . . . I'm as disappointed as you. Probably more so. I feel mostly to blame, for leading you into it."

"But there were so many trucks! Full trucks, Albert. Isn't *somebody* making money off of this?"

Albert removed his hat, pointlessly crimped the brim several times, and pulled it tightly back onto his head. Shoulders slumped, he had the air of a defeated man.

"Yes ma'am. Somebody probably is. Just not us."

They continued to talk, pouring over the numbers, but I'm certain that's the last I heard, and the last I was able to see, for quite some time.

So this is what society was trying to tell me. This is what my city-born father, and his father before him, was so afraid of, what my entire culture had been trying to tell me for years:

Forget about it, kid. It's a fairy tale. A nursery rhyme. There's no "family farm" anymore, just huge corporations with tractors as big as houses.

Do you see now? Do you get it yet, hayseed? We told you so. Now go get a haircut and a suit, and find a real job before it's too late.

I had dropped out of school, abandoning a steady, reliable career as a teacher. And for what? All those trucks filled with corn and soybeans? At the end of the day, they had made us enough to buy a bag of corn chips and a glass of soy milk. At least I could afford some tap water to wash the bad taste out of my mouth.

Yes, I replied. Yes, I see how it is. Anger boiled within me, waves of shame and humiliation. If Albert had handed me the eighteen dollars at that moment, I would have torn it into shreds and tossed it into the wind.

Yes, I understood now. Our family farm was broken. I made up my mind that, somehow, we were going to fix it.

Chapter Two

I t came to my attention rather quickly that I had no idea what I was doing.

As I laced up my work boots the following morning, I didn't even know where to begin. The harvest was complete, and Albert was finished with our farm for the season. With my parents away at their day jobs, I had now volunteered myself as our sole worker, manager, and problem-solver-in-chief. I had no one there to guide me, no experience, and no money. Regardless, I quietly burned to prove the skeptics wrong, convinced that we could save our farm through sheer force of will.

Those first days, I did the only things I knew how to do. We still had our cows, about fifty head, and I focused my energy on making sure we'd have a successful calf sale the following spring. I fed them hay and checked on them twice a day, and replaced old posts in our perimeter fence. My arms and face became deeply suntanned, and I lost the ten pounds I had brought home from college. As winter approached and the days shortened, I took a catering job at night to help pay the bills, serving shrimp kabobs, cucumber sandwiches, and champagne. The contrast of lifestyles wasn't lost on me. Each morning, my cummerbund and bow tie discarded at the foot of my bed, I stretched and looked optimistically out the window at the fields but had no clear idea of what I really should be doing.

The landscape, at least, was familiar. After all, I had been raised on the farm and had lived there most of my life. The hills and pastures, the barns and buildings were the playgrounds of my youth. In the eighties, when my grandfather passed away, the property had been split into several pieces and divided among his children. The portion of land that came to my mother was nearly three hundred and fifty acres of gently rolling hay fields and aging apple orchards. Roughly square in shape, the borders flowed from one state into the next, from Clarke County, Virginia, into Jefferson County, West Virginia. The ability to be in both states at once while standing in the middle of a cow pasture had been a novelty to me as a child.

After returning from Seattle, my parents had built their house along a distant edge of the original farm, several miles from the property we had inherited. Now I moved out of their home and onto the farm proper, into a derelict brick house that had been uninhabited since the 1940s. My electricity arrived via an extension cord I plugged into the barn's lone outlet, supplying power to my reading lamp and a hot plate. I cleaned squirrel nests from the closets, disposed of a blacksnake skeleton I found curled inside the defunct toilet, and spent my first night beneath the rough-hewn rafters of a rusty tin roof.

I had briefly known my farmer grandfather, when he was a very old man. The farm had been passed to him in 1915, while he was still a teenager, and he had done the best he could to simply survive. He never received more than a high school education.

Eighty-two at the time of his death, he had farmed through two World Wars, the Great Depression, and the unpredictable stagflation of the 1970s. All the while, the farm had remained debt-free, productive, and profitable. To me, barely twenty-two and with my entire farming career in front of me, it seemed like an impossible résumé to emulate.

Before the land was parceled out to my grandfather's children, my grandparents' farm had comprised just more than two thousand acres. As a rough comparison, the property was nearly three times the size of New York's Central Park. The land was contiguous, and we could easily drive for an hour over potholed, muddy farm roads without ever crossing the smooth asphalt of the public highway. The meadows and orchards literally stretched for miles.

It was along these rough country roads that Betsy and I learned to drive a truck before we were ten, bouncing and bumping over the groundhog-pocked cattle pastures. Just able to reach the pedals, I practiced the three-part harmony of clutch, gas, and stick shift. When I finally got the rhythm down pat, the feeling was exhilarating.

If it seems implausible to say that, as a child, I roamed freely over most of the farm, exploring the woods and creeks, pretending to be a knight, or a movie hero, walking for miles through tall grass in a quest to discover what was waiting over the next hill, then that's understandable. Recalling those days, I marvel at the liberty I was granted, tied to nothing more than my punctual response to the front porch dinner bell.

But it was precisely those carefree, unsupervised hours that allowed me to connect to the land, and it was the resonance of that freedom that made farming seem so important as the years began to pass. Now I wanted to recapture that feeling, sculpting it into a greater sense of purpose. If I could somehow make the farm profitable once again, it would give me a legitimate reason to remain on the land I had grown to love.

The Shenandoah Valley, where my ancestors settled, is famous for its natural beauty. Stretching from Roanoke to Harpers Ferry, the valley is roughly forty miles across, bounded by the Blue Ridge Mountains on the east and the West Virginia border to the west. The land is softly sculpted with wooded hillsides, and the Shenandoah River winds serenely through the lush valley bottom. Appreciating the vista from the heights above Harpers Ferry, Thomas Jefferson once remarked, "This scene is worth a voyage across the Atlantic."

On a clear day, Jefferson might have been able to see my ancestors' farm. Tucked into the northernmost section, here the valley was truly in full splendor. The sloping hills were crisscrossed with hand-hewn locust fences, with green pastures extending into the horizon. Clusters of mulberry trees, loaded with sweet purple fruit, shaded the cool limestone outcroppings. Sheep dotted the clover-thick meadows, miniature reflections of the expansive white clouds above. Broad silver springs laced the pasture floors with plumes of crisp watercress waving just beneath the surface, and crayfish darted between submerged stones. The springwater was cold to the touch, even on the hottest of summer days.

Early settlers quickly realized the potential of the valley and began cultivating the rich soil in earnest by the mid-1700s. Many of these old farms endured, passed down as family heirlooms, and as a child I explored their barnyards as my grandmother gossiped with her octogenarian peers. Comprising little more than a whitewashed farmhouse and a barn or two, these farmsteads were rustic and pragmatic, aesthetically lovely to behold, and framed by the genuinely azure Blue Ridge Mountain supine on the horizon. Free to explore the cobwebbed corners of these venerable farms, I recall the clean smells of hay, well-tended livestock, and fresh, sun-warmed earth.

Most spectacularly, the roads of our counties were flanked by thousands upon thousands of apple trees. In the mid-twentieth century, our corner of Virginia was nicknamed the "Apple Capital of the World." Half-forgotten varieties such as Winesaps, Yorks, Grimes Golden, Northwest Greenings, and Rome Beauties stretched into the horizon. Reciting the names of these apples was like poetry in advance of the harvest. In late April, with the apple blossoms in full pink-and-white bloom, the perfume was nothing short of intoxicating.

As far as I could tell, the Shenandoah Valley was full of farms just like ours. And why wouldn't it be? The summers were rarely hot for long, and rainfall was usually plentiful. The climate and the soil were ideally suited for agriculture, from vegetables and fruits to grains. The sweetly sloping hills were the perfect setting for pastured livestock. It was as though our valley awoke each morning ready to produce, to thrive, to grow. The land was so gentle and fecund, so perfectly temperate, that it tempted farmers to try to grow a little bit of everything.

Neighboring farms filled in the blanks. Dairies and horse farms, in particular, abounded. In the 1980s our farm was bordered on three sides by dairies, with dozens more scattered about. Nearby, the Charles Town racetrack ensured steady opportunity for local horse breeders, and less than a mile from our farm, a dozen Thoroughbreds were born and raised each year. I watched them each morning, racing across the pasture, keeping thunderous pace with our car as they galloped past the wooden fences.

My grandfather had been an orchardist and a cattle farmer. Where he didn't plant apple trees he planted fence posts. With miles of grass, water trickling from the rocks, and always a tree or two for shade, he grazed thousands of cattle in his lifetime. On nearly every corner of his farm, on each distant hillside, in every lush meadow, drinking from the edge of a spring-fed creek or drowsing in the shade of a hackberry and sassafras thicket, were cows.

Cattle flourished on my grandparents' farm, grazing the abundant pasture that volunteered from the rich valley soil. These animals were fed only grass and clover, grain being far too precious for animals that had been bred for grazing. It was the simplest of recipes, and my grandfather made a sixty-five-year career out of it.

He raised Herefords, a breed of cattle brought across the ocean generations earlier from England. Their coats were a deep, rusty red; their faces, feet, and the tips of their tails titanium white. The cows

My grandfather Robert R. Smith Jr., with his herd. Circa 1950.

seemed to enjoy the pastures most when it was cool and overcast, like a stereotypical British day, with an intermittent, penetrating drizzle.

Even into his dotage, my grandfather would clamber each day into his doorless Scout International and check each cow in the herd, making certain that everything was just so. These animals meant more to him than just a job or an investment. Husbandry, the practice of raising healthy animals, was my grandfather's passion.

Still, as idyllic as it might sound, raising livestock came with much physical risk. As a boy I had seen one of our farmhands, a man in his late forties, get mauled by an angry bull, caught from behind as he tried to flee from the enraged animal. The bull charged, lowering his head just as the man reached the fence, tossing him like a doll fifteen feet in the air. Turning a cartwheel, the farmhand's arms and legs searched for midair handholds that didn't exist. He no sooner hit the ground than the animal was on top of him, a cloud of saliva and dust, grinding him into the dirt with his broad, powerful head.

The man screamed and curled into a ball, pleading in vain against ferocity unleashed. I turned my head away, unable to watch. When the bull was finally satisfied, the other farmhands rushed into the corral and pulled the broken man to safety. Strong as a locust post, the twenty-year farm veteran suffered cracked ribs and a concussion, but a few weeks later he tipped his cap to me from the seat of his pickup as he headed back to work in the fields.

A few years later I had my own brush with death, but mine came from behind the steering wheel of a tractor. I was fourteen, just old enough to be trusted with farm equipment. We had recently finished making hay, and the landscape was dotted with scores of enormous round bales, cylindrical rolls of sun-dried grass that stood five feet high and weighed close to one thousand pounds apiece. For years I had watched the men move the hay with hydraulic-powered tractor spears, effortlessly lifting them into the air before transporting them, one bale on the front and another behind, to the shelter of the barn. Now, at long last, I had been asked to participate.

In my teenage mind, I saw nothing especially complicated about the work. I already knew how to drive a tractor, and operating the hydraulic controls was child's play. When I was finally offered the keys to the tractor, I fired up the engine with feigned nonchalance, secretly excited to take my place among the men.

The afternoon went smoothly, and I fell into the cadence of the work, the vibration of the motor lulling me into daydreams. At last, only one bale remained. I threw the tractor into high gear and raced across the field before one of the older men could get to it first. As I approached the bale, now fully confident in my abilities, I slowed the tractor just enough to gracefully lift the bale with my front spear without even stopping. Triumphant, I raised the final bale high in the air as though lifting a trophy, making sure that everyone could see. I shoved the throttle into full steam and the tractor engine roared as I headed down a steep hill toward the barn.

Without warning, the front of the tractor rocked forward, carried downward by the tremendous weight of the hay. As the bale struck the earth, the tractor pivoted on its front tires, raising the rear of the machine completely off the ground, the back tires spinning in midair. The force of the impact wrenched my grip from the steering wheel, catapulting me upward. I would have been hurled into the air but luckily my boots hooked beneath the steel pedals, the clutch on one side, the brake on the other.

An instant later the impact of the bale caused the tractor to ricochet backward, slamming the rear tires against the ground. For a split second I thought the danger was over, but as soon as the spinning tires found traction, the sequence was violently repeated anew: *Slam . . . bang!* The tractor pitched forward again.

I grasped the steering wheel with both hands as, this time, I came clean out of my seat, suspended helplessly with my knees above my ears. It was like a carnival ride without safety restraints. I held on for my life.

Ahead of me, a thick copse of trees waited at the bottom of the hill. Everything was happening too fast; I couldn't think, couldn't act. Every muscle tensed as I braced for impact with the trees.

From my periphery, one of the old farmhands raced across the pasture, shouting, "Jump! Jump! You're gonna hit the trees! Jump!"

Jump? My teenage hubris had been consumed by total panic. Jump? Yes! Of course! As the rear tires hurtled toward the earth, I set my feet against the pitted steel of the floor and flung my body as far as I could.

I hit the ground, rolled, and watched as the tractor bucked and bounced straight into the trees. A second later, it careened off a walnut tree trunk, swung like a protractor to the left, and slammed head-on into a towering sycamore. Covered in scrapes and bruises, completely humiliated but otherwise okay, I was awarded the honor of changing the oil and meticulously greasing each of our five tractors for my poor judgment.

As much as I admired the men who worked on the farm, I never dreamed in those days that I might someday become a farmer myself. The land had been in our family for more than a hundred and fifty years, and I took it for granted that someone else would always be there to look after it. Generation after generation, someone had always shouldered the responsibility. In my childhood mind, our farm existed independent of time and place, much the same now as it had ever been, or might ever need to become.

By the 1990s, however, I couldn't ignore the fact that the lights of suburban Washington, D.C., were growing brighter on the eastern horizon. Each night a pink nimbus pulsed above the top of the Blue Ridge, an otherworldly electric cloud. These were the lights of a quarter million new homes, just over the mountain. The suburbs had finally reached our doorstep.

All at once our local economy, based for generations on agriculture, experienced a dramatic transformation. Enticed by higher paying jobs just an hour's commute over the mountain, young people began choosing careers in Washington over a life of farming. Our rural towns became "bedroom communities," places where people returned to each night, but only to sleep.

My own father was a perfect example of this shift. Having convinced himself that farming was a dead-end job, he awoke each morning at four, carpooled to a commuter train, and didn't return home until nearly eight o'clock at night. Although some families tried their best to pull it off, balancing a life of farming and working in the city was a nearly impossible task.

Over the next ten years, fewer and fewer people my age began careers in agriculture. An entire generation of young farmers traded in their blue jeans for khaki pants, filled up on gasoline and coffee, and disappeared over the mountain. The highways operated like a bloodstream, conveying our rural youth to the beating heart of our nation's capital.

As older farmers retired, no one stepped in to replace them, and by the mid-1990s, Shenandoah Valley farms began disappearing en masse. Even as a teenager, I could see the consequences. Driving into town on an errand, I witnessed fleets of earth-moving equipment carving the green hills into graded plateaus; hundred-year-old farms were bulldozed down to bedrock in a day or two. The family farms of my childhood were becoming an endangered species.

I struggled with this emerging reality. How could centuries of tradition change so radically over the course of a generation? This was still the same productive land, the same rich soil that had provided sustenance and income for two centuries. Farming simply couldn't become obsolete over night.

As I considered a career in agriculture, right from the outset I saw nothing but red flags. No one in our community, not even the final die-hard farmers, encouraged my farming dreams. Farms were pushed over for houses; I never saw a single house pushed over for a farm. I wanted to believe that, like my grandfather before me, hard work could turn our future around. But as I witnessed these other farmsteads vanish one after the next, I questioned whether I was being stubbornly naive, or perhaps even foolish.

What good was hard work if there was no money left over at the end of the day? As much as we loved our land, we hadn't made a profit since Jimmy Carter was president. Who could blame the young people, my peers, for taking jobs in the city and safeguarding their futures? They were forced to look beyond an agricultural system that couldn't compensate them for their efforts.

Increasingly I found myself lost in an imaginary debate, sparring with my devil's advocate. I listed the pros. Where else could I have the freedom to grow my own food? Work outside in the fresh air? Set my own schedule? Be my own boss?

You don't have any farming experience, the contrarian voice countered. You don't even know where to begin.

Where will you live?

What will you grow?

How will you pay the bills?

Sometimes the voice asked even harder questions.

What if you fail?

What if, by following your dream, it ends up costing you the farm?

Outweighing my optimism, tempering my ambitions, these questions sat heavily in the pit of my stomach, churning. *What if you fail?* the voice kept repeating. I had no good answer.

Chapter Three

Our finances were even worse than I had imagined. Not only had my parents poured every nickel of their income into the farm, they had managed to accrue a staggering amount of credit card debt. Out of desperation, my father had developed a strategy of continuously rolling his monthly totals onto new cards, taking advantage of zero-interest introductory offers before flipping the balance onto yet another card before the offer expired. All told, they were now fifty thousand dollars in the hole.

"How did this *happen?*" I asked, floored by the discovery. With the pittance I made at my catering job, the number might as well have been a million.

My father shrugged. "Equipment. Repairs. Fuel." He regarded me bleakly with his pale blue eyes. "Son, if you haven't figured it out yet, farming's a money pit."

I shook my head, unprepared for any of this. "But what are we going to do? How are we going to pay this off?"

"What are *we* going to do?" he replied humorlessly. "I can tell you what *I'm* going to do. I'm going to be in debt for the rest of my life."

As difficult as this was to hear, I knew he believed it.

Helpless to change anything overnight, I decided to take stock of our assets. We still owned a small herd of cattle and a few dozen chickens. But after the fiasco with the corn and soybeans, our herbicide-sprayed pastures needed to be replanted. Of course the farm itself was worth money, but the thought of selling even a small parcel of our land remained anathema; once it was gone, chances were we would never get it back. I sat down one winter evening and wrote a long list of moneymaking ideas, hoping to create a temporary source of income until a permanent solution revealed itself.

Sifting through Albert's pile of bills was more useful than any economics class I had taken in college. Under Albert's way of farming, the first people to be paid were the seed salesmen, the fertilizer suppliers, the fuel distributors, the truck drivers, and the insurance agents. There was money to be made, certainly, but by whom? We were not only the very last to be paid but also the ones most likely not to be paid at all.

We needed to put any profits, however modest, directly into our own hands, and less through a siphoning series of middlemen. Eighteen dollars and sixteen cents could never again be an option. My list prioritized self-reliance, immediate returns, and low-input enterprises. Predictably, my father greeted my first idea with a negative shake of his head.

"Firewood?" he repeated. "Absolutely not. I've thought about it before. It's hard work, little return. You'd be better off mowing people's lawns."

Mowing lawns, I countered, wasn't the same as using the already available dead trees littering the farm. Trees died naturally like anything else, and on a farm the size of ours, it wasn't unusual for two or three to expire each year. It had been a decade since anyone had managed the woodlots on our property, where dozens of decaying trees currently stood out among the healthy ones. Many had already fallen over, and they needed to be cleaned up as a matter of general pasture management. Turning them into salable firewood, I suggested, seemed like a good way to multitask.

He folded his arms over his chest. "It's dangerous, too. Especially doing it by yourself. And I'm not just talking about the chain saws. A falling tree can kill you before you even know you're in trouble."

"I wasn't planning to fell any trees," I told him. "I was just going to cut up the ones that get knocked down in storms or fall down on their own."

My father had been a forestry major in college and spent twenty years working as a bureaucrat for the USDA Forest Service. Each autumn he stockpiled cords of hardwoods to burn in our stoves, and I had learned to split wood by watching his technique, a combination of muscle, steel, and confidence. After he had chainsawed a fallen tree into smaller rounds, it was my job to stand each section on its end in preparation for splitting. My father wielded a thirty-pound splitting maul with the ease of swinging a Wiffle ball bat, cleanly cleaving each round with a mighty karate chop. As a boy, my knees buckled trying to lift this monstrous maul, a solid wedge of steel welded to a long metal pipe. Now, having finally mastered its heft, I felt as powerful as a demigod.

As I explained my reasons for selling firewood, he countered at each turn with information that I hadn't seen coming. Was I aware, he wondered, that most species of trees on the farm, particularly those that blew down, weren't very good firewood producers? Sycamore, hackberry, tree of heaven, white pine, and cherry all either burned too quickly, deteriorated rapidly once cut, or put out little heat. Other trees, such as oaks, hickories, black walnuts, and mulberries, took at least a year to properly "season," the process by which the moisture evaporates from the wood. If the wood wasn't properly seasoned, not only would it be difficult to ignite, but it could cause dangerous flammable residues to build up in the chimney.

He lectured me on chain-saw horsepower and blade-sharpening considerations. Finally, he pointed out the fact that we didn't have access to a hydraulic wood splitter or a truck that was properly suited for deliveries. Give the old man credit, I acknowledged begrudgingly. There were a lot of things I hadn't considered.

In spite of all this, though, I had to do *something*. Selling firewood might not be the solution to all of our problems, but it was a necessary, practical job, requiring little more than gasoline and time as overhead. If I worked hard, by the end of the winter, I could actually make a tidy profit.

I privately resolved to try it. By my reckoning, there were enough already downed, properly seasoned, good-burning hardwood trees scattered across the farm to keep me busy for at least a season or two. The following morning I sharpened my saw, knocked the sawdust out of the air filter, and selected a handful of likely logs that were ready to be cut into firewood.

I enjoyed the work right away. It was especially satisfying to clean up the farm as I went, removing a windblown tree from the pasture and watching as the cattle gobbled up the suddenly available grass previously hidden beneath the sprawling branches. I had an affinity for the smells associated with cutting wood—the peppery aroma of hickory, the loamy, sweet odor of oak, and the musky perfume of black walnut. At the end of each day, I'd turn my pockets inside out and let the multi-hued sawdust tumble to my boots.

Perhaps most of all, I enjoyed the sweat and the sore muscles. These were reminders of why my body was here to begin with, and what it could accomplish. After an hour of work, the maul began to feel like an extension of my body, and with each impact a deep vibration traveled up my arms and across my shoulders. Nothing was more satisfying than executing a perfect swing—*thwack!*—and watching as the oak leaped to life, cartwheeling across the autumn leaves. When the truck was loaded high with freshly split wood, the grain streaked with the bright yellows and salmony pinks of honey locust and hickory, the sense of accomplishment was tangible. At the end of the evening, I was tired but happy.

Naturally, I also planned to make money. I had worked it up on paper that I could truck as much as six loads of wood per day, anticipating an average delivery distance of forty miles, round-trip. My mornings would be spent cutting and splitting wood, loading, planning my routes, and making the delivery. I'd then return home to load up again.

My little Toyota pickup truck could carry only about half of a cord at a time, and since a cord (eight-by-eight-by-four feet of stacked wood) was more or less the professional standard, I figured I would lower my price just a bit, hoping to differentiate myself from the other suppliers.

My ad in the local classifieds looked something like this:

FIREWOOD
Seasoned hardwoods, split and delivered
$40 a pickup load (1/2 cord)
Local delivery to Berryville/Winchester area

Looking back on it now, how I imagined, even in the mid-1990s, that it would be economical to deliver all this wood for forty dollars, I honestly can't recall. Comparing it to another delivery system, the neighborhood pizza restaurant, I was transporting a thousand pounds of wood for the same price as a couple of pounds of flour, cheese, and tomato sauce. The pizzas would make a customer happy for one meal; the firewood would heat a house for a month. Relatively speaking, my firewood delivery was the value of the century.

That being said, there's simply no substitute for hearing the phone ring and having a customer on the other end of the line. When I came in from work at lunchtime to find the answering machine blinking with a half dozen messages (this was before the age of ubiquitous cell phones), it was truly exhilarating. It might only be forty dollars, but I was now completely in charge of my own success or failure. Part of me now felt less like a child, and a little more like an adult.

Off to cut wood, fall of 1996.

My first customer was an elderly lady who lived near Front Royal, Virginia. I had been to Front Royal dozens of times, and even though I knew better, I convinced myself the delivery was no more than a twenty-minute drive from the farm.

Allow me to explain how this might have happened. When one lives in the country, everything seems closer than it actually is. This phenomenon seems to occur, oddly enough, because everything is actually pretty far away. Distances are judged by how well our car radios maintain a signal; when the music becomes staticky, chances are we've traveled a long way.

Rural folks build up tolerances for traveling long distances, and gradually it throws our sense of time and mileage neatly out the window. School might be a half hour away in one direction and the hospital forty-five minutes in the other—or "right down the road." Since these destinations are necessarily part of our lives, we never quantify how long it takes us to get there. We just start driving, and after a while we're there.

Hence, my first major business mistake: I had vastly misjudged distances. Front Royal was *not* twenty minutes right down the road. By the time I arrived at the woman's house, which was on the far side of the town, I had driven nearly fifty minutes one way. As I pulled into her driveway, I already realized I had some major rethinking to do.

"Good morning, ma'am!" I greeted her, waiving broadly. Not exactly certain what a wood salesman looked like, I had tried my best to dress the part, choosing a pair of broken-in coveralls and a plaid cap pulled snugly over my head. The temperature was in the upper fifties, and frankly a little warm for the outfit, but at least I felt professional. "Where would you like me to drop off your wood?"

Her house was built into the side of a very steep hill, and the parking lot where I was standing was at the bottom. She stood just outside her door, looking down at me from a front porch supported by stilts.

"I need it stacked around back, on my deck." She moved with the assistance of a walker, and as she spoke, she gestured up a long set of stairs landscaped into the hill. The wooden steps climbed the sharp incline, paused at a landing, then continued to rise as they turned left and disappeared behind the house. From my vantage point, I couldn't even *see* the deck.

"I've just had a bone spur taken off of my heel, and I'm all alone, so I need it stacked nice and neat right outside my door. I don't suspect I'll be able to carry in more than one stick at a time." She squinted down at my truck, covering her eyes against the glare. "You didn't cut it too big, did you? Too big is just no good for me. I need small pieces."

Had I cut it too big? I asked myself. I didn't think I had. It was the same size we had always burned in our own home.

"No ma'am," I responded sincerely. "It's really nice wood. Perfect pieces. I split it all myself."

She continued to peer wordlessly at the load, expecting to find, I feared, blocks whittled to the size of tongue depressors. I began to have a sinking feeling about the whole transaction. The thought of hauling and stacking all that wood, particularly under such arduous conditions, had never factored into my plans.

"Where . . . how . . ." I stammered, walking a line between professionalism and economic calamity, "how do I get my truck back there? Where's the road that leads back to your deck?"

"Your truck?" the old woman said. "Oh, there's no place to back up a truck. There's no road. Besides," she added, gesturing with a roundabout motion of her arm, "I've got my rhododendrons back there, and my peonies. Not to mention my lilac bush."

"So," I replied, my spirits sinking, "it's up the stairs."

"Up the stairs." She nodded. "To the landing. Then up the stairs again, to the deck. You can't miss it." With her walker positioned carefully in front of her, she began a slow orbit toward the comfort of her house.

"Oh," she added, over her shoulder, "and don't stack the wood right up against the wall. It'll dirty the paint. The delivery man did that last year, and I had to call to get my money back. That was a real inconvenience for me."

I mumbled an impolite response beneath my breath, then smiled. "Yes ma'am. I'll be very careful. One load of firewood, coming right up." Literally coming right up, I amended silently. I stacked five or six wedges of wood onto my arms and started up the stairs. Look at me, I thought ironically. I'm finally climbing the noncorporate ladder.

An hour later, drenched in sweat and just short of exhausted, I trundled the last armload of firewood up the steps. The final few sticks capped a tidy pyramid right outside her sliding-glass doors, and

I couldn't help but admire my flawless stacking, an entire morning of exertion transformed into a functional work of art. She had watched me working the entire time, standing with her walker just behind the glass doors. I motioned to her that I was all done, and she opened the door a crack.

"What do you think? Looks nice, huh?" I asked, hands on hips, breathing heavily. I was hoping for a compliment, or better yet, a cool glass of water.

Either she hadn't heard or chose to ignore me. "How much did you say it was again?" she asked, in a suddenly small voice.

I wiped sweat from my forehead with a bandanna. I had shed my coveralls by the second load, and my T-shirt, saturated, clung darkly to my chest. "Forty dollars, ma'am," I replied, still catching my breath just a bit.

"Oh. Oh, my." She paused. "Really? That seems like an awful lot. Can't you do a little better than that? Say, thirty-five? It doesn't hurt to ask, you know."

Doesn't hurt to ask? Who was she trying to fool? The old bat was sparring like a veteran prizefighter, working the body, then going for the upper cut.

"Ma'am, forty dollars is already ten below the next lowest price. You can check for yourself. I was really hoping to get what I advertised."

"Well," she replied, disappointment playing a mandolin tremolo in her voice. "If that's what you have to have, then that's what I'll have to pay." She furrowed her brows, reached into her purse, and produced a ball-point pen.

"Since I'm all alone, I don't carry cash. Thieves," she added, loudly, as though the word might scare a robber straight out of her peonies. "To whom should I make the check?"

Nearly four hours after I had left the farm, I pulled into my driveway with a tiny piece of paper that may, or very well may not, have been worth forty United States dollars. I prayed that her check wouldn't bounce.

Taking stock of the day, I had burned five gallons of gas in my truck, another gallon between my chain saw and rented wood splitter, and I'd spent the morning exhausting myself on the grueling hill. I had expected to be back hours earlier and had already booked three additional afternoon deliveries. By the time I was finished with my day and pulled my truck back onto the farm, it was after eleven o'clock at night.

Across the course of the winter, I delivered more than one hundred loads of firewood. After expenses, this left me with a profit of nearly two thousand dollars. It wasn't a fortune, but at the end of a long, arduous season, one where I had simultaneously managed our cattle while selling the wood, the balance looked really great on my bank statement. The sense of accomplishment I felt far outweighed any lingering hard feelings I had toward ornery little old ladies.

It all fell apart faster than I could have imagined. Spring arrived, and with the warmer weather, firewood sales wrapped up for the season. Hard work had transformed my physique over the course of the season, and for the first time in my life, my upper body sported real definition. Still, I had worn myself down with an endless string of seven-day workweeks, and with summer haymaking right around the corner, I knew I needed a break.

I took a rare day off and spent the afternoon in town, enjoying a luxurious lunch and taking in a movie. As I headed home later that afternoon, I entertained myself with thoughts of investing the two thousand dollars, buying a few more cattle for the herd or perhaps a better chain saw for the upcoming season. Things felt like they were looking up.

I had just pulled into traffic, less than a hundred yards from the theater, when my engine began to rev alarmingly. It seemed to be getting plenty of fuel, but as I pressed the accelerator, the truck barely moved. Cars began to pile up behind me as, despite my best efforts, the truck decelerated from thirty-five to barely above five miles per hour. Gratefully, as I manually downshifted into second gear, the engine responded. I limped back home along country roads going no more than twenty miles per hour.

A few days later the transmission mechanic summed up my problem very poetically. "I don't know how you did it," he said, "but you pulled the guts clean out the tailpipe. I'm damned impressed you drove it up here."

I knew the deliveries had occasionally pushed the truck to its limits but had no idea I had overworked it to the point of collapse. The strain of a winter's worth of firewood caused the metal timing chain to carve into the motor, allowing oil to flow freely with transmission fluid. The resulting caustic mixture caused both the engine and the transmission to fail. Permanently.

In order to get my truck rolling again, the mechanic estimated it would cost $4,600. I swallowed hard.

Chapter Four

Selling firewood may have been a financial debacle, but the failure hadn't been a result of poor planning. My idea had more or less worked . . . right up to the point where my engine exploded.

My dad received the news of my truck's infirmity with an expression that wordlessly proclaimed, "That sounds about right." Nancy, now studying at Chapel Hill, visited the farm one weekend and studied the broken-down Toyota forlornly. "You know," she said, half seriously, "the only reason I ever agreed to go out with you was because of that truck." I resolved to get the engine fixed as quickly as possible.

We sold some cattle that spring to help pay our bills, but much of the money went toward replanting the barren fields that Albert had sprayed with herbicide. After reseeding the pastures, my parents and I placed a strict moratorium on any additional farm purchases. The following month, when their credit card debt plateaued for the first time in years, their sense of relief was undeniable.

With the cold days of winter behind me and my itch to sell wood now officially scratched, I looked forward to spring, and new opportunities. It wasn't long before something came my way.

Albert was now managing another farm right next to us, and he had planted fifty acres of wheat in a nearby field. Rain had fallen steadily that spring, breaking the previous year's drought, and this new crop was copious, an ocean of gold waving against the foothills of the Blue Ridge. It seemed as though he would have the bumper crop we had wished for the previous year.

Perhaps it was simply for financial gain, or perhaps it was out of a misplaced sense of guilt from the failed partnership, but Albert offered me a fifty-fifty stake in selling the straw left over from the wheat. Our farm had a large barn for storage, and tractors and wagons to help move it. It was an arrangement that required only my time and hard work to turn a profit, and I didn't have to think long before agreeing.

When wheat is harvested, only the seed, or grain, is captured. The rest of the plant passes through the back of a large combine, a specialized tractor that harvests and threshes simultaneously. The combine is able to differentiate between the desired wheat and the rest of the chaff, and sorts the two in separate directions.

The grain accumulates in a large hopper until the bin is full, at which point it is augered into a waiting transport truck. This is then hauled away to a processing mill and ultimately turned into basic ingredients for food, such as flour for bread. Meanwhile, the bright yellow stalks are forcefully blown from the back of the combine and deposited into long, fluffy windrows. These stems, which just moments before had held the seed head aloft, can now be gathered by another machine and transformed into rectangular bales of straw.

Though the two are commonly confused, straw is very different from hay. The clean, quasi-soft golden stems of wheat, similar in shape to a drinking straw, are used for things such as animal bedding or landscape cover. Straw is mostly composed of air and carbon, and it has little nutritional value for animals. Hay, on the other hand, is the sun-dried blades of grasses and legumes. Good-quality hay is packed with nutrients, and it's intended for animal feed in the wintertime.

Dad hauling round bales with tractor.

The light, airy stalks of a bale of straw are also much, much lighter than a similarly sized bale of hay. These sorts of distinctions can be extremely important.

When I was fifteen, I took a job on a neighbor's farm, helping him bale alfalfa hay. I never had made hay before but was told in advance by my sister Betsy that it was very hard work, and to be prepared. Since I had helped bale straw once before and mistakenly thought hay and straw were basically the same thing, I told her I wasn't too worried about the challenge. Glancing at my toothpick arms and scrawny torso, she shook her head in silent disagreement. Her little brother would have to learn his own lessons.

The morning I showed up, the old man who ran the farm told me that his regular helper had called in sick, so I would be alone on the back of the hay wagon. No problem, I thought. Ever since my bale-hauling fiasco on the tractor, I had been waiting for another chance to prove I could do a grown man's job. I climbed onto the wooden wagon that was linked behind the tractor and the baler, and we set off, bouncing and swaying across the field.

Nothing could have prepared me for the difficulty of the job. The first bale was so heavy, I wasn't sure I could even move it. I tugged, strained, redoubled my efforts, and somehow cajoled the bale across the wagon, flipping and sliding it more than actually carrying it.

By the time I got it situated, another bale was already waiting. It was at least as heavy as the one before. The old man and the tractor chugged placidly along, while I used every ounce of my 135-pound body to keep up with the pace. Somehow, I managed to finish the row. I started a second layer, then a third.

All at once, the baler shut down with an earsplitting *craaack!* A rumbling shudder ran through the machine, as though the beast had been shot and was suffering its death throes.

The old farmer quickly turned off the tractor and clambered to the ground, expectorating a rust-colored jet of tobacco juice onto the stubbled field. He dropped to one knee, peering into the dark tines of the pickup, and then made his way to the back, where another bale sat waiting to wrestle with me. With an exploratory grunt, he lifted the bale off the slide. As the bale tipped toward him, he nearly fell backward with surprise.

"Jesus Criminy!" He dropped the bale to the ground with an audible thud and recovered his balance. "That's gotta weigh close to a hundred pounds!" He bent over and gave it a second, disbelieving tug. "Maybe more than a hundred, even. Good lord, son," he said, studying the bales I had already stacked, "are they *all* this heavy?"

I nodded. He gave a low whistle and shook his head.

"For Pete's sake, why didn't you say something? It's a wonder you didn't kill yourself back there."

I was too embarrassed to tell him I never had made hay before. I knew other boys my age who had already been helping with hay for years. Plus, I was afraid that my inexperience might have caused the machinery to break.

"I was just trying to get the job done. I figured we'd keep rolling till we got the wagon full."

"Not with bales like that," he said, shaking his head. He cut the strings on the bale with a pocketknife, frowning as he examined the alfalfa. "This hay's too wet to start with. Needs another day to cure. If we put these bales up, they're liable to catch on fire."

I had heard stories of moist, uncured hay gradually building heat until it spontaneously combusted, burning down the barn in which it was stored.

"No," he continued, ruefully, "we'll have to cut the strings on these and let them dry out. I'll pull the wagon along, and you shake them off the side, back out onto the field."

All my hard work had gone for nothing. We spent the next half hour spreading out the wet alfalfa, then repairing the broken shear bolt on the hay baler. He let me go home for the rest of the day, certain that with an extra afternoon of sunshine, the windrows would be properly dried by the following morning.

That evening, as I stepped into the shower, I nearly fainted as I looked down at my abdomen. A bulge the size of a fist was protruding just above my groin. I pushed against it gingerly, and the entire mass disappeared back inside my body, only to pop out again when I took my hand away. Gathering what little nerve I had left, I called for my dad.

He couldn't hide the look of surprise on his face.

"My word." He put his hand to his mouth, pensively. "I'm guessing that's a hernia." My father, never much of a nurse to my sister and me when we were sick, appeared several shades paler than normal. "I think we ought to take you to see a doctor. Right now."

My hundred-pound alfalfa bale experience came to an abrupt end.

One hernia surgery and seven years later, I was now enthusiastic to handle a field full of thirty-pound straw bales. Albert and I hashed out a deal. He would provide the straw, the equipment, and a man to drive the tractor, and I would stack the bales on the wagon and unload them in my barn. Additionally, I would be in charge of marketing, and as the straw was sold, I would pay him one dollar per bale. We estimated that the field would produce several thousand bales, and at the going rate of $2.50 a bale, there was enough money in it for each of us. Like many deals between farmers, the promise of a profit and a firm handshake was all it took to finalize the arrangement.

The day arrived when the wheat had been harvested and the straw was ready to be made. Acre upon acre of gleaming, golden stems stretched across the open field, sculpted into graceful rows that accentuated the contours of the hills. The goal was to load the straw onto the wagon, trundle it to the barn, unload it, then head back into the field for another round. With an average wagon accommodating roughly one hundred bales, the process would be repeated again and again . . . twenty times, at least. Bandanna tied around my head, water bottle at my side, I climbed over the fence that divided our fields, ready to work.

Albert greeted me with his easygoing smile. "Forrest, this is Jim Hester. Have you two met before? No? Jim, Forrest. Forrest, Jim."

I shook hands with the man. Short and wiry, somewhere in his mid-fifties, he was dressed in thin navy coveralls and tightly laced leather boots. He carried himself in such a way that it seemed he might break into jumping jacks at any moment.

"Jim'll be driving the tractor. You're set to be on the wagon all day?"

"I think so," I replied agreeably.

"You think so?" Jim Hester said. He widened his stance and crossed his arms over his chest. "Have you ever worked a baler with a kicker before? You'd *better* be ready."

My expression must have revealed my confusion, because a moment later, Albert repeated Jim's question. "*Have* you ever worked with a kicker?" he asked, not unkindly.

I had made hay earlier that summer with our own square baler, but I had never heard of a "kicker" before. "I don't think so," I replied, noncommittally.

Jim snorted. "Buddy, you'd *know* if you'd been around one." He rubbed his hands together, flashing yellow teeth in Albert's direction. "Oh, boy. We're gonna have fun today."

I had barely met the man yet already sensed an air of menace about him. I consoled myself with the knowledge that Albert, whom I knew to be reliably genial, would be there as a counterbalance to Jim's strange energy.

"Well," Albert said, snapping a small salute from the brim of his feed cap, "y'all take care. I'm gonna get back to work over at the other farm. Be back around noon to check in."

Jim Hester grinned. "Well, then," he said, striding briskly toward the tractor. "What are we waiting for?"

I climbed into the bale wagon as he fired up the motor. This particular wagon was cage-shaped, with twelve-foot-high bars enclosing the sides and back. It was a very different sensation from the open-sided wagons I normally used, and being in a cage felt like an especially ominous beginning. Jim swiveled on the tractor seat and shouted above the noise of the throttle.

"The kicker can be a little squirrelly sometimes," he hollered, squinting against the bright morning sunshine. "Let me know if they're coming out too high."

Wait a minute, I thought. Wasn't I the rookie here? How was I supposed to know what was too high, or too low, for that matter?

Jim let out the clutch, and the chain reaction, from the tractor through the baler to the wagon, sent me lurching backward. A moment later, he flipped a lever, and the baler began gobbling up a gleaming windrow of straw.

The kicker must have been invented by the same person who created the baseball launcher at the batting cages. I had no idea that a bale of straw would come flying at my head like a small airborne hippopotamus.

The first bale caught me squarely on my right shoulder, spun me into a pirouette, and knocked me off my feet. The bale tumbled awkwardly to the side of the wagon. I wasn't injured nearly as much as I was stunned, and extremely embarrassed. Jim's high-pitched laughter lilted over the roar of the tractor.

"You're not s'posed to catch 'em!" he hollered. "You're s'posed to stack 'em! Let the kicker pitch it all the way back!"

He hadn't slowed the tractor, and as he shouted, a second bale sailed over my head. Fortunately I was still on one knee, or I would have taken it straight in the face.

"Just stand in the back," Jim yelled, tossing advice over his shoulder. "They'll damn near land where they're supposed to, if you take my meaning!"

Eventually, I did take his meaning. The kicker launched the bales with varying degrees of intensity, sometimes in a smooth, graceful arc, and other times with the speed and precision of a laser beam. I was gradually able to modify my technique, directing the bales in midair so they landed in the proper spot. After a few loads, the rhythm and flow became increasingly satisfying, and the work became easier. By the time Albert came back around noon, we had all three wagons loaded up.

"Looks like y'all made out pretty good without me," he said by way of greeting.

"Yeah," Jim said, climbing down from the tractor. "After that first bale knocked him on his ass, he got the hang of it pretty quick. I reckon you know what a kicker is now, don't you?"

We unhooked the baler and linked the wagons behind the tractor. In another hour and a half, we had unloaded most of the straw into the barn, had a quick lunch, and headed back into the field. By the time the sun had set that evening, we had put away close to one thousand bales.

The weather held dry and fair, and by the third day, we were done. The field yielded more than we expected, nearly three thousand bales. I stumbled to bed that evening utterly exhausted and fell asleep in my clothes, passed out on top of my blankets. The next day I slept straight through my alarm and woke up around noon. Famished, I ate an enormous breakfast, drank several glasses of cold water, and a short time later felt completely refreshed and rejuvenated.

I called in my ad for the straw, and waited.

This time, the third call I received was the jackpot. They wanted everything I had, as soon as possible, and didn't even haggle over the price. It was a contractor working for the National Park Service, and his landscaping company had run out of straw the previous week. They were planting grass seed at a large new park that was opening along the banks of the Shenandoah River and wanted the straw as a mulch cover.

Not only did they request all the straw that I had, they needed an additional 2,500 bales the following month. Sorry, I told them. I wished I could, but I was happy to sell them what I had.

Armed with a genuine opportunity, I phoned my dad in his office in Washington, D.C., and explained the situation.

"So," he deduced after a few moments, "I'm guessing you're going to need my truck."

Indeed. A truck with a working engine would be supremely helpful.

My father's pride and joy was a burgundy-red GMC 1500 long-bed extended-cab pickup, purchased new off the lot. He had installed a custom-modified captain's chair, complete with armrests, drink holder, and electric butt warmer. A year after purchase, the truck was still without a single scratch, door ding, or speck of mud. It was the ultimate tony ride.

"I'll return it just like I found it, Dad. I promise."

"The man said he wanted all of it? Every last bale?" He hesitated. "How many trips will that be?"

"Twelve. A hundred and seventy-five on the trailer, and twenty-five in the back of the truck. Should be able to knock it out in two days."

"Hmm." I could tell he was intrigued. Although my father remained skeptical of my farming ambitions, he had never been one to pass up quick money. "So you get two-fifty a bale, minus a dollar per bale, times twenty-five hundred . . ."

"It's three thousand, seven hundred and fifty dollars," I interjected.

"Gross," he countered, "not net. Still . . . you'll probably end up making a little money off of that." He paused. "So. Not a scratch, right?"

"Not a single scratch."

Two days later, I returned my dad's red behemoth unscathed, the job completed on time. So far, after working on the farm for slightly over a year, I had managed to generate more than ten thousand dollars in cash. After expenses and a new truck engine, however, I had retained precisely zero in profit. In fact, the only thing keeping my personal bills paid was my occasional catering and bartending stints.

As I reflected on my first year on the farm, something felt lacking. Even if I could make additional money selling firewood or straw, those things no longer felt like the right fit. I wasn't concerned about the hard work or the long hours. Instead, the idea was dawning on me that, as a farmer, I should be raising *food* for a living.

It was during one of those straw deliveries, after stopping for lunch at a fast-food restaurant, that I suddenly had a clear sense of where our farm should be headed. For years I had been indiscriminate in my food choices, consuming any and all food that was put in front of me until I was satiated. My vegetarian friends in college marveled at the way I devoured fifty-cent beef burritos, using the microwave at the local 7-Eleven to transform frozen entrees into mouth-scorching infernos of beef and cheese. While they loaded up on chickpeas and rice, I wolfed down sausage strombolis and buffalo wings. Why should they care what I ate? Food was food, and I was a poor, hungry college student. Now in my twenties, I still hadn't stopped to consider what I put in my mouth.

Famished from loading hundreds of bales of straw, I was three bites into a fast-food cheeseburger when something irrevocably shifted for me. After a year of raising my own cattle, tending to their daily needs, and being able to recognize every cow in our herd at a single glance, I suddenly realized how anonymous this cheeseburger was, how little I knew about the animals I was now eating. How had they been raised? How had they been treated? I stared at the gray patty in my hand and realized I had no way of knowing whether one of my own animals was among the thousand different cattle ground into the wan, tepid disc. Now that I was directly involved in the food chain, my ignorance felt deeply hypocritical. As the realization washed over me, the meat turned to ash in my mouth. I crumpled the sandwich in its wrapper and threw it away.

This was the autumn of 1997, and it was the final time I purchased factory-farmed meat. I vowed that if I was ever to eat meat again, I would raise it myself. I would rebuild my grandfather's cattle herd, and I'd raise the animals on grass just like he had done—no corn, no feedlots. If he could do it, then so could we.

I excitedly told my parents of my new ambitions. "Well," my father said, after I had rested my case, "I can't say it's your finest idea, but it sounds more promising than your firewood business already."

"You know," my mom said, "it's funny. I just read about an organic farming conference in West Virginia. It's a long way, almost all the way to Ohio, but they'll be talking about grass-fed livestock and . . ."

"I'm in," I said, not giving her a chance to finish. I had now shifted all my enthusiasm from firewood and straw into raising cattle, and I could hardly wait to get started. A farming conference was the perfect opportunity.

"I was going to mention," she continued, addressing my father, "that Joel is going to be there, teaching classes."

My father's ears perked up immediately. "Salatin will be there? Hmm," he added after a moment's consideration. "Alright then. I'm in, too."

"Hold on," I said. "Really? Aren't you the guy who hates farming?"

"That's just it," he replied. "When you hear Joel talk about farming, it doesn't sound so . . . so completely *miserable*. I can't explain it exactly. But somehow he makes the work seem almost enjoyable."

Farming? Enjoyable? I had never heard those words spoken together in my entire life. Even at its very best, farming seemed like hard, if gratifying, work. That this speaker, Joel, had somehow managed to curtail my father's long-held cynicism was extraordinary in and of itself. Now that I had a year of farming experience under my belt, I was eager to hear what Joel had to say. The next morning we reserved three tickets to the conference and began planning an unexpected detour to the distant hills of Jackson County, West Virginia.

Chapter Five

My parents had met Joel Salatin a decade earlier, in the late 1980s, long before his farming practices became widely touted in the sustainable food movement. A deeply passionate and persuasive advocate of farming, Joel was a speaker at a conference in Morgantown, West Virginia, and my dad, in attendance, had been immediately impressed. The topics of Joel's presentation ranged from direct marketing and self-reliance to sustainable agriculture and food politics. It was just the sort of impassioned polemic that ignited my father's imagination. When he learned that Joel would be giving a second presentation later that evening, he insisted my mother drop whatever she was doing and listen to this self-described "lunatic farmer."

They attended the conference with hopes of learning new strategies, something better than the mainstream notions our hired managers, educated in agriculture schools, had brought to the farm. Inspired, they returned from the conference with several exciting, innovative ideas, but these new suggestions fell on deaf ears. Their managers dismissed all talk of sustainable agriculture, calling it economically unproven and little more than a temporary fad. Discouraged, my parents returned to the grind of their city jobs, their brief dreams of alternative farming drifting into hazy nostalgia.

Even so, Joel had made enough of an impression that, one day, my father decided to take me for a visit to his farm near Staunton, Virginia, a few hours away. All the way there, Dad chattered with an enthusiasm that ran deeply counter to the attitude he normally held about farming. Something about Joel's passion had persuaded him that agriculture might be worth a second look.

At age fifteen, very much into comic books and video games, I surely had mixed feelings about a farm tour. The idea of agriculture interested me, but I was only a sophomore in high school; in my mind, farming was the occupation of old men in overalls. I was still recovering from my hernia surgery and happy to be liberated from farm chores and responsibilities while I convalesced. Besides, I told myself, weren't all farms pretty much the same?

Arriving at Joel's place confirmed my teenage suspicions. It *did* look like a typical Shenandoah Valley farm. Green rolling hills, open meadows, a tidy farmhouse. Functional barns and sheds, warm sunshine illuminating the barnyard. It was a beautiful setting, no doubt. But so was nearly every farm we had passed on the way there.

In fact, in many ways, it looked just like my grandparents' farm. The scattered buildings carried a utilitarian, weathered appearance. There was nothing exciting to see, no shiny tractors, no larger-than-life diesel trucks idling in the parking lot. Although I had no criteria for knowing what a successful farm should look like, my cultural intuition told me it should look flashier, somehow more ostentatious. Perhaps, in my 1980s mind, I was expecting neon lights.

Still, something told me this was my sort of place. Much like my grandparents' farm, with its wide, open pastures and sun-drenched, inviting barnyard, Joel's farm simply felt *clean*.

Growing up as a 4-H'er, I had visited dozens of farms in our area. These farms weren't untidy or disorganized. In fact, many of the operations I visited functioned with such a level of complexity that cleanliness and order were paramount. What made these farms different from Joel's, or my grandparents', was more than just a matter of cleanliness. On a tour, with a dozen other 4-H kids, it was common to catch the odor of chemical fertilizers or sprays wafting on the breeze, or the uniquely pungent and acrid smells of confinement animal manure. As a child, after a couple whiffs of these unpleasant smells, I really couldn't wait for the tour to be finished.

It's not to say these farmers were doing anything misguided, or that something was inherently wrong with their methods of production. Black-and-white absolutes never crossed my mind. Instead, it was more of a visceral reaction, perhaps even on a molecular level, of what "clean" felt like. Clean wasn't a sharp breath of ammonia gas, or rank odors bubbling from a manure lagoon. Even if I had consciously wanted to, I couldn't ignore what my senses were trying to tell me.

On my grandparents' land, farming meant open spaces and towering trees, diverse wildlife and fields of grazing cattle and sheep. I sensed a balance in these methods, where cultivation and wilderness abutted in an intentional compromise. As I walked across the parking lot with my father, whatever was going on here at Joel's farm felt comfortably familiar.

Joel was in the middle of slaughtering a large group of chickens, his shirtsleeves rolled to the elbows. Absorbed in his work, he slowed down only a moment to greet us, and then he spoke over his shoulder as his knife flashed.

The chickens had just come off pasture, he explained, where they had been grazing grass alongside his cattle. His crew consisted of his family and a few summer interns, there to learn his techniques. Later that afternoon, dozens of customers would show up to buy these fresh chickens and take them home to their families.

His processing facility was the definition of modest. The shelter where they worked was an open-air pole building, designed more for shade and protection from rain than anything else. As he worked, Joel said that fresh air and sunshine were his

Six years old, in my grandparents' garden.

greatest allies in sanitation, and they had designed the building to maximize their usefulness.

At one end the chickens waited in crates to be slaughtered; at the other they bobbed fully processed in a bath of ice-cold water. In between, it was carefully organized mayhem.

The birds were killed by hand with a quick slash of the throat. Once drained of blood, they were dunked in a hot-water bath for roughly a minute, a process known as "scalding." This loosened their feathers. As one batch of chickens was being scalded, another batch was being slaughtered. The process was very fluid.

After the hot-water bath came the "plucker." A drum-shaped, clothes-dryer-type of machine, studded with hundreds of three-inch-long rubber "fingers," it sent the scalded carcasses spinning in a mesmerizing free-for-all of steam, feathers, and flesh. Remarkably, when the machine was turned off and the chickens tumbled to a clumsy stop, the birds were picked entirely clean of feathers and undamaged in any way. The person who invented the chicken plucker must have had a fascinating imagination.

Down the line they were passed. Off with their feet, slice slice. On to their wide breasts, removing the small oil gland above the tail. On to their backs, slice slice, to have their entrails removed in three brisk, successive motions. The offal went into waiting buckets to be composted into soil, right there on the farm. When a bird was fully cleaned, it was dunked into cold well water, bagged, and readied for pickup by customers later that afternoon.

Even as a teenager, this process made total sense to me. I could see the logic behind raising food this way and understood why a customer might seek it out. At the time I probably imagined that most farms operated like this. Quite the contrary, as I learned over the ensuing years, this type of farm was nearly the lone exception, not the rule.

As I stood watching the process, my mind whirling from the activity, a little boy stepped up beside me.

"You can't be afraid to do it," he told me matter-of-factly.

"Can't be afraid of what?" I asked. He must have been all of seven or eight years old.

"To kill them," he said. "You can't be afraid of the blood and stuff like that. You've just got to do it."

Being psychoanalyzed by a seven-year-old made me feel slightly defensive. "I'm not afraid," I replied. "I'm just watching. I've never done it before."

"Well," he added, precociously, "you've got to start sometime."

Joel passed by with three cleaned chickens in each hand and eased them into the ice-water bath.

"That's my son, Daniel," he said with a nod. "Daniel's a big help around here. He already knows how to do most of this stuff. Don't you?"

His son nodded. "Now," Daniel piped, leaving no doubt that his conversation with me was concluded, "it's time to get back to work." He strode, as much as a seven-year-old can stride, over to the crated chickens and began methodically placing them into the stainless-steel kill cones.

It was, very clearly, business as usual for this family farm. Each of the members hummed along separately, with the assembled whole creating a synchronized harmony. The process was smoothly practiced and polished, just short of theatrical. It wouldn't have surprised me if they sold tickets for people to come and see their show. Watching them work, I realized that my father and I were still very much a part of the audience.

Now, nine years later, my parents and I pulled into Cedar Lakes Conference Center in Jackson County, West Virginia. Joel, it turned out, was the keynote speaker at the conference. His son, Daniel, now a teenager, was presenting his own seminar on raising rabbits, a business he started himself. Clearly, they had kept busy in the intervening years.

My parents and I headed over to the banquet hall for the evening's presentation. We found our placards and introduced ourselves to other attendees seated around us. A general buzz of optimistic conversation filled the packed room.

I shook hands with the man on my left, a nondescript, seventy-something farmer type with a balding head of white hair. He wore a plaid flannel shirt and suspenders and introduced himself as Bob. As we ate, a man named James, seated across from us, told us about his career as a tree farmer.

My forestry-trained father forged an immediate connection with James, and together they spent the majority of the dinner relating anecdotes about woodlot management. Next to me, farmer Bob ate quietly, occasionally smiling at a joke my father told, or listening politely as James elaborated about lumber price fluctuations. The talk was pleasant enough, but not what I had hoped for. By the end of the meal, I was unequivocally bored with boards.

Finally, Joel took the podium.

"It's my honor to be your keynote speaker this evening," he began, "and an even greater pleasure to present a special unannounced guest. I was just telling my son, Daniel, how delighted I am that he'll get to meet a true American icon. When I was a young man, I once had the opportunity to meet the famous Colonel Sanders. Obviously," he said, adjusting his glasses and smiling, "you can imagine what an impression that left on a chicken man like myself." A twitter of laughter rippled through the crowd.

"So, I'm delighted that my son will get to meet a similar legend tonight, and brush shoulders with restaurant royalty. Without further ado, may I introduce a direct marketer extraordinaire, and an inspiration to all of us. Ladies and gentlemen, Mr. Bob Evans, founder of the eponymous restaurants."

Everyone in the room, myself and my parents included, looked around the banquet hall, trying to locate the celebrity in our midst. I was turned toward the front door, expecting the restaurant mogul to walk through to some sort of fanfare, when I noticed that, next to me, old farmer Bob had risen, carefully pushed in his chair, and was now walking toward the podium. Joel smiled broadly, vigorously shaking his hand. As the crowd applauded, I was just adjusting to the fact that I had been sitting next to a world-famous millionaire for the past hour.

Bob Evans adjusted the microphone on the podium.

"Thanks for inviting me. It's a true honor. You know, it's great to look out on a crowd of this size and see all the farmers and young people here starting out, heading down a direct-marketing path.

"When I first started this business, I was like many of you in this room. Most folks don't know this, but I got started by selling my sausages right here, in West Virginia. I had a little refrigerated truck, and I'd load it full of sausage and drive from Ohio over into West Virginia, visiting the coal-mining towns, and selling to the stores where the miners and their families shopped. I did that for many years. I've always been grateful to the folks around here, for believing in my product. They helped my business get off the ground."

This was surreal. Bob Evans started his business by selling sausages, door to door, in West Virginia? I could hardly believe my ears. It wasn't exactly firewood or straw, but nor was it a total stretch by comparison. Still, from selling sausages from the back of a truck to owning five hundred restaurants? It couldn't be possible.

"Now," he continued, "I'm especially encouraged that so many of you came to learn about grass-fed beef, and raising animals on pasture. I've believed for a long time that grass-finishing is how successful farms will operate in the future, and I'm delighted that you're about to get a full weekend learning about it. There are some real experts here, so be sure to take advantage of it."

The crowd murmured in approval, but I was still wrapping my mind around the situation. A restaurant millionaire showing up at an out-of-the-way conference and preaching agricultural sustainability?

This man was either truly ahead of his time or this was some sort of elaborate hoax. Perhaps a celebrity imitator was part of the evening's entertainment? Part of me sat waiting for the punch line.

"I'll conclude by saying that I'm very happy to be here, to see so many people interested in the future of agriculture. As a farmer myself, I consider the company of fellow farmers to be the best company in the world. I'll be around for the next hour or so if any of you have any questions you'd like to ask."

He bowed his head with a little nod and stepped away from the podium. The crowd applauded and gave a standing ovation. If that was the punch line, I told myself, then somehow I had missed the joke.

During the next two days, my parents and I split up and attended every seminar that was offered. We passed one another in the hallways between classes, giving a thumbs-up or a thumbs-down, trading notes, providing feedback. My father appeared reinvigorated. He had just attended a seminar about growing native plants, and he was almost giddy at the thought of growing ginseng in our woodlot. Ginseng? I thought to myself. Where had *that* come from? Even if it was only fleeting, I was happy to see the fire return to my father's eyes.

As the conference wore on, the speakers who captured my interest were the ones who told stories of direct marketing. Even though I had already struck out on my own a little, these farmers were light-years ahead of me. Many of them were selling out of everything that they were able to produce, with customer demand craving more than they could supply. Of course, especially interesting to me were the farmers who raised livestock and sold meat, eggs, and dairy products directly to customers. This was how I envisioned our farm's future—a cycle of sustainable production, clean food, and motivated customers. I spent the final day attending only these presentations.

I listened, engrossed with the speakers' personal experiences. As questions and ideas bounced around in my head, I jotted down notes in a longhand scrawl, dividing my thoughts into two basic categories:

RAISING ANIMALS

—*Stay with the cattle we already have, or raise different breed/ species?*

—*How big/old do they have to be?*

—*Is one type/age/sex of animal better than another?*

—*How many animals should I be raising?*

—*What about veal? Can it be free-range?*

—*Does our farm have enough pasture? Do I need to make more hay?*

—*How do I load and transport? What's the best way to handle them en route?*

—*What about laying hens/eggs? Dairy? Pigs/sheep/turkeys, etc.?*

SELLING MEAT

—*Who/what is my market?*

—*How many different cuts of meat?*

—*Regulations (health department . . . county/state/federal)?*

—*Frozen or fresh?*

    —*what kind of refrigeration will I need?*

    —*different types of freezers, chest/walk-in?*

—*How do I find a butcher?*

    —*figuring out which butchers are the best?*

    —*are there different types of butcher shops?*

—Transporting meat from butcher back to farm?

—refrigerated truck?

—does the butcher provide this service?

—Farm store/restaurants/farmers' markets/CSAs/Internet?

Each question, reliably, led to additional questions. As the hours passed, I was persuaded by the speakers' enthusiasm, yet I couldn't imagine even a rudimentary strategy to begin doing what they were already doing. As the final presenter concluded his talk, I was the first to raise my hand.

"So . . . how did you start? I mean, I totally buy into everything you've said. But what's the first thing you need to do to get going?"

"How do you start?" he repeated. "That's the most difficult, and the easiest, part of the whole ordeal. You start," he said, "simply by starting."

A few snorts and guffaws emanated from the crowd. The speaker held up his hands in mock self-defense.

"Now, now. Wait a minute. I know that probably sounds esoteric, or even cliché, but I mean it. It really *is* the hardest and the easiest part at the same time. Let me explain.

"It's hard," he continued, picking up a piece of chalk, "because of words like these." He wrote with bold strokes on the chalkboard: *Fear. Uncertainty. Doubt.*

He turned back to us. "What else?"

"What other people think," someone suggested.

"Yes. Other people's opinions, especially our peers in the agricultural community. It's amazing how others can hold us back from trying something new. Any more?"

"Inexperience."

"Good. And the funny thing about inexperience is . . . we're usually the ones keeping ourselves from getting the experience! Next?"

"How about feeling completely confused, lost, and clueless?" I volunteered.

Several people laughed, a few raising their hands as if to say, "Me too."

The farmer laughed as well. "I can certainly understand *that* feeling." He gestured over his shoulder. "So, look. Those are the hard parts with getting started. Now comes the easy part. Let me see a show of hands. How many of you are here because you love to farm, or love the idea of being a farmer?"

Every one of us held up a hand. The speaker took a long appraisal of the results.

"Keep those hands up a minute longer. Look around the room. *That,*" he said, "is what makes getting started so easy. It's because we genuinely love what we do.

"How many people can say that? How many places in the world can you go, and ask that question, and have every single person hold up his or her hand? And you guys didn't even have to think about it for a second."

It was a powerful observation. As we slowly lowered our hands, he picked up the chalk again.

"*We Love What We Do,*" he wrote, then underlined it.

"When we believe in this," he said, tapping the chalk several times against the blackboard, "then it makes all of this 'hard' stuff seem a lot less important."

He looked at me. "So, back to your question. You already know the easy part, that you love to farm. Now, you just start by starting. When you do that, the hard stuff gradually falls by the wayside."

"So what you're saying is, once you start, it just sort of takes care of itself?" I asked.

The farmer smiled enigmatically. "Yup. More or less."

For reasons I couldn't explain, I believed him. Later that afternoon, I met up with my parents, and we packed our belongings in the car.

"You know," I said, after we had been on the road for an hour, "I've been thinking about our farm's name."

"We've *always* been called Smithfield Farm," my mother quickly interjected, a defensive note in her voice. She had been born a Smith, and considered the family name a particular point of pride. "Even after they moved the farm in the early 1800s, after the original farmhouse burned down, they kept that name. You know, there's a street in Winchester named 'Smithfield,' where the first farm used to be."

"I know," I said. "I'm not saying we should change the name of the farm. But if we start our own label, I think we should call it something different. Something that says a little more about who we are, what we're trying to do."

"How about 'Pritchard's Pastured Products'?" my father suggested, an eager participant in this new game. "No, wait, better yet: 'Farmer Forrest's Free-Range . . . Free-Range . . .'" He searched for the right alliteration, his mouth silently enunciating words as he drove. "Hmm. Have you ever considered raising pheasants?" he asked at last, apparently at a loss.

"I was thinking 'Smith Meadows.' It's simple, and to the point. It's kind of a combination of the past and the future."

"'Smith Meadows,'" my mom repeated, testing the sound. "You know, it never occurred to me that we should have a different name. But now that you say it out loud, 'Smith Meadows' has a nice ring to it."

As the words lingered on the air, I liked the sound of it, too. I leaned back in my seat, watching the blur of passing scenery, my head swimming with ideas. A few miles later, Dad suddenly spoke up.

"'Forrest's Finest Filets?'"

"No, Dad."

"How about 'Forrest's Famous Farm-Fresh Flavors?'"

"Edward." My mother shook her head in the passenger seat. "Please."

He drove on in silence for a few minutes. "So. Plain old 'Smith Meadows,' huh?"

"I think so," I said.

"Okay," he replied, his inner poet doffing his cap in concession. "But if you ever change your mind, then I get to pick the next name."

I knew I couldn't allow that to happen; there was already too much suffering in the world. From that moment forward we became known as Smith Meadows. It was a name that would endure.

Chapter Six

As we navigated the winding roads home, my parents reminded me I had more marketing experience than I realized.

From the age of twelve until well into high school, I had spent several weeks each summer picking sweet corn and selling it along the highway of the local truck-stop diner parking lot. Each year, along the outermost edge of our expansive family garden, we planted a dozen rows of sweet corn. These were long, finely kerneled, creamy white ears, so delicious they were almost as good raw as they were boiled or roasted. My sister and I would race, choosing our rows and trying to fill our burlap sack before the other. Several years older than me, and with seasons more practice, my sister always won.

We constructed a large plywood A-frame signboard, and painted on it the words *Sweet Corn "Silver Queen" $3/Dozen* in large green and yellow letters. Occasionally, with the tractor trailers breezing past at sixty-five miles per hour, an errant gust would topple the sign, leaving it spinning and skittering on the dusty gravel of the parking lot.

People routinely told us it was the best sweet corn they had ever tasted. And looking back, why wouldn't it have been? It was picked between three and four in the afternoon and available for sale by the five o'clock rush hour. We usually sold out well before the sun set around eight. By then, most people had already eaten it for dinner. Our corn was the definition of fresh and local.

Sometimes, when sales were slow, I held an ear of corn in each hand and stood right beside the highway, waiving them like an air traffic controller's flashlights. As a car came toward me, I'd dramatically point the corn at them, then at the sign, then back again, enthusiastically directing them into the parking lot. The brown, silken allure of the corn's tassels must have been effective, because I persuaded many smiling drivers to stop this way. Customers picked through the corn we had spread across the tailgate, and they were always sent home with a free bonus ear as a lagniappe of gratitude.

My sister and I used this money to buy our back-to-school clothes each autumn. I purchased my first pair of floral Jams shorts this way, as well as a Vision Street Wear T-shirt. For a farm kid from West Virginia, I was officially styling.

I recalled that my parents had direct marketing experience, as well. Despite his adamant protestations about the farming life, every so often my dad temporarily relented. Throwing his hands in the air, he'd announce that he was finished with his grueling commute once and for all, insisting that even the cash-strapped life of a farmer must be better than the Washington, D.C., rat race.

These episodes were few and far between, but one in particular stood out. Frustrated that yet another farm manager had failed to turn a profit, my dad decided that our next enterprise would be to grow free-range chickens and butcher them ourselves. Evidently, free-range chicken farming was his self-prescribed therapy for gridlock on the Capital Beltway. Sitting in endless traffic does strange things to people.

Perhaps our visit to Joel's farm convinced him he could emulate the methods he witnessed there, or perhaps he just had a chronic entrepreneurial bug, an itch that needed to be scratched every so often. It's even possible that he wanted pocket money to buy his own pair of XXL flowered Jams. Whatever inspiration seized him, one thing is clear: This episode of our family farming experience is unanimously remembered as the most harebrained, ill-conceived, and poorly executed enterprise we were ever wrangled into.

On a small farm, plans always start out innocently enough. Farmers cultivate their dreams in winter, when nothing else can grow. By the time spring rolls around, they are changing the oil in the motor, cleaning mouse nests out of the planter, and preparing for the first day of spring when the air is just barely warm and the ground firm enough to support tractor tires. Innovation begins with a seed, a sapling, or a sprout.

My father's agricultural vignette began serenely, too, with the arrival of baby chickens. Nothing on any farm, anywhere, is quite so adorable, cuddly-looking, and downright lovable as a fluffy, bouncy, peeping yellow chick. As a grown man, I feel no compunction in writing this. They are, without a doubt, the epitome of cute.

So it seemed like a great idea when, through the assistance of the local post office, we received a hundred of these frenetic puffballs with legs. We placed them in the safe confines of a large, empty livestock trough in our garage, carving a space between our old bicycles, stepladders, spare tires, and garden tools. I spent hours watching them dash from one end of the tub to the other, tumbling over themselves, hopping and bobbing, flapping futilely with dander fluff for wings. They were mesmerizing to watch, completely absorbed in their own busy world.

After less than a week, they grew wing feathers, and a few days later, petite tail feathers distinguished themselves. Their legs thickened from toothpicks to pencil-widths. By week three, they were looking distinctively chickenlike, with supple red combs crowning their white-feathered heads. They had also nearly outgrown their home.

My dad and I spent an afternoon building a bottomless pen where they could live outside on pasture. Looking more or less like an enormous shoe box turned upside down, the sides were made of chicken wire to admit plenty of light and fresh air, and the top was plywood capped with metal sheathing, to keep the rain out. The "floor" was all pasture. This is where our chickens would live and eat, safe from harsh weather and predators. Their carpet would be clean, nourishing grass and clover.

As the chickens grazed the fresh vegetation at their feet, they would litter the ground with their manure. By moving the pen twice a day, the chickens would fertilize the soil as they went, and verdant pasture would always be in front of them. We knew that, with enough chickens, some farms successfully fertilized entire fields without ever using a tractor.

It all sounded great, and I was more than willing to help with the carpentry project. My dad gave me measurements, twelve-by-twelve feet, and I cut boards and stapled wire to his specifications. By the time the sun had set, we had built our first pastured chicken pen.

There was only one problem. It was too heavy. Way, way too heavy. I stood at one end, my dad at the other, and we tried to pick it up. Dad managed to lift his end off the ground, but my sixteen-year-old arms still resembled chicken wings. If this was going to be a two-person job, my father would have to replicate himself.

"Well," he said, hands on hips, "looks like we'll need to make some modifications."

We started again the next morning, taking off the metal roof and removing the layer of plywood reinforcement. That was a start, but still not enough. Next, we eliminated the heavy four-inch base and replaced it with lighter lumber. Now I could lift it, but I could move it only with wobbly, encumbered steps. If I tripped even slightly, I was likely to drop the whole thing on my foot. Finally, we removed the solid wood back and cut it down by half to serve as a windbreak. This did the trick.

Twenty bent nails, six improperly cut two-by-fours, a jammed staple gun, three hammered fingers, and two full days of my life went into making that pen. We practiced raising and lowering it in a "one-two-three-lift!" cadence, Dad walking blindly backward, me stumbling forward wheelbarrow-style. After much effort, we synchronized the rhythm. That wood-and-wire chicken pen became our personal embodiment of blood, sweat, and tears.

It was all worth it once we finally placed the chickens inside. Watching them in the old water trough had been fascinating, but seeing them gobbling up grass, scratching the dirt for insects, and sunning themselves in the clover was absolutely sublime. My father studied the scene, his arms crossed, a hint of a smile playing across his lips. He appeared to be enjoying the moment nearly as much as the chickens themselves were.

By the next morning they had munched down the entire sward of pasture, leaving behind a sheet of manure in their wake. It was time already to move the enclosure. Dad and I flexed our muscles, bent at the knees, and got ready for our first move onto fresh grass.

Looking back, I'm not exactly sure what we were thinking. Did we imagine the chickens would remain under the shelter, marching in a square-shaped formation as we lifted the pen over their heads? I had never stopped to consider how I would react if a giant hand lifted the roof off my house as I was inside, reading a book, or cooking macaroni and cheese. Suffice it to say, I probably wouldn't stick around to find out which way my roof was headed, much less jog beneath it as it floated through the sky. Instead, much like the chickens did, I would positively freak out.

We no sooner raised the pen than chickens were running everywhere. They squawked, startled and terrified, fleeing as fast as they could, desperate to get away from their levitating house. In seconds, nearly all one hundred of them were out, many of them headed for the camouflage of taller grass along the edge of the pasture. Seeing what was happening, we hastily lowered the pen, only to realize we had pinned at least three chickens under the base. Utterly flustered, we raised it again, freeing the trapped birds. They dashed into the tall grass with their brethren, apoplectic with fear but apparently unharmed.

"Quick," Dad shouted, "let's get this thing moved before those chickens end up in Berryville! Ready? One, two, three!"

We both lifted for a third time. I took approximately two frantic steps before my feet slipped on the thick icing of manure. Losing my balance, I dropped my end, sailed parallel with the ground, and landed with a splat in no less than a hundred fresh chicken turds.

"Oh, gross!" I stood, my chest and pants absolutely painted with poop. "Aww, man! This . . . this *sucks!*"

"Well," Dad said, unable to resist a pun, "it's a shitty job, but somebody's got to do it."

I wicked a glob of manure from the corner of my eye, intentionally flicking it in his direction. "Can summer vacation be over now? Please?"

More than an hour later, we accounted for every last chicken, my dad muttering poultry-related insults as he carried them in ones and twos by their hind legs. We gradually adapted our method of moving the pen by lifting it only about three inches off the ground. This way, the momentarily panicked chickens safely bounced off the wire like balls in a pinball machine while we slowly guided them to their new destination. We built a second pen, to give the birds more room. Day by day, our skills improved, and the chickens began to grow. Now, we needed to find some hungry customers.

I spent hours that summer at the public library, using the community computer to create a trifold brochure. On it, I touted the merits of our pastured chickens, how fresh, delicious, and nourishing they would be, the sustainable story of how we raised them, and the ease and convenience by which they could be purchased. I printed these out on taupe-colored paper, for what felt like an earthy touch. The final third of the brochure featured a tear-off order form to be sent back to us with the customer's name, phone number, and the number of chickens desired.

This was in the early nineties, well before printers were common household fixtures, so I saved it to a floppy disk and took it to our local copy center. I ordered about two hundred and fifty copies, at five cents apiece. For the next few weeks, I dropped these off at health food stores, farmers' markets, fitness centers, and yoga studios. I tried to think of places where people went to eat healthy, be healthy, or become healthy. These were the people, I figured, who were more inclined to buy their food straight from the farm.

The birds continued to grow. In fact, they grew beyond expectations, flourishing on the verdant clover and bluegrass springing from our farm's fertile soil. An old photo we have from those days shows mature chickens with red top clover growing *above* their heads, allowing them to nibble the nutrient-rich leaves and seeds without so much as craning their necks. By always having fresh grass in front of them, they also remained immaculately clean and healthy. If there was a more delicious, sustainable, or humanely raised free-range chicken to be found in our area, you could have knocked me over with a feather.

As the days passed, we wondered if we would be overwhelmed with requests. If demand outstripped supply, we could always start a second batch, creating a waiting list for later in the summer. Just to be safe, we placed another call to the hatchery, hedging our bets by ordering only fifty additional birds.

With two weeks to go before the first slaughter date, we checked the mail each day for orders. None had arrived, but I wasn't worried. I ordered a second print run of two hundred and fifty brochures, and made my rounds again. Nearly all the original pamphlets were gone; clearly, people were picking them up. It would be only a matter of time.

An early flock of free-range chickens on pasture.

With a week to go, however, not only was the mailbox still empty, but the phone hadn't rung, either. What did people want, we asked ourselves. Pre-stamped envelopes?

Slaughter day arrived, and we had amassed exactly zero orders. The birds were mouthwateringly plump, and there were far too many for us to eat by ourselves. Moreover, fifty more were already on the way, and not a customer was to be seen. At the end of the slaughter, my mom, dad, sister, and I looked at one another, blood-splattered and covered in feathers, and wondered where it had all gone wrong.

As we cleaned up, part of me still hoped to hear the sound of crunching gravel in the driveway, a vanload of customers in the parking lot, each requesting ten chickens apiece. It was not to be. One by one, we carefully placed the bagged and dressed chickens into a large chest freezer as we brainstormed about a backup plan. Dad was the first to speak.

"Well, I could always try selling them at work. You know, take four or five at a time, and go cubicle to cubicle."

Cubicle to cubicle? Somewhere between demoralized and exhausted, we laughed a little too loudly. Now *that,* we decided, was truly the modern manifestation of the door-to-door salesman.

My father had recently changed jobs and now worked at the US Information Agency, as a contractor for Voice of America. Hundreds of people worked in his building. Selling chickens cubicle to cubicle . . . it sounded crazy to say it out loud, but it was more than we had going for us at the moment. If it didn't send people screaming for the elevators, we figured, it probably stood as good a chance of succeeding as anything else. It was settled.

Each morning for several weeks, Dad rode the commuter train with a cooler full of frozen chickens on his lap. Arriving at Union Station, he toted them onto the Metro, trundled them up and down escalators, and navigated them along crowded sidewalks. There, in his office building on Third Street, he sold them chicken by chicken, cubicle by cubicle, day after day, week after week. His coworkers were bemused, sometimes skeptical, and they frequently flat-out turned him down. Still, he never came home with any chickens, only money.

The people who tried them absolutely raved about their flavor and quality, and they often convinced their office mates to go out on a limb and try one for themselves. They brought leftovers into work the following day, sharing a piece of cold fried chicken or a chicken salad sandwich, inspiring their intrepid chicken monger to keep the deliveries coming. Our chickens tasted like the ones their grandmothers used to make, they told my dad. When was he bringing more?

My father was motivated by these delicious bribes, and sales went so well that we moved all of our birds this way for the rest of the summer. We never received a single order from any of the pamphlets we passed out. Evidently, taupe-colored paper wasn't getting the job done.

My father, naturally, quickly became known as the Chicken Man. People stopped him in the hallways, or leaned into his cubicle, offering a good-natured ribbing.

"Morning, Chicken Man! Cock-a-doodle-doo!"

"Everybody look! Chicken Man's crossing the office . . . now he's on the other side!"

"Hey, Chicken Man! When are you going to give the supervisor the bird?"

My father, who had grown up in the city and had spent a sizable portion of his life avoiding farm work, had unintentionally become a farming mascot for many of these people. It seemed like no matter how much he wanted to disassociate himself from a life on the farm, he kept getting pulled back in.

One morning the train conductor was unable to contain his curiosity any longer. He punched my father's ticket and then asked him what he had been carrying in the large cooler all summer.

"Six whole, frozen chickens, of course," my father replied, as though it were the most natural response in the world. "Would you like to buy one?"

The conductor returned the ticket stub wordlessly, stared at my dad for quite some time, and shook his head. Evidently, not everyone was familiar with traveling chicken salesmen. From that day forward, the two men avoided eye contact as much as possible.

Chapter Seven

I t probably goes without saying that there's no three-credit course
at any major university for selling meat off the back of a pickup
truck. Yet, during the weeks following the conference, this was precisely what my parents and I hashed out. I would buy a small chest
freezer, put it on the back of my little Toyota, and sell frozen, free-
range, grass-fed beef. The details of where, when, or to whom we
would sell were still complete unknowns, but we all agreed on one
thing: We could rule out the local train conductor.

An examination of a half-dozen local farmers' markets revealed
that no one was selling grass-fed meat in our local vicinity. In fact, no
one was selling meat of *any* kind at these markets, leaving me without
a model I could imitate or modify as I started my own operation. What
seemed like such a great concept—providing customers with local,
organic meat—either hadn't caught on yet or wasn't such a superb
idea after all. I had no way of knowing it at the time, but in 1997 the
excitement I felt was just barely penetrating the consciousness of the
food world at large.

I asked the manager of the Berryville farmers' market if they'd
be interested in having our free-range meat at their market. Just give
a week's notice, she replied enthusiastically, and she'd be happy to
make space for us. Her response immediately boosted my spirits.

A few weeks later I visited Nancy in North Carolina and told her of my new plans.

"I think I've finally found a direction," I began. "I'll sell meat at the farmers' market. The operation will be totally transparent. Organic. Natural."

"It sounds great," she nodded. "But how are you going to do it? You don't have any freezers, or a refrigerated truck, or . . ."

"Money," I said, finishing her thought. "I know. I still have a lot to think about. But I've got cattle, and lots of pasture. Now, I've got my first farmers' market. It's a start."

Later that evening, Nancy's stepfather, an eighty-year-old Venetian named Luigi, described what he had recently seen at the markets in his native Italy.

"In Veneto," he explained, in his robust Italian accent, "they have the big trucks, everything automatic. Is fantastic."

No Italian story would be complete without dramatic hand gestures, and he wove a tapestry of emphasis in the air between us as he spoke.

"The farmer load the truck [lifting and placing motions], drive to the market [hands on imaginary wheel], push the button [a meaty index finger jabbed at an imaginary target], and boom! Is all done. Automatic." He leaned back, his fingers laced comfortably behind his head, a faraway look in his eyes. "Yes," he concluded wistfully, "is fantastic."

"Wait a minute," I said, intruding upon his reverie. I understood the loading and the driving, but the button-pushing part had lost me. "What do you mean, 'automatic'?"

"Is all automatic," he repeated, as though this clarified everything. My future father-in-law had mastered the skill of regarding me as if I had cannoli filling for brains if I didn't understand something the first time.

"What is to not understand? You push the button [again, the hand gestures, but this time a little faster, and more forcefully], boom, out come the canopy for shade. Another button, boom, table. Third

Father-in-law Luigi Contin, in his hometown of Venice.

button, ice chest for display. All electric refrigeration. When market is done, you push button again, it all go away, *tutti*. Is fantastic."

Wait a minute, now it was three buttons? This was getting complicated. I glanced sidelong at Nancy, who acknowledged the inconsistency with a subtle squint of her eyes. We prudently kept this observation to ourselves.

A truck like that would immediately solve a lot of my logistical problems, I conceded. There were plenty of stories of tents somersaulting through market on a windy day; a turnkey type of marketing truck would be amazingly helpful. Although tempted, I refrained from asking if the driver's seat came with an automatic eject button.

Refrigeration, of course, was a major concern. I needed a way to keep the food cold on-site, especially on a hot summer day, and having built-in electricity would be a real problem solver. At a minimum, I should see one of these trucks in person to get a basic understanding of how other farmers used them.

"So," I asked, "where's the best place to see one of these trucks?"

He held up his hands. "Oh, nothing around here. No, is only in Italy. And expensive . . . poof!" He shook his hands three or four times, as though flicking water from his fingertips. "Expensive, these trucks. Like you wouldn't believe. No," he concluded sadly, "I dream for you this truck, but is terrible expensive to import."

That settled that, I told myself. At least I wouldn't have to worry about getting all those buttons mixed up.

Returning home, I took stock of my available resources. As far as meat storage was concerned, my parents owned two cavernous, but already filled to capacity, chest freezers they kept in their garage. The freezers were our family's version of the Bermuda Triangle; food mysteriously vanished into their frozen, uncertain depths, often never to be seen again. Only the very uppermost four to six inches of ice-rimmed packages ever received any real attention.

I devoted one afternoon to digging through the contents of the freezers, organizing my excavations into two piles. The first group was stuff that I could actually recognize as food: pizzas, half-eaten boxes of ice cream, homegrown beans and corn with pack dates less than five years old. The second group was things that were so mangled, freezer-burned, and shapeless that they might have been frozen prehistoric monkey heads for all I could tell.

Pile one was neatly reorganized and placed back in the freezer. Pile two went straight to the compost heap. When I was done, I had secured an entire freezer for my own use.

My second and only other significant asset was the very truck I had gutted and rebuilt just months before. My first idea was to put the empty chest freezer on the back and hold it in place with a ratchet strap. I imagined loading the freezer full of meat, plugging it in overnight, and driving the whole kit and caboodle to a farmers' market the following morning. The frozen meat would certainly stay cold enough until I made it back home later that afternoon.

A few tape measurements later, I quickly discerned this wasn't going to work. The bed of my truck was far too small to accommodate such a large freezer, leaving one end hanging alarmingly over the edge of my tailgate. Moreover, there was no remaining room for a tent, table, or anything else I might need at the market. I realized there was no way to make the large chest freezer work, at least not on the back of the truck. It was time to go shopping.

In the months following the truck repair, I had saved about four hundred dollars from my various catering gigs, and I decided to use this money for a new, smaller freezer. A seven-cubic-foot freezer, I learned, fits perfectly across the back window of a Toyota pickup truck. I wiggled it into its new location, strapped it in, and plugged it up to an extension cord. Mobile refrigeration, check. The plan was all coming together.

For a twenty-three-year-old with a new freezer, a rebuilt truck engine, and a driver's license, there was really only one thing left to do: take it out for a joy ride. I didn't make it very far.

In hindsight, I never considered wind resistance when I positioned the freezer on the back of the truck. Like most people, I had experienced the "umbrella phenomenon," when a gust of wind changes directions so abruptly that one's umbrella is turned inside out. Needless to say, as long as the umbrella is always pointed the right way, everything remains more or less hunky-dory.

I was sailing along in my truck, the new engine and transmission beneath the hood, a sparkling white freezer on the back. Brimming with pride, it was with equal parts disbelief and resignation that, at sixty miles per hour, I heard a loud *whumph!* directly behind me. From my side-view mirror, I witnessed the lid of my new freezer spinning through the air, flipping and twisting like an Olympic gymnast before landing with a belly flop against the highway asphalt.

I had inadvertently placed the freezer lid directly in the line of wind shear, instead of turning it the other way and allowing the air to cascade harmlessly over the hinges. Behind me, cars swerved around the obstacle, spraying gravel and dust as they careened onto the unpaved shoulder. I made a hasty U-turn and rescued the lid moments before an eighteen-wheeler would have pulverized it into oblivion. Wedging it into the cab, I spent the rest of the afternoon repairing the bent and twisted hinges as best I could.

It took the better part of the evening, but I finally repaired it close to its original condition. Aside from an arabesque of abraded paint and a large crimp down the middle, I had dodged a catastrophe right out of the gate; I counted my blessings that no one had been injured. After raising and closing the lid a few times, I acknowledged that the job wasn't perfect, but it was serviceable. Just to be sure, I left it plugged in so I could check the temperature the next morning.

That night, it poured. As a grass farmer, nothing is as important to the vitality of my pastures as a good, soaking rain. I'm even superstitious about ever saying there's been "too much rain," thinking I might somehow jinx the farm into another drought. But two inches of rain on a lush, well-managed pasture is one thing. Two inches of rain falling into the back of a pickup truck, equipped with a plugged-in freezer, is another matter entirely.

During the night, the bed liner had trapped every last drop and, due to the slight downward pitch of the truck, transformed the deluge into a five-inch-deep puddle. When I checked on the freezer the next morning, the motor was less than a centimeter away from being submerged. The plucky little freezer hummed along indifferently, oblivious to the threat of its own electrocution. I hastily unplugged the extension cord, drained the water, and wondered what could go wrong next.

Inside the freezer, a form-fitting, three-inch-thick rectangle of solid ice had materialized at the bottom. The dented freezer lid had acted as a funnel, redirecting water along the smooth metal top and draining it into the interior. I imagined myself at the farmers' market, opening the lid for a T-bone steak and finding my entire inventory ensconced in a solid chunk of ice.

"Here's your T-bone," I'd say. "And it comes with these seventy-five other cuts of meat. That'll be five hundred dollars. Would you like a complimentary stick for your meatcicle?"

With my savings now exhausted, I knew the rest of my market setup would have to be extremely modest. An extensive scavenger hunt through my family's disorganized basement yielded an aluminum folding table and a red-checkered tablecloth. I also found a wooden chicken silhouette (onto which I affixed an index card with my egg price) and an ancient, rusting set of kitchen scales. These scales, I imagined, would tie the ensemble together, creating a feng shui of true farmers' market professionalism. My dad sarcastically suggested all I had left to do was to put on my cowboy hat and have the customers organize themselves into a neat and orderly line.

As soon as my market stall was complete, I turned my full attention back to the farm. The terrible drought we'd endured when I returned home from college had convinced me that pasture was the best way for our farm to thrive. Far more resilient than corn and other row crops, grass practically grew itself; once established, it appeared as if by magic each spring and spread its seeds on the wind. With such minimal costs, and so little capital to work with, the price was undoubtedly right.

The following spring, in 1998, I implemented rotational grazing for the first time, cobbling together information I had gleaned from books and lessons I had brought home from the conference. Each morning I divided our preexisting pastures in half, or even into quarters, allowing the cattle to graze an area for only a day or two before moving them onto fresh grass. These paddock shifts gave the cattle all the grass and clover they needed while allowing weeks of pasture regrowth as the animals rotated their way across the farm. The system was incredibly simple: All it took was some reusable, portable fencing and a movable watering trough.

In the past, some areas of our farm had been overgrazed, eaten down to the dirt, while other areas had hardly been grazed at all. The decrepit fences separating the fields were mostly in poor repair, and sometimes nonexistent. When I arrived back at the farm from college, our three hundred and fifty acres was basically one gigantic pasture. Everywhere I looked, dusty cow paths crisscrossed the hills, leading to the stream bottoms where the cattle drank. By the middle of summer, under relentless grazing pressure, the close-cropped grass simmered beneath the hot sun. The cattle stood in the creek all afternoon, taking solace from the unrelenting heat.

By dividing our fields, the pasture now had time to rest and recuperate. Long blades of grass shaded the soil, keeping the surface cool and moist. The dusty paths, created from cows wandering from one end of the farm to the other, gradually disappeared. I fenced off the creek and installed remote watering lines. Cow manure, rich in nutrients for the soil, now stayed on the pasture instead of ending up in the stream, bound for the Chesapeake Bay. Slowly, month by month, the land began to heal itself.

Decades of farming mismanagement, practices that stripped vital nutrients from our soils, couldn't be corrected overnight. Slowly, I began to understand that nature didn't give a hoot about our debilitating financial crises, our frantic sense of urgency. These problems could be solved, but only through patience. Plant roots regrew at precisely the rate they were supposed to, and grass-fed cattle grew at their own pace as well. I was determined to rebuild the soil naturally, avoiding the world of chemical shortcuts. This kind of farming was the very definition of "hurry up and wait."

The amount of knowledge I was absorbing was more than I ever imagined. How had my grandfather done it? Beyond raising cattle, he had also successfully managed a thousand-acre orchard. In two years' time, my most memorable accomplishments had been blowing up my truck and nearly destroying a brand-new freezer.

That summer I catered a party where several other farmers were in attendance. Between serving trays of bacon-wrapped scallops and olive tapenade bruschetta, I found myself talking with an older couple who raised cattle.

"I was wondering. Do you guys ever let your cattle graze your hay fields?"

The farmer looked at me as though I were batty. "Why would I do that? So they could eat all my hay?"

"No, so they can fertilize it in between cuttings."

"Between cuttings? If we let them graze it, there wouldn't *be* any cuttings."

I was probably blushing a little. "What I mean is, after the first cutting. Do you let them graze off what *would* have been the second cutting?"

The farmer's expression turned completely askance. "That's what pastures are for. Cattle graze the pasture, not the hay field."

"So, do you ever drop a pasture out of rotation and then use it later as a hay field?"

He was now clearly exasperated. "What kind of question is that? A pasture is a pasture. A hay field is a hay field."

"Well, I was reading how the Amish consider everything to be a pasture, and only make hay from a field when they have extra pasture. Then, they won't make hay off of that field again for several years, to let it recover."

"Extra pasture? Extra pasture?" he repeated, disbelievingly. He turned to his wife and laughed. "What's 'extra pasture'? How do *I* get some extra pasture? I've been looking for that my entire career!

"Look," he continued, struggling to remain cordial, "if you're managing your farm correctly, you never *have* extra pasture. That's what more animals are for. And as far as recovery goes, that's why they make fertilizer. From what I've been told, the Amish don't use the stuff."

"They use cow manure," I said. "That's why they keep everything as a pasture, so the fields get manure each year."

The man snorted, folding his arms over his chest. "That's all well and good, if you're not trying to make a living. Sure, you can try all that natural, organic stuff for a while, but eventually everyone finds out it doesn't work. Farming's no different from anything else. You've got to spend money to make money. You find someone who tells you otherwise, check back in with me in a few years. They'll be out of business before you can turn around twice."

I thanked them for their time and continued my rounds with the hors d'oeuvres. I understood that I was just starting out and was barely entitled to any opinions about agriculture. This farmer was obviously experienced, and perhaps he was even correct. Yet, for some reason, his advice rang hollow. What might be right for his farm, I decided, didn't have to be right for ours.

My parents, resigned to their city jobs, were buying me all the time they could, hopeful that I might decipher these conflicting messages. I had listened attentively to the advice of my fellow farmers, but many of their ideas didn't resonate with me. If I could only remain patient, tuning out the words of pessimism and negativity, I might come to understand what the farm itself was trying to tell me.

As I served the old farmer another appetizer, I wondered what he would think if he saw me out in the pasture one day, my ear pressed to the ground, listening. I shook my head; I had caused his blood pressure to rise enough for one evening. The more I thought about it, though, imagining his red-faced consternation, the more I smiled. Fortunately for both of us, we lived on opposite sides of the county.

Chapter Eight

I spent no small amount of time considering the fact that if our farm was eventually successful, I would be personally responsible for the slaughter of hundreds, perhaps even thousands, of animals throughout the years. This knowledge weighed heavily on my conscience.

The pros and cons of livestock farming became a constant tug-of-war in my mind. Throughout my life, the fact that I loved to raise animals and also had an appetite for eating meat had never felt like a contradiction. Now, as I watched our cattle grazing contentedly in the field, peacefully living out their existence, my decision became increasingly conflicted.

I had grown up in a culture where meat was the centerpiece of each meal, and where animal husbandry was a celebrated skill. Even my city-born father had learned how to hunt as a young man, and he killed a white-tailed deer each autumn for our family to eat. I can vividly recall freezing-cold Sunday mornings when, after the carcass was skinned and gutted, I watched the steam rise in smoky tendrils from the fresh meat. Venison sloppy joes were a culinary staple in my childhood home.

I understood that there was a difference between hunting wild game and personally raising an animal destined for the slaughterhouse. As a farmer I would be the one selecting each head of beef, loading it onto the trailer, and delivering it to the butcher shop where the animal would be killed. Once the processing was complete, I'd also be handling the packages, passing them over the counter to the customer.

The fields were reseeded and established, and I now found myself with hundreds of acres of pasture to manage. Even if I had wanted to do something other than grow grass and cattle, I had no money to do so; if I was to pull our family farm out of debt, then photosynthesis, rain, and luck would have to be my primary assets.

Before I made my mind up once and for all, however, I spent a long time considering other options. Most vegetable farms I had visited were capable of growing tremendous amounts of food, but they achieved these yields on only a few intensive acres. Even if I had been trained to raise vegetables, our farm was simply too vast for one person to effectively manage the miles of spinach, carrots, and potatoes our soil could produce. Aside from keeping a garden for my personal use, I crossed vegetables off the list.

Fruit trees were perhaps a more sensible use of large acreages, but growing fruit required many hands at harvest time, and specialized equipment and storage facilities that we couldn't afford. Of course, my grandfather had managed large tracts of apples, pears, and cherries, but he always employed dozens of experienced men throughout the growing season. If I had been born a decade or two earlier, perhaps I might have become an orchardist under his tutelage.

Looking across the waving fields of orchard grass and clover, I finally decided I had only one sensible choice. I would convert this perennial pasture, fueled by nothing other than sunshine, soil, and rain, into human food. People couldn't eat grass. But they could eat grass-fed meat and eggs.

The more I learned about it, the more grass-farming seemed to hint at a larger promise, one that eclipsed the boundaries of traditional economics. Suddenly more than being just a farmer, I felt as though

I could be a collaborator, a participant in a system that not only sustained itself but also actually improved the earth year after year.

Modern grass-farming borrowed heavily from anthropological traditions, reaching into antiquity when migratory peoples followed herds of roaming animals and hunted them for sustenance. For millennia, prairies had been grazed, trampled, and fertilized by bison, buffalo, elk, and antelope. These were creatures that lived and died on the grassy plains, enriching the soil in a never-ending circle of life. Grass-farming intentionally mimicked these natural cycles, allowing our farm to reconnect with an ancient biorhythm. The message made too much sense for me to ignore.

Still, as I considered the implications of my decision, I never tricked myself into believing that just because the animals would be raised in a free-range environment, their death would somehow be more noble or high-minded. These were living, sentient creatures, and I was raising them to be slaughtered. The cows and chickens on our farm would be turned into food for human sustenance, and in my mind this demanded the highest respect for their sacrifice.

But just as important, to me, was the knowledge that our meat would be purchased by people who genuinely cared about how our animals were raised and treated. By opting out of the conventional system—one of feedlots, antibiotics, and growth hormones—our farm provided customers with a genuine alternative to industrially raised meat. Farmers' markets seemed to be the best way to establish a loyal following. These markets provided a deeper connection to the philosophies behind the food, something that the local supermarkets, stocked with anonymity, could never replicate.

In the spring of 1998, I selected my first steer, a large red-and-white Hereford that had been a calf the summer I arrived back home from college. Although I had no real experience choosing cattle for slaughter, I had listened carefully to the various speakers at the conference, looking for visual clues to aid my decision. This animal

My mother, Ruth, with our cow Maybelline.

had the shiny coat, fully formed haunches, and uniformly blocky body that suggested superior grass-fed beef.

As beautiful as this animal was, though, spending his days munching mouthfuls of bluegrass and white-top clover, I couldn't take him to a farmers' market like that. Our cattle had to be transformed from eleven-hundred-pound, four-legged grazers into neatly packaged steaks, roasts, and hamburger patties. There was a critical component that was still missing: I didn't have a butcher.

Finding a butcher whom I could trust would be crucial. There was no point in raising animals this way only to have them end up at the point of an electric cattle prod, or forced to stand all afternoon baking in the sun, their final hours spent in a concrete holding pen. Death was inevitable, but suffering was entirely avoidable.

Decades earlier, nearly all the towns in the Shenandoah Valley had had a butcher shop located within their city limits. Business was once in such high demand that both Charles Town and Berryville, the towns closest to our farm and less than ten miles apart, each had its own abattoir. These shops had their own sausage recipes and uniquely eccentric personalities, and they were a thread in the tapestry of small-town life.

Times changed. As fewer people raised their own animals for slaughter, these small shops had a harder and harder time staying in business. Regulatory paperwork mounted. Most slaughterhouses either closed or became seasonal, processing only deer. By the mid-1980s, both of our local butchers were out of business.

When I searched the phone book for the nearest processor, I was dismayed to find that there wasn't even a header for an entry. Butcher: nothing. Abattoir: zilch. Slaughterhouse: nada. I wondered if I was somehow looking in the wrong part of the directory. Perhaps the terminology had changed over the years? I looked under meat processors and packers. Still nothing. It was hard to believe there was truly no one out there.

I went to my agriculture extension office for help. A butcher shop? Nearby? Blank stares circulated around the office. They promised to look into it for me and give a call when they found the closest shop. A day or so later, they gave me the number of a shop that had once processed cattle but now mostly handled deer. It was at least worth a call.

Ring ring. Ring ring. Ring ring. On about the ninth ring, a man answered the phone.

"Hello?" He was breathing heavily and sounded extremely annoyed.

"Yes, hi. My name is Forrest Pritchard. I got your number from my local extension agent. I'm interested to know if you still do custom slaughtering. And if you do, do you vacuum pack and offer custom labeling?"

There was a long pause, with more heavy breathing. Finally, "Who did you say you were with again?"

"Who am I with? I'm just a farmer. My name is Forr—"

"And what do you want?" he asked, cutting me off. "Are we talking about deer, or cattle, or what?"

"Oh, cattle would be great," I said, trying to remain unrattled. "Do you still process beef? The man who gave me your number wasn't sure." Heavy breathing. I felt as though I could smell his sweat coming through the receiver.

"Well," he said at last, "we're mostly set up for deer now. And you said something about some kind of 'vacuum packing'?"

"Yes sir. I was wonder—"

"We don't do none of that," he said without preamble, "and I'm sick and tired of people asking!"

Boy, had I sure touched a nerve. I wasn't certain how to continue the conversation, or even, quite frankly, if I wanted to.

Neither of us spoke for several moments. More accurately, I should say that the silence was broken by the cadence of his exhalations, a noteworthy rhythm of chug and wheeze. Perhaps we had simply gotten off on the wrong foot. Surely the etiquette skills I had learned in college, cultivated from a year in the French House, could effectively bridge our communication gap.

"Okay," I said demurely, "maybe we should start over. Basically, what I'm looking for is—"

"I don't want your business!" the man interrupted, and hung up the phone.

Ouch.

I kept looking. I followed several more leads, but they were all dead ends.

Hearing of my difficulties locating a shop, a friend good-naturedly suggested that I start my own slaughterhouse, running an end around the whole process. I took his idea with a grain of salt and an appreciative nod and made a rough mental calculation of the amount of capital it would take to open a custom processing plant. I lost track somewhere in the high hundreds of thousands of dollars. Instead I tried another phone number, this one in another state.

Ring ring. Ring ring. "Hello?" a voice answered, not unhelpfully. I liked it better than my first attempt already. "Can I help you?"

"Yes, sir. My name is Forrest Pritchard. I'm trying to find someone who'll do custom slaughtering. Labeling, vacuum packing. That sort of thing."

"Well . . ." He paused long enough for me to imagine him hitching up either side of his trousers and settling into a chair. In the background I could hear a white noise of machinery clanking, and an occasional moo or bleat. "Maybe," he continued. "What kind of volume are we talking about?"

What kind of volume *were* we talking about? I had no idea, really. After all, I was just trying to get my first steer slaughtered. If the business were successful, I'd obviously need to increase production. But how I would determine that, or even begin to form an educated guess, remained completely up in the air. I decided to play it safe.

"One?" I volunteered, guardedly. "I think . . . just one steer, for now. Then maybe go from there, once we see how it all works out."

I held my breath, already conditioned for emotional turpitude to erupt from the receiver. "Does . . ." I added, cautiously, "does that sound possible?"

"One?" The voice on the other end sounded equal parts relieved and incredulous. "Oh, sure. We can handle one. We can do *that*." The white noise was now accompanied with the rustling sound of shuffled papers, and the click of a ballpoint pen. "This will be for resale, right? So you're going to need inspection and a label."

Finally, someone was speaking my language. It was as though I had accidentally stepped off the train at Hillbilly Hollow but was now arriving at my appropriate destination, Professionalville.

"Yes, sir, I'm going to need labels." I could hardly contain my enthusiasm. "I've even got a logo."

If he was interested to know what my logo looked like, he didn't let on. "We do minimum print runs of a thousand labels, but you get a price break starting at ten thousand. I'd suggest you start at ten, and see where that takes you."

Okay, I thought. That sounded reasonable. I had already figured that one beef would require several hundred labels in and of itself, by the time everything was packaged down to one-pound portions. Ten thousand labels wouldn't be cheap, but I had already learned the hard way that little, if anything, was going to be cheap.

As we discussed label specifications, packaging options, and cutting instructions, the conversation bordered on fun. At last, we got down to scheduling, and I let him know that I planned to attend our local farmers' market, and that opening day was less than a month away. Ideally, I wanted to deliver the steer that Thursday or Friday, giving me plenty of time to make sure I was ready for market.

His response quickly derailed my enthusiasm. "Thursday or Friday? *This* Thursday or Friday? We're booked up solid for the next six months."

I struggled to find my voice. "Really?"

"Yeah. In fact," he said, and I could hear him flipping pages in a notebook, "our first opening is actually in November. Should I put you down for then?"

"November? That's eight months away. You don't have a single opening before then?"

"Well, we might get a cancellation, but not usually. I could always keep your number by the phone and give you a call if something shakes free."

This sounded, for the moment at least, like my best and final offer. "Okay," I replied, beyond disappointed. "Yeah. Give me a call if you get an opening. I'd appreciate that."

I was about to hang up when a thought crossed my mind. "One more question?"

"Yeah?"

"I've spent the last week and a half calling around trying to find someone. Is there anyone you'd recommend, someone I might not have heard of, who can fit me in?"

"Hmm. Nobody comes to mind. I mean, unless . . . hold on a second." He covered the phone with his hand, but I could still hear his muffled voice quite clearly. "Hey, Frank! What's the name of that place up in Pennsylvania? The place Donny bought. Huh? Lowery's? Lowell's. You sure? Lowery's or Lowell's? Alright, alright." His voice returned to normal.

"Try a place called Lowell's, up near Gettysburg. One of our employees took it over a year or two ago, and they might be looking for new customers. Ask for Donny. Tell him Gary said to call."

Donny. Gary. Lowell's. Gettysburg. Got it.

"Thanks. Do you have their number?"

"Not handy. But they shouldn't be too hard to find."

Famous last words. It took a good bit of searching to locate the phone number. This was well before the Internet was an especially useful tool, and uncovering information in those days was a complex recipe of detective work, diplomacy, and general good fortune. It turned out, after several dead ends where I insisted that the name was Lowell's, it was called Lowery's after all.

Ring ring. Ring ring.

"Yup."

"Hi, is this Lowery's Meats?"

"Uh-huh."

"I'm calling for Donny."

"That's me."

"I was told to tell you that Gary gave me your number." Well, close enough anyway.

"Okay."

"Right. I was wondering if you do customer slaughter, labeling, vacuum packing. That sort of thing."

"Yup."

I waited, expecting more information to be forthcoming. When none was, I realized I might be dealing with a man of few words.

"Do you have an opening anytime soon? I need to get a steer slaughtered by next week."

"Alright."

"Say, this Friday?"

"We slaughter on Mondays."

"This Monday? The one coming up?"

"Uh-huh."

"And you can fit me in? And you're inspected, and I can do a label, and everything?"

"Yup."

The thought of actually getting this accomplished made me slightly giddy. "Cool. Excellent. Alright." Shut up, Pritchard, I told myself, don't put your foot in your mouth. I climbed down from my trampoline.

"What do I do next? Do you need my information?"

"Just show up. We get going at six."

It was all that simple. In a few weeks, I would have my own steaks and roasts, and perhaps be eating my first grass-fed hamburger. It had taken about fifty separate phone calls, dozens of false leads, and several grumpy conversations. But now I had an appointment.

In hindsight, it was one of the easiest parts of my farming career. I could never have anticipated what an adventure simply getting my first steer to the butcher was going to be.

Chapter Nine

Throughout my childhood, loading cattle on our farm meant sorting the animals through a rickety wooden corral and cajoling them single file through a splintered and patched loading chute, all the while sweating, pleading, and somehow convincing them to climb a hard-packed dirt ramp onto our cattle truck. The process started early in the morning, when the air was still cool and the cattle were more inclined to move, before the hot sun crested Blue Ridge Mountain.

It started then, but rarely concluded swiftly. Inevitably a stubborn heifer would break a board or jump a gate, or a steer would spin interminable circles in front of the entrance to the chute. Most predictably, a troupe of brood cows would balk at the bottom of the loading ramp, rolling their eyes in a synchronized refusal to climb. The bovine line would be thrown into a catastrophic reversal, and the entire process would have to start anew.

Before we ever accomplished much of anything, early morning often slipped into lunchtime, and by the time we were actually done, drenched with perspiration and generally furious at the universe, it was midafternoon. All in all, it was a reliably crummy job.

This particular form of self-inflicted torture was a family tradition dating back at least forty-five years. I knew this because, in our

Mom and Dad, sorting cattle in the mid-1990s.

ancient wooden filing cabinet, there was a sales receipt for our 1958 cattle truck, bought brand-new for two thousand three hundred and thirty-five dollars. The receipt had the words "Customer Requests No Radio" double underlined, as though, in an attempt to make cattle loading as miserable as possible, my grandfather had regarded listening to music as too great a luxury. Perhaps, as he drove his big International truck to the livestock sale, the sound of mooing cattle was music enough for his ears.

Now it was my turn to drive the truck, delivering my first steer to the butcher. My father and I opened the barn doors, studying the unwieldy jalopy in contemplative silence. We brushed hay dust and pigeon manure from the windshield, checking for black snakes beneath the seats. It was my first time driving it, and I tried to imagine what my grandfather must have felt nearly half a century earlier, bringing it home new from the dealership. I climbed into the cab, wrapping my hands around the expansive wheel. The interior carried an odor of chewing tobacco and old leather—pleasant, musty smells. It all felt right.

"You know, I'm just remembering," Dad said from the passenger seat, interrupting my reverie, "when I put this thing away last fall, it didn't have any brakes."

That didn't sound too serious, I said to myself. Once I got going, I'd just be sure not to stop. Ever.

"What do you mean, 'no brakes'? And why are you just telling me this now?"

"Because I just remembered right now. I kind of wanted to forget about it at the time."

I thought back, recalling that the truck's last trip had been over the mountain to neighboring Purcellville to pick up a load of grain and lumber. The Blue Ridge was a steady, steep grade in both directions, and wrecks from out-of-control vehicles were, unfortunately, a common occurrence.

"When did you realize it needed brakes?"

"On my way down the mountain into Purcellville."

"On your way down the mountain?" I spluttered. I had assumed the brakes failed after he was already back at the farm. "What did you do?"

He shrugged. "Well, naturally, I panicked."

"I can imagine! Seriously, how did you keep it under control?"

"First, I tried the hand brake, and I got a little response from that."

"The hand brake . . ." I said, looking down and to my right. "This one?"

He nodded. "The very same. That got me going *just* slow enough to gear down into third. The transmission didn't like it, but I was pretty grateful it agreed, if you take my meaning. Made a terrible noise before I finally jammed it home. Anyway, I put on my hazards, and kind of limped down the mountain."

"But . . . but . . ." I shook my head, disbelieving. "But Dad, I remember you driving it *back* here last fall."

"That was the easy part." He removed his hat and smoothed a few loose, wispy hairs. "I already knew I didn't have brakes, so I just kept it in first, hit my flashers, and crept on home."

"Kept it in first? You must have been going . . ."

"About seven miles an hour," he said with aplomb. "I think I might have ticked a few people off."

There were only two instances when my father actually enjoyed farming: when he could dream and when he could drive a vehicle on an errand. All the details in between, the setting of posts and the baling of hay, the painting of barns and the raising of livestock were intolerable nuisances to be avoided at all costs.

His imposing physique would have certainly lent itself to physical exertion if he had applied himself to that kind of work. When I asked him once why he didn't become a farmer, he told me his ideal life involved an air conditioner, a recliner, and a television. He was on a quest for maximum personal comfort, and on that score, at least, his sedentary office job in Washington suited him perfectly. The position required no strenuous effort, and he had a buffet of fast-food restaurants within easy walking distance. I had recently asked him why he put two straws into his milk shake. His pithy response? "So I can get it in my face faster."

My dad was also a subscriber of that patently American nostrum known as the "get-rich-quick scheme." At home after work, he passed untold hours conceiving half-baked farming enterprises, convinced that he could formulate a recipe of nearly effortless agricultural profits. He didn't buy lottery tickets. He didn't try out for game shows. Instead he fabricated farm-related Rube Goldberg machines in his mind.

I first noticed this pattern when I was five. In the depths of our cool, shadowy basement, I helped him fill an oversized *Alice in*

Wonderland-esque mailbox with potting soil. Following his directions, I dumped pail after pail of dark dirt into the cavernous opening. The metal mailbox, which he stood on its back end with the lid on top, was at least as tall as I was. Raised on tiptoes, with the lid opened, I could barely glimpse the black and fragrant soil, mysterious in its moist, loamy depths.

Where this humongous mailbox came from, or why he chose to use it instead of a conventional trash can, I can't say. As with many of his ideas, the strategies were vague, and execution was haphazard at best. We sprinkled the soil with night crawler cocoons, which arrived in a padded envelope via the mail. The worms were to be raised and sold as fishing bait, and Dad told me I could sell them for as much as one dollar for every Styrofoam tub I filled. With that kind of money, I envisioned completing my action figure collection in no time at all.

Dreams sometimes dry up and fade away, and, evidently, so can worms. After weeks of carefully moistening the soil, watching the worms hatch, and feeding them grass clippings and vegetable scraps, one day we apparently forgot about the whole project. Although I can't remember how or why this happened, I'm reluctant to place the burden solely on my five-year-old attention span. When the night crawlers were finally remembered a month later, the open lid revealed a desiccated wasteland where vermiculture had become an impossibility.

Stolidly resolute, my father embraced and then abandoned his dreams one poorly executed notion at a time. His next idea was a microscale red maple tree nursery, which lasted until the family dog knocked the seedlings off the front porch. This was followed by a custom rototilling service for small gardens, lasting for three separate gigs before crescendoing in a rodeo wheelie where, as a nine-year-old, I nearly flipped the tiller onto my head. A year later, he mapped out a custom hunting reserve for trophy pheasants. By the following spring, pheasants forgotten, he swooned over the possibility of raising shiitake mushrooms. We went on field trips to several fungi farms to see their production methods, but the idea never took hold.

We would raise crayfish. Better yet, trout. Erase, erase. Bottled springwater would make us millions. Into the car we went to visit a bottling plant owned by an old college friend of his. "Hmm," he said, standing along the edge of our spring. "I wonder what the market is for watercress?"

After yet another weekend farming conference, he became convinced there was a fortune to be made planting paulownia trees. He explained how the timber would be milled into ceremonial Japanese kimono boxes. By next summer, the five hundred trees we planted were overgrown with weeds and forgotten. He had already jettisoned the idea of growing ginseng, his most recent fascination.

It wasn't that his plans were inherently flawed, or that they didn't deserve further consideration. In fact, most of these endeavors were perfectly feasible, and he might have been successful, even working only nights and weekends. The problem was, he never saw anything through to completion. Raising the flock of chickens was as close as he ever came to following through on a project he started, and that lasted for only three months.

When I told my father I wanted to start farming, I immediately understood that he had projected these previous failures onto me. However, as the months passed and I dutifully showed up to work each day on the farm, I began to sense a grudging respect from him. My enthusiasm for grass-farming had even rekindled a small spark behind his eyes, and we had talked more than once about the details of getting the new business off the ground.

The old cattle truck, we both agreed, would have to play an instrumental role. With no operating capital, and my meager savings already spent on the tiny chest freezer, the old truck had one important thing going for it: we owned it free and clear. But now that

I had learned the truck had no brakes, I suddenly felt my own dreams slipping away, foiled by my lack of foresight.

"So," I said, climbing out of the cab. "You're telling me the truck's out of commission."

"Unless you've got a spare set of 1958 International brake pads, and you went to automotive school when I wasn't looking. Some brake fluid might help, too." He smiled humorlessly. "That is, if the lines aren't dry-rotted."

"My appointment's tomorrow morning, Dad. What am I going to do?"

"I'm all out of ideas," he said, his face downcast. A ghost of a smile played across his face. "But you *could* use the trailer your mom and I bought for you yesterday. We're picking it up this afternoon."

Ah, the morale-boosting miracle of new equipment! The appearance of a useful farm apparatus has the magical ability to lighten moods, buoy spirits, and make you want to spontaneously kiss your three-hundred-pound father. After double-checking that he wasn't pulling my leg, I performed a little happy dance right there in the barn. A new trailer! I could hardly believe it.

That evening, we hitched up the new trailer, a twelve-foot silver beauty that arrived gently used via the classified ads. Despite our moratorium on expenditures, my parents had scratched up eighteen hundred dollars for it. "You've got to have a way to safely move these animals," my mother replied matter-of-factly when I later asked her about the surprise purchase. "I won't have my child driving a fifty-year-old truck with no brakes. Common sense has a role in this business, too."

Bypassing the rickety corral, the steep loading ramp, and the truck with no brakes, my steer could now step an easy six inches onto the back of the trailer. After generations of commendable service, and a hair-raising ride down the side of a mountain, the old International was finally granted a dignified retirement.

Dad and I loaded the steer calmly and easily and parked the trailer beside the barn to keep him out of the wind during the night. As I got out of the truck, though, he motioned to me.

"You don't have any trailer lights," he said. He pulled the plug, reinserted it, and gave it a firm jostle. "Probably just a bad connection. Try it again."

I turned my lights on and off. Nothing. No taillights, brake lights, or turn signals. It was now dark outside, and we crawled beneath the truck with a flashlight, examining the wires. Like any good farm vehicle, the underside was encrusted with a dried mélange of soil, manure, and grass. We knocked away the dirt chunks, squinting against the dust, until we had a reasonable idea that everything was in proper working order. Next, we checked the fuse box.

The fuses appeared fine. As a last resort, we applied electrical grease to the socket, boosting conductivity. Nothing worked. Cold, dirty, and exasperated, we stood in the darkness, discussing our options.

It was too late to call a mechanic or ask someone to custom-haul for us. There was no getting around the darkness; dawn would have barely broken by the time we crossed the state line into Pennsylvania. Without trailer lights, we would look like a shadow moving down the highway.

Faced with the ethics of being a public safety hazard, coupled with the likelihood of being pulled over by the police, my father defaulted to a plan that was almost, nearly, and—fingers crossed— possibly destined not to fail: the cockamamy scheme.

Here's how he scripted it. The truck had headlights, so no problem there. I would drive the truck and trailer, and my dad, in his 1984 Camry, would follow closely behind, illuminating the back of the trailer with his headlights. It was his job to stay close and not let anyone get between us. Since I had no brake lights, he would use his self-proclaimed catlike reflexes to apply his brakes in case I had to suddenly stop. Close, but not too close, was the goal.

We picked a route that we knew had three mandatory stops. The first two were stoplights, but the third was a four-way stop sign in the heart of Shepherdstown, West Virginia. I slept fitfully that night, and we set off at four the following morning.

Everything was going great. At that hour there was hardly a car on the road, and we made it all the way to Shepherdstown without incident. I began congratulating myself on our cleverness, our ability to overcome adversity. One more stop, and we were nearly home free. I sang along with Freddie Mercury's voice on the radio. *"We are the champions, my frieeeeeend . . . and weeeeee'll keep on fighting . . . till the ennnnnd . . ."*

As I pulled to a stop at the four-way, a police cruiser eased up the hill from my right. I was going straight, and the cop put on his right-turn signal. He would be following me. My falsetto trailed off.

I hesitated, futilely waiving him on in the darkness. If I waited long enough, I told myself, he might take my cue and turn in front of me. No dice. I waited until I couldn't wait any longer, realizing the cop was about to smell a rat. With a deep breath, palms sweating, I drove through the intersection, prepared for red-and-blue flashing lights as he pulled me over.

My dad, who could clearly see what was about to happen, gunned his engine, ran the stop sign, and cut off the police officer's car. Dumbfounded, I watched from the side-view mirror as the cop swerved out of the way, avoiding a collision.

He was taking one for the team, I marveled. Despite all his complaining about farming, all his doubts and pessimism, *the old man was taking one for the team.*

"Woo-hoo!" I cheered. "Go, Dad!" My pulse was racing.

Almost immediately, the police officer was in pursuit. Pulsing red-and-blue lights strobed behind my father's car, and the scream of the siren was distinct above the roar of my motor. Behind me, I could see my dad slowing and then pulling over. With only a moment of second thought, and a bittersweet mixture of pride and determination, I accelerated into the darkness.

Seconds later I crossed the Potomac River into Maryland, the police lights a distant halo in my wake. Another forty-five minutes of carefully navigating back roads, and I arrived at the butcher. I had just finished unloading the steer and was turning into the parking lot when Dad pulled up beside me.

"Well," he said, laconically. "That was something."

"Dad! That was . . . that was *awesome!* I don't believe you did that!"

He smiled. "Looks like you made it alright."

"So you're not pissed I kept going?"

"What would the point have been otherwise? He never would have let you go."

I laughed, relieved. "What in the world did you say to him? I mean, what did he say to *you?*"

"He said, and I quote, 'Sir? Excuse me, *sir?* Are you *blind?*'"

We burst into laughter. Tension melted out of the air, carried away by his deadpan good humor.

"Did he give you a ticket?"

"It was like this. I told him you were my son, up ahead with the trailer. I said we had just gotten done loading the meanest, nastiest bull I'd ever seen. He'd damn near killed the both of us this very morning, you know." He winked. "I was so wound up, what with nearly being killed, and worrying about how *you* had almost gotten killed, that I hadn't seen the stop sign." Smiling, he added, "I also told him I was very, very sorry."

"Wow." I shook my head with admiration. "You thought all that up on the spot?"

"Of course not," he said. "I already had my story straight, just in case."

I laughed. "Wait a second. Didn't he wonder why I didn't stop for you?"

"Naturally."

"What did you say?"

"I told him the truth. That you had to make your appointment."

"And he let you go?"

"Obviously."

"Without a ticket?"

"That's right."

"And that's *it?*"

"Well, he told me to be more careful. I promised him I would."

And that was that. We entered the butcher shop, but not before vowing to get the trailer lights fixed.

Chapter Ten

Despite being raised on a livestock farm, I knew next to nothing about butchering. Of course, I knew that animals were raised on a farm and meat appeared at the grocery store; in between, I had only vague impressions of men in white coats with sharp, flashing knives. As hard as it was to admit, beyond these generalizations the entire process remained shrouded in mystery for me.

At the conference in West Virginia, I had been told that grass-fed beef should be "dry-aged" for at least two weeks. This meant that after the steer was slaughtered and the hide removed, it was hung in a very cold but not freezing cooler, allowing frigid air to circulate around the carcass. This old-fashioned process allowed the meat to "age" in the cold, "dry" air. According to the speaker, it was the way that beef had been handled for generations.

Increasingly, modern-day processors had shifted to a technique called "wet aging." Here the beef was immediately cut into large portions and then vacuum-packed and boxed. This type of aging created an enzyme marinade, the beef stewing in its own juices as it traveled around the country in refrigerated tractor trailers. Arriving at a grocery store, it was then unsealed, giving off a belch of nose-wrinkling gas that butchers likened to the smell of rotten eggs. This was a streamlined process, allowing the beef to get to supermarkets more quickly, and it satisfied a population that demanded a cheap and endless supply of meat. It also eliminated nearly all the artistry and nuance of traditional dry aging.

Chefs and food aficionados swore that properly dry-aged, grass-fed beef was an unforgettable eating experience, one of the simplest and yet most memorable pleasures of life. After a few weeks of hanging, the meat became noticeably more tender, and a concentration of unique flavors emerged to create a nirvana for the palate. In short, dry aging was culinary alchemy, able to transform an average piece of meat into something truly special.

Nancy and I tested this theory one weekend when I drove down to North Carolina to visit her. Inquiries at grocery stores for dry-aged, pasture-raised meat garnered little more than furrowed brows, followed by tentative calls to the manager. After several failed attempts, we tracked down a dry-aged sirloin at an organic food co-op, and we hurried our treasure home with an accompaniment of porcini mushrooms, a head of garlic, and a bottle of Cabernet Sauvignon the manager swore was the finest he had ever tasted. With her steady paychecks from two part-time jobs, combined with her Italian heritage, Nancy never took shortcuts when it came to food.

In no time at all, she had her tiny apartment kitchen smelling like a five-star restaurant. Fragrant mushrooms simmered in garlic and butter while she seared the sirloin, pre-warmed to room temperature, a few seconds per side in a cast-iron skillet. The meat sizzled and popped beneath her scrutinizing eye. Next she drizzled the steak with olive oil and black pepper and placed it in the broiler. Through some workings of her own internal clock, she knew exactly when to rescue it from the oven. She sliced it lengthwise, allowing it to rest untouched several minutes on the countertop while it continued to steam in its own savory juices. Much like dry aging, properly cooking grass-fed meat was a process that required patience, but my stomach had a hard time rationalizing this fact.

Just when I didn't think I could wait any longer, Nancy plated the food in simple rustic fashion: a palm-sized portion of steak, crisp and peppered along the edges, pink and succulent in the center, with the mushrooms ladled over one side. It was a melody of garlic, porcinis, and beef. I poured the wine.

From the first bite, my palate sang praises I never could have anticipated. The delicate crunch of the caramelized exterior was perfectly balanced with the lightly earthy flavors of the rarer meat beneath. My tongue identified forgotten tastes and smells from my childhood, distinctive notes of black walnut and warm oak leaves, a bouquet of orchard grass on a sunlit day. And when I swallowed, the meat left my mouth feeling clean, invigorated, satisfied. Lost in our food reverie, we nearly forgot about the Cabernet.

I couldn't have known it until that moment, but I had been missing this food my entire life. There was no substitute for what I was experiencing; this meat clearly deserved a category unto itself. Nancy and I wordlessly devoured the steaks, communicating our satisfaction only through occasional, blissful eye contact.

As we cleaned our plates, using our final slices to shepherd garlic and mushrooms into our mouths, Nancy's roommate Catherine entered the apartment.

She stopped in the threshold, frozen. "Oh, no," she said, sniffing the air. A look of pure disappointment crossed her face. "Nancy's cooked something. She's cooked something amazing, and I missed it."

I was about to apologize when Catherine brusquely cut me off. "No," she said, holding out her hand like a stop sign. "Don't even try. Whatever she did, whatever it was . . . I'd just rather not know." She shouldered her backpack and marched sullenly to her room, locking her door with an audible note of reprimand. If I hadn't felt so wonderful, I surely would have felt bad.

On the drive back home, I thought for a long time about that meal, and what it might mean for the future of the farm. It was foolhardy

Nancy, cooking up a delicious meal.

to think we could somehow bring the past back to life, altering the direction of a food industry that prioritized speed and anonymity. But perhaps we could take the best aspects of our food heritage and give them a modern reincarnation. If grass-farming and dry aging were to be part of the solution, then finding the right butcher would be my next great challenge.

———————

Donny's butcher shop was a sprawling building located behind an aging industrial park. The expansive interior was partitioned off with temporary walls that didn't quite reach the ceiling, and the metal exterior had been constructed without windows. It appeared to have been a modified garage or warehouse of some sort, and indistinct noises echoed throughout its tinny, hidden depths. Dad and I waited in the fluorescently lit sales room until Donny, the man with whom I had spoken on the phone, appeared from the other side of a partition.

We introduced ourselves, passing along our labeling information and filling out a worksheet of cutting instructions. "Can I ask you a few questions about dry aging?" I asked him when we were finished.

"Alright." Donny was probably in his early fifties, dressed in blue overalls with a green hat. He had what could only be described as a very, very large gut.

"We'd like the steer to hang for two full weeks before cutting it. Dry aging, I think it's called."

"Dry aging?" he repeated, his expression inscrutable.

My dad spoke up. "Dry aging. You know, as opposed to wet aging, the way most people do it."

"Alright. I'll dry-age it."

"And, will two weeks be okay?" I asked.

"That'll work."

"Great. Then we'll see you in two weeks. Or a little later, I guess, since the beef has to freeze."

"Yup."

My father and I drove back home, playing the same follow-the-leader game as before, but this time with less urgency.

That afternoon I got a call from our local newspaper, which had heard through the grapevine that we were about to start direct-marketing our beef. The timing was absolutely perfect. I would meet with the reporter the next day.

"What do you feed your cattle?" the reporter asked, as we walked across the pasture toward the herd.

"They're completely grass-fed." I stooped slightly as we walked, snatching a handful of seed tops from the belt-high grasses. "Their entire lives, they eat exactly what they'd be eating out in the wild. We just work with what nature already provides, and they do the rest.

"Here," I said, showing her the seeds in my hand. "Orchard grass, fescue, timothy. And down below," I added, dropping to my heels, "clovers, and alfalfa. Weeds, too. You know, a lot of what we think of as 'weeds' are actually super-nutritious plants. The cows are free to select whatever they want. Sometimes they eat things we might normally consider a weed."

"It's really beautiful out here," she said, allowing her fingertips to drift over the bowing grass. "I grew up on a farm in Indiana. Not as big as this, but we had cows, too. It was an old-fashioned farm, like the one you have."

Her eyes drifted across the pasture, becoming dreamy as she spoke. "My grandparents ran it, until they passed away. I always thought it would be great if we had kept it somehow, maybe do something like you're doing. I don't know." She shook her head.

"It's just a dream now," she said, snapping back into the present. "So, when do you feed them corn?"

"We don't give them any grain at all. They're raised start to finish on pasture."

She paused. "No corn? I mean, we used to graze our cattle, too, but we always gave them some corn."

"Well," I said, good-naturedly, "they can't get corn in the wild, and somehow their ancestors survived. Our animals might not be as large as a grain-fed steer when it comes time for slaughter, but they're not as fatty, either. A lot of that grain just turns into excess weight. What we're raising here is lean, heart-healthy beef. Totally organic, too."

"But isn't it gamy-tasting? I've always heard that if you don't feed grain, it tastes gamy. Tough, too."

"It's a totally different eating experience," I explained, recalling my amazing meal with Nancy in North Carolina. "Some folks think they can taste the actual flavor of the soil, like a famous vintage of wine. The French even have a word for it: *terroir.*"

We were quite close to the herd now, and the two of us stopped to watch them grazing in the bright afternoon sunshine. Light glinted off their shiny backs as they ducked their heads beneath the waiving grass, grazing white-top clover. "As far as toughness goes, I've never met a steak I couldn't eat. That's what our teeth are for, right? To chew?" I smiled.

"I mean . . ." she said, writing notes onto a spiral-bound pad as we talked, "you're simply turning the cattle loose onto pasture. They're just eating what grows wild in the field, and that's it."

"Yes. Basically." I hesitated, wanting to elaborate. "I mean, there's a lot of complexity to—"

"So, at the end of the day, you're not really growing anything, then. I mean, you're raising animals, but you don't plant any vegetables or crops. Right?"

"I'm growing pasture first and foremost. Every year that passes, our fields get stronger, more productive. And when the year is through, we produce a crop of cattle."

She looked at me skeptically. "But that doesn't really count, does it? I mean, grass grows on its own. You don't have to plant anything."

I wasn't sure whether I needed to feel defensive. "I'm a livestock farmer, yes. Not a vegetable farmer. I mean, the cattle won't grow if they're not properly fed, right?"

She wrote quickly. "And so, basically, what you're doing is what everyone else is already doing, but just not giving them corn at the end."

"Well . . ." Now I *was* feeling a bit defensive. "It's not quite as simple as that. I'm managing pasture. If the pasture isn't properly rotated, fertilized, and rested, then the animals won't grow. It's a chemical-free, natural system. There's no antibiotics, dewormers, hormones . . ."

"Wait. What happens when the animals get sick?"

"They rarely get sick in this system. It promotes health and vigor. The whole farm is set up as a preventative against bacteria and infection. In the rare instances of illness, we use homeopathic—"

"But what about all the manure? Isn't that where bacteria builds up?"

"What manure?" I asked, puzzled. "With a proper pasture rotation, it just turns into soil."

"The manure in the feedlot." She tucked the pad of paper under her arm and smoothed her windblown hair. "When I was growing up, you could smell the feedlots from a mile away. We would be driving, and we'd have to roll up our windows and turn on the air-conditioning. In the summers, especially, the smell was just awful."

I shook my head. "We don't have a feedlot. This," I said, gesturing to where the cattle were contentedly munching mouthfuls of fresh grass, "is our 'feedlot.' If you notice, there's no bad smell."

Her eyebrows lowered in confusion. "You mean . . . ? Oh! I see!" She brightened considerably. "So, you don't put them in a feedlot at all, do you? They just stay out here all the time. I get it now." She scribbled quickly, flipping pages as she wrote. "But what about in the winter? You have barns for them? What do they eat in the barn? There's no grass in there."

"They stay outside year-round. When we need to, we feed hay. But if the pasture is properly managed, they'll have grass until around mid-February. We usually feed hay about only six weeks a year."

"Wow," she said, not looking up. "That's a lot of hay."

"Well, to give you perspective, before we started managing our farm this way, we'd feed hay for six *months*."

"Uh-huh." Her head was buried in the notebook. "And you'll be selling this meat . . . when? And how?"

"The first beef will be available in a couple of weeks. We'll be selling it by the pound, or people can order a quarter or a half at a time."

"A quarter or a half of what? A half pound of beef?"

"No, of a steer."

"Half a steer! How much is that? That must fill up a school bus!"

"It's usually about two hundred pounds or so."

"Two hundred pounds?" She laughed. "It would take me, like, ten years to eat that much."

"Well, it's intended for families. And like I said, we'll also be selling it by the pound."

"Alright. I think I've got it." She continued writing for several more moments before finally looking up. "Great. Fantastic. The piece should be out sometime next week. Do you mind if I get a couple pictures? My photographer should be here any minute."

I was flattered. Here I was, barely a farmer, and I was getting my picture in the paper. "Sure," I replied, doing my best to act nonchalant. "I mean, if you want."

———————

A few days later, on Friday, the phone rang.

"Hello?"

"This is Donny at the butcher shop. Your steer's ready."

"What?"

"I said, your steer's ready."

"But it was supposed to dry-age for two weeks. I just brought it up on Monday."

"Well, it's ready. And I'm gonna want a check when you come."

"But . . ."

"Alright then." He hung up the phone with a click.

What happened next is so memorably odd that it is etched into my mind, word for word. I arrived at the butcher shop later that afternoon and met Donny in his office.

"I'm not sure if there's some confusion," I began, as politely as I could, "but I thought we agreed to dry-age that steer for two weeks."

"Yup. It was two weeks."

"But I just dropped it off on Monday. And today's Friday."

"Huh." He stood and studied a large calendar pinned to the wall. "Let's see. Last Monday was the ninth. And today's the twentieth. So that's two weeks."

"But this past Monday was the *sixteenth*."

He gestured at the calendar. "Last Monday was the ninth," he repeated, pointing at the date. "See?"

"Yeah, but I didn't drop the steer off then. I dropped it off on the sixteenth."

"You've got the dates mixed up."

All at once, I felt a little hot under the collar. "I'm one hundred percent certain. You can ask your guys out back, if you want."

He lifted his hat slightly and rubbed his temples. "Well, still." He counted the days, tapping his finger against the calendar as he spoke.

"Monday, Tuesday, Wednesday, Thursday . . . That's still ten days. That's almost two weeks."

I couldn't control myself any longer. "What are you talking about?" It came out a little louder than I might have liked. "That's not ten days! That's *four* days!" I looked around for someone to commiserate with, but it was just the two of us. I wished suddenly that my dad had been able to come with me, but he was at work in Washington. "This doesn't make any sense at all!"

He held up his hands. "Whoa, whoa, whoa! Easy, partner. Easy." He thumbed at the calendar again. "That's ten days, right there. Okay, maybe nine, maybe ten. Now look, there's no use arguing about it, it's already cut up and packaged. Let's just call it even."

I was fuming. How could I work so hard only to have my work compromised simply because someone couldn't count? To top it off, I had to pay him for a job done incorrectly, or I couldn't even have my own beef back.

The meat came out in large boxes, which I loaded into the freezer on the back of my truck. Removing the lid on the first box, I immediately realized there was a mistake. A quick check of the other boxes confirmed my suspicions.

I tracked down Donny for the second time. He seemed less than thrilled to see me again.

"I think there's been another mix-up. All my packages have Not For Resale marked on them."

"Yeah?" He appeared utterly indifferent.

"Well, you said you'd custom-label it."

"That's right."

"But my label's not on these packages, and, on top of that, it's marked wrong anyway. I'm planning on reselling all of this."

He stared at me wordlessly.

"I mean, what am I supposed to do? Can you repackage it?"

"Not after it's been frozen."

I was only seeking some sort of compromise, some small concession on his part. "But, why did you mark it all Not For Resale? I gave you my label instructions."

"Label machine broke."

"So, instead of putting it in plain bags, you put it in Not For Resale bags?"

"Gotta put it into something that's clearly marked. That's USDA rules."

"But why didn't you tell me? I would have waited until the machine was repaired . . ."

"Rules is rules," Donny said. He folded his arms over his chest and gave me a stern look. "You don't want me to break the law, do you?"

I felt defeated. Shoulders slumped, I returned to my truck, transferring my non-dry-aged, mislabeled meat into my freezer. No, I said to myself, I don't want you to break the law. I just want you to do what you promised me you'd do. As I drove back to the farm, I resolved to find a different butcher as soon as possible.

The following Tuesday, the article headlined page B1 of the paper. I eagerly turned to it, more than ready for some good news. A large photo showed me standing in the foreground near a fence, with gorgeous waves of pasture rising up behind me. It read like this:

> *Farmer Forrest Pritchard, a recent graduate of the College of William & Mary, is taking his family's farm in a new direction: back to the future. At Pritchard's farm Smith Meadows, cows don't eat corn, but have a totally natural diet.*

"They eat a lot of weeds," said Pritchard, pointing to his pastures. "Our cattle never get fat. You can taste dirt in the meat."

Even though conventional wisdom says cattle raised this way are tough and gamy, Pritchard disagrees.

"You have to chew a lot," he explained. "That's why we have teeth."

The farmer describes his practices as "growing pasture." He doesn't raise crops or vegetables, but still considers this type of work to be agriculture.

"Our feedlot is over there," he said, pointing into the distance. "You can't smell the manure from where we're standing."

Pritchard's beef will be available soon for purchase. Please call the farm for more details.

Chapter Eleven

E vidently, weed-fed cattle with meat that tasted like dirt had a certain appeal after all. Over the next few weeks, half a dozen brave souls ventured out to our farm, most of them buying a forty-pound sampler we dubbed the "Family Pack." This was a mixture of all our available cuts: ground beef, steaks, roasts. After a brief explanation, customers took the labeling fiasco in stride. The transactions were friendly and appreciative on both sides.

Priced at $2.50 a pound, our average sale was right around a hundred dollars. As customers passed me checks, I let them know that I was genuinely grateful for their business. My sister, with her reliable salary working as a nurse, had loaned me the money to pay Donny's butchering fee. Now, not only was I able to pay her back, but I also had managed to put away some modest savings. These first sales provided tantalizing hints of economic sustainability.

Just as gratifying as the actual transaction was the interest the customers expressed in what we were doing. They wanted to learn more about the farm and the way the animals were raised. Often they had a farming story of their own to share. At the end of the day, selling food that I had personally raised was far more satisfying than being a straw or firewood salesman. I even managed to squirrel away a pound of ground beef for myself when no one was looking.

There were still dozens of kinks to work out, but finding a different butcher now topped the list. Our local farmers' market started the following week, and even though I had half a steer left to sell, I doubted that it would last long. Going back to Donny's shop was out of the question. If he was to be my only option, I was going to have a very short career.

There was one phone number I had picked up along the way that I hadn't called. It was in an out-of-the-way town in north-central Maryland, a place I had never heard of. Still, they were USDA inspected, and that in and of itself was worth a phone call.

"Schoen's Meats, Harold Schoen speaking. May I help you?" The man's voice sounded world-weary. It was a tone, I was beginning to sense, that butchers everywhere shared.

My spiel was fairly well-rounded by now. I explained who I was, what I was about, and what I was after. I then held my breath, conditioned to expect rejection arriving in one form or another.

"Let me make sure I understand you," Mr. Schoen replied. "You want us to vacuum-pack and freeze your meat. And it'll be available for resale."

"That's right."

"And you'll want your own label on it. Not ours."

"You got it."

"You know," he said after a short pause, "no one's ever asked me this before. Can you hold on a minute? I need to ask the floor inspector a few questions."

Sure, I told him. I could hold on. I consoled myself that this was better than a flat-out "no," but I was beginning to wonder. Could we be the only farm out there trying to do this? The premise seemed basic: Raise our own animals. Have them processed. Sell the meat. It all seemed so natural, so intuitive, that I increasingly feared I might have overlooked some major stumbling block.

Aside from the handful of speakers at the agricultural conferences, perhaps there really were no other farms marketing their food this way. As far as I knew, all the other farms in our area sold their cattle to the commodity market, the animals packed into freight cars and tractor trailers, ending their days in a confinement feedlot. But the grain and concrete model had been such a resounding failure for us, it seemed impossible that we were the only farm opting out of the system.

In my more idealistic moments, I imagined a small army of farmers like myself, a loosely connected tribe, each producing what we could reliably grow and each selling directly to our surrounding communities. Although we might not know one another personally, collectively we supplied food with a local provenance, a viable alternative to supermarket fare. It hardly seemed like an intellectual stretch.

Perhaps it was all simply too difficult. Too many steps, too many challenges and obstacles. I had no way of knowing how many other farmers had previously attempted what I was now trying to do and had simply failed. If it were as easy as I imagined, wouldn't there be a meat vendor at every farmers' market?

A few more moments passed, and I could hear a low murmur of conversation above the buzz of the receiver. Eventually Mr. Schoen's voice emerged from the earpiece.

"Mr. Pritchard? Yes, the inspector says that should be fine. But since we've never done this before, he needs to call his supervisor."

"That sounds reasonable. When's your next availability? I'd like to bring up, say, one steer."

I could hear him flipping through a few pages. "We could fit you in in about two weeks. Do you think you can you bring your label up sometime soon? We'll need to get a copy of it over to the folks who do our printing. It's all part of the process, I'm sure you can imagine."

It felt as though I were starting over again from scratch; what had seemed like progress with the first butcher was now clearly a total waste of time. Still, something in this man's tenor sounded encouraging, and my expectations were now so low that almost any butcher shop would have to be better than Donny's. I drove up to Schoen's that same afternoon.

After an hour of dodging traffic, I exited from the ferocious energy of the interstate, drifting into the nearly flat farmland of north-central Maryland. I passed tidy farms with well-kept barnyards, many of them with a small garden near the road. Women in black bonnets hung laundry on lines; the cars I passed were jet black, driven by men wearing black hats. They waived as I passed, and I returned the gesture. As I drove by a large, nondescript brick church, it dawned on me that I had entered a Mennonite community.

The butcher shop was an unassuming cinder-block building, painted white and tucked between a large green barn and a limestone farmhouse. The sign at the end of the road was printed with stark, black letters:

SCHOEN'S MEATS
8 TO 5 MONDAY THROUGH SATURDAY
CLOSED SUNDAYS

More black cars were in the parking lot. These were sturdy-looking four-door sedans, gleaming in the bright sunshine, not a speck of dirt to be seen on them. A line of waiting customers trickled out the door of the shop's deli. Inside, the ladies behind the counter wore simple prairie dresses with delicate floral prints, their hair drawn into tight buns and capped with miniature bonnets. They weighed large scoops of ground beef and ropes of fresh sausage and solemnly sliced wedges of bright yellow cheese.

Directly behind the counter, an enormous glass window revealed the inner workings of the butcher shop. Through the glass, half a dozen men stood cutting large blocks of meat. They were dressed in neat white coats and matching white paper hats, and they worked beside a long stainless-steel table. Carcasses of beef hung on hooks, suspended from above by a metal track on the ceiling. The men employed their knives in graceful, sweeping arcs, slicing off entire quarters at a time for further processing.

I was immediately struck by this transparency, which seemed entirely intentional. Everyone who walked in was able to see exactly what was happening, how the meat was handled, and the artistry involved in its preparation. One of the men glanced up, caught my eye, and sheathed his knife as he made his way toward me.

"I'm guessing you're Mr. Pritchard," he said. He was at least a foot shorter than I was, and very fit. His cheeks retained the ruddy glow of physical exertion.

"Mr. Schoen?"

He smiled. "I'd shake your hand," he said, holding up an arm covered in beef blood, "but in my line of work, things get a little messy." He made his way to a hand sink and worked the soap into a vigorous lather. When he was done, he doffed his paper hat and replaced it with a crisp black fedora. The transformation from butcher to businessman was instantaneous.

"A proper handshake," he said, by way of introduction. His grip was firm and callused. "You've brought a label for me, correct?"

"Yes, sir. Right here."

He took the paperwork and studied it appraisingly. "Mmm-hmm. Mmm-hmm. That's a handsome drawing," he commented. "I like the mountains in it. Okay, I don't see why we can't work with this. We'll get this over to the printers, and add our plant number to it." He glanced at the clock. "Are you in a hurry? I could give you a tour of the shop, if you'd like."

A tour of a real, working butcher shop? After months of phone calls, dozens of ambivalent and dismissive conversations,

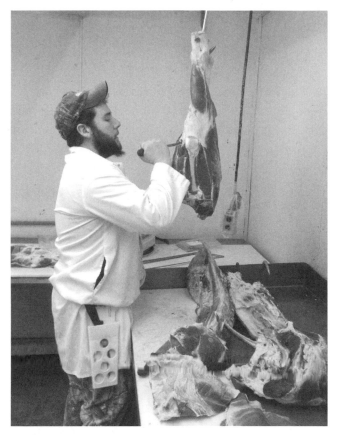

Working on a side of dry-aged beef.

I had given up hope of actually seeing the inner workings of a professional shop.

Why, yes, I replied. Since he mentioned it, yes, I would.

We started out back, where the animals were unloaded. The pens were clean and airy, a mixture of shade and dappled sunshine. Each section had its own waterer so the animals could drink, and a large scale was built into the floor to record their weights. A fresh pyramid

123

of sawdust was piled to one side, to be used for bedding. Based on the reputations of slaughterhouses, I was impressed with how sanitary and orderly everything appeared. It was actually cleaner than many farms I had visited.

The butcher took in the view for himself. "There's not much to it, really," he said. "When we designed it, we tried to make it functional. My dad started this business more than forty years ago, and we've pretty much been doing the same thing ever since. I'm hoping my own boys will want to take it over when I'm done." He turned, gesturing for me to follow him. "Come onto the kill floor, and I'll introduce you to my sons."

Mr. Schoen introduced me to his three boys, each progressively shorter and younger mirror images of himself. They sported the same white cotton coats and paper hats that seemed to be their uniform. Small, bright flecks of blood spotted their clothing, evidence of a morning's work. Each shook my hand in turn.

Even the youngest, no older than fourteen, exhibited the practiced ease of a craftsman in his element, leaning casually against the wall, absently cradling his knife. It was as though the family butcher shop was where these young men were truly destined to be.

The atmosphere here was a complete departure from that of the first abattoir. Donny's assistants had been surly middle-aged men sporting heavy-metal T-shirts. They lit cigarettes as I backed up my trailer, yelling and prodding at my nervous steer before hustling him through a dark network of poorly hung gates and cobwebbed alleys. Treating my animal this way had seemed to border on cruelty.

Here, as we walked through the slaughter room, there wasn't a spot of blood or mess to be found. Grown men in white aprons washed the blue-tiled walls, thoroughly sanitizing the area from floor to ceiling. The concrete floor was worn smooth from decades of use, and the room carried the air of practical hard work.

Mr. Schoen led me through his large walk-in freezers, an arresting negative ten degrees where our breath froze the moment we exhaled. Here, packaged cuts of meat were stacked on wheeled metal carts, ready for sale. We emerged into the processing room, where I first had seen the men carving the beef. After every few cuts, a knife flashed across a hand-held sharpening post, *scritch-scratch-scritch,* almost faster than I could see. In less than five minutes, they had completely broken down a half side of beef. The demonstration was spellbinding.

I again could see through the large window, but this time from the butcher's perspective. I made eye contact with several of the customers who were waiting in line. How remarkable, I thought.

One of the white-aproned ladies walked by, pushing a large vat of fresh hams. She opened a side door, and a mouthwatering smell of hickory smoke billowed into the room.

"Do you raise hogs, Mr. Pritchard?"

I quickly put two and two together. If I raised hogs, I could enjoy this smell wafting from my own skillet. "No," I replied, repressing a disappointment that, a moment before, I hadn't realized existed. "My grandfather did, but I've never tried farrowing any myself."

"That," he said, pointing at the door, "leads into our smokehouse. We make all sorts of things in there. Hams, bacon. Smoked ring bologna."

"Can you make any of that with just beef?" I asked, hopeful that there might be some sort of magical "beef ham" that had escaped my notice my entire life.

"Well," he replied, politely, "you could *possibly* do a bologna made only out of beef, but you probably wouldn't want to. There's something about adding the pork fat that just makes it too tasty to miss."

I believed him. A second-generation butcher with opinions about fat ratios and their subsequent smoky deliciousness automatically demanded my respect. More important, I trusted him. In an industry where blood and gore were an inescapable matter of fact, Mr. Schoen's business seemed almost impossibly clean and straightforward.

As I drove home, I realized how the butchers' mannerisms at Schoen's, both their words and their body language, contributed to an atmosphere of integrity. It had taken just one brief negative experience for me to learn how easily my trust could be violated, and what the cost could be. I wouldn't underestimate its value again.

Chapter Twelve

As far back as I can remember, chickens have been in my life. It's been a blessing, with occasional cursing.

When I was three years old, I recall playing in my grandmother's henhouse, a solid, gray cinder block building that sat a few hundred feet from the front porch of her house. Though the coop had a human-size door, I was fascinated by a tiny, ground-level wooden opening built into the wall. This little door was no more than twelve inches square, big enough for two hens at a time to pass through on their way to their daily constitutionals. Watching them come and go, appearing and disappearing through this little dark hole in the wall, felt hypnotic. It was something akin to the cadence of counting sheep.

Lithe and flexible, I made this little opening my entrance as well. Inside, the floor was bedded with bright golden straw from wheat harvested on the farm. A dozen laying boxes were nailed along one wall, stuffed with clean pine shavings. Nearby, a rickety roost was engineered of rough sawmill lumber, a perfect perch for the twenty-five hens my grandmother kept.

A year later, when I could no longer contort my body through the tiny opening, she put me to work gathering eggs twice a day. Since there were never more than fifteen or twenty to gather at one time, I was given a small galvanized bucket she called her "tin pail." This little bucket suited me perfectly, as it was directly proportionate to my five-year-old stature.

I was just tall enough to unlock the rusty latch holding the door, and I shoved my weight against the heavy wood. Inside, I stood on tiptoes, peering over the edge of the nesting boxes. Many of the nests were empty, but every other box or so held several large, brown eggs nestled into the soft bedding.

I gathered these one by one, gently placing them in my pail. There were always one or two hens still on the nest, and the birds allowed me to reach slowly beneath them, groping through soft belly feathers for eggs they had tucked away. These eggs were warm orbs of pleasantness, fitting smoothly into the rounded cup of my palm.

Occasionally, as I reached toward them, the hens would strike at me with the velocity and precision of a snake, a painful reminder that they were defenders of their nests. With practice, I began to identify these birds ahead of time. Certain hens carried a malevolent expression in their eyes, subtly cocking their heads in anticipation of my offending hand. Thirty years later, I would grimace as my own son received his first peck on the fingers, an experience that always hurt more from surprise than from the actual bite.

The eggs were occasionally oddly shaped, sometimes elongated like gherkins, or as round as a golf ball. Beautiful speckled patterns danced across the shells. I came to appreciate the heft and balance of a bucket filled with large brown eggs, the pressure of the handle an indicator of how well the hens had laid that morning. Although the job unquestionably felt like a chore, there was a satisfaction in fulfilling my responsibility and playing the role of farmer.

When I became a farmer myself, I realized this childhood satisfaction came with a context. The coop had been built in advance, protecting the birds from predators and bad weather. Daily labor involved hauling feed and water, as well as providing oyster shell and granite grit for eggshell development. The floor needed constant attention, lest manure became a sanitation problem. At the end of the season, older birds were culled from the flock and replaced with younger hens. These younger hens, raised from chicks, wouldn't begin to lay eggs until they were nearly six months old. The chores, I realized, literally never stopped.

Perhaps more than any other animals on a farm, laying hens are creatures of habit. They have no issues with the same scenery, the same schedule, the same routine day after day after day. Descended from jungle fowl, their chicken ancestors never flew south for the winter because everything they needed was right around them, year-round. Modern chickens seem to have inherited this trait from their ancestors. As long as they have food, water, and a place to roost, they appear remarkably content to spend their lives on the same piece of real estate, no Caribbean vacations required.

With this in mind, I always suspected that the worst punch line ever written was actually conceived by a chicken. Everyone knows the joke: Why did the chicken cross the road? To get to the other side, of course. Funny? Never. What human comedian could ever write such insipid material? He'd be grouned off the stage.

"Why would I even *want* to cross the road?" I can imagine a chicken comedian musing. "I mean, I guess if I absolutely *had* to (not that I'm considering it, mind you—this is purely for the sake of discussion) I would probably cross it because . . . for some *unimaginable* reason . . . I needed to get to the other side. Ridiculous. [Shakes her head and pauses.] Hmm. [Thoughtfully scratches her wattles.] You know, the more I think about it, it's not only ridiculous . . . it's hilarious! Why did the chicken cross the road? To . . . *get to the other side*. Cackle cackle cackle! Take my rooster, please!"

Of course, chickens *do* wander around a little bit, chasing after beetles and scratching their way across a grassy pasture, but they journey only so far. As soon as evening shadows lengthen, they punctually stop whatever it is they are doing and immediately head toward their coop. They seem to have not only an inner clock but also an internal homing device. Within minutes they are in bed, beak tucked snugly under a wing.

In the morning, they wake at the first hint of sunrise. There is no such thing as "sleeping in" for a chicken, and certainly no snooze alarm. When the sun is barely a pink smudge on the eastern horizon, she is already up, stretching, preening, and doing her chicken yoga. She's the proverbial early bird, ready to go get those worms.

A coop of chickens is a lot like high school, where a large part of each day is spent maintaining the pecking order. This is rather the exact opposite of Facebook. Instead of "friending" their fellow hens, chickens will posture, peck, and downright clobber each other, demonstrating their individual superiority within the flock. Their goal is to preemptively "unfriend" as many hens as possible, ensuring a wide berth around the feed trough, or a prime perch on the roost. It's like a social network for egg-laying bullies.

Yet, somehow, they always manage to sort themselves out and enjoy the day. Happy hens are easy to identify. They are the ones who are "singing," a peculiar blend of clucking and cooing that melds into a single, stretched soprano note of *baaaaaaawck, bawck, bawck, bawck.* A henhouse filled with singing chickens is a joyful sound, and it's a sure sign the chickens will lay lots of eggs that day.

Birds that aren't laying eggs, on the other hand, are silent and jittery, and they take a long time to settle down once startled. Once a chicken gets out of her routine, she becomes just like that office mate who has had way, way too much coffee. But it's amazing how a favorite song can brighten a mood. If they had lips, our hens would undoubtedly whistle while they worked.

For a 4-H project the summer I was twelve, my father and I built a henhouse on the edge of our yard and started our own small flock of laying hens. That August I crated up three brown hens, a gorgeous Rhode Island Red rooster with extravagant green tail feathers, two cackling guineas, and a large Pekin duck and entered them in our county fair. I also submitted a dozen eggs, painstakingly sorted, based on uniformity of color, size, and shape.

In a community still heavily aligned with agriculture, and out of the hundreds of hens, ducks, and roosters that were exhibited that week, each of our birds won a blue ribbon, and our eggs received Best in Show. I had always assumed there was nothing especially remarkable about how we raised our poultry, and I certainly didn't expect to garner special recognition. But at that Friday night's awards ceremony, I was awarded the trophy for Best Overall Poultry.

A 4-H'er herself, Betsy was named Horticulture Queen the same year. It was 1986, and we were thrust into the spotlight of local agricultural celebrity. I felt like the Tom Cruise of chicken farmers.

Free-range chickens simply belonged on our farm, fitting in as naturally as a sunset on the horizon. By the time I graduated from college, though, I understood that there was an enormous difference between the way my grandmother had taught me to raise chickens and how most birds were grown.

My father had several friends who owned gigantic poultry barns, raising meat chickens in the steep hills of West Virginia. They fattened these birds, tens of thousands at a time, in windowless, automated confinement buildings. This type of farming was described as a sideline to what they considered their real jobs, such as school superintendent, or highway department administrator.

I listened as they complained bitterly of electricity bills and grain prices, the cost of labor, and the meager profits they received for the chickens they raised. While my dad commiserated with them, hands shoved into pockets, hats pulled low over their eyes, the only thing I could wonder was how anyone could live with the *smell*.

As one of my dad's friends put it, his daily chore was to "put on a gas mask and pick out the dead ones." The look on his face carried no trace of humor or irony. He was merely stating a fact.

The odors emanating from these confinement houses were, to be generous, nose-wrinklingly pungent. Elevated levels of ammonia burned my sinuses, triggered headaches, and left me physically nauseated. My nastiest memory is of a confinement shed that had been recently cleaned, where months of manure had been bulldozed into a mountain of excrement and feathers. Dozens of dead chickens, in various states of decomposition, protruded from the heap. Even from fifty feet away, the putrid odor was staggering. I knew that if I were to ever have a farm of my own, it wouldn't look anything like that.

Instead, once I was out of college and had fully made up my mind to farm, I began studying alternative, old-fashioned production models. There were dozens of early twentieth-century techniques describing chickens on pasture, methods that improved upon the pasture pens that my father and I had engineered. After reading these books, I could now envision our birds genuinely free-ranging, enjoying the liberty to roam and forage. If we were going to keep chickens, I resolved this was how we would raise them.

As I turned various ideas over in my mind, I realized I should talk to my resident chicken expert while I could still get her advice.

"To be honest," my grandmother began, after I had explained my model to raise a hundred laying hens on pasture, "I like your ideas about cattle a whole lot better."

I tried to take this backhanded compliment in stride. Had she forgotten that a mere twelve years earlier I had been Jefferson County Poultry King?

"But people love free-range eggs," I reminded her. "I learned that from helping you."

"Oh, yes. That's certainly true. And eggs are so nutritious. Very healthy, a completely balanced diet. You know, when I was in nursing school . . ."

I resisted the temptation to roll my eyes. My grandmother, now close to ninety, somehow managed to steer nearly every conversation back to her days as a nursing student.

I intercepted her thought. "You were taught that eggs were the perfect food, and you fed them to patients recovering from tuberculosis or swine flu or whatever horrible disease was around back then. *And . . .*" I added, stretching out the "and" as she tried to interrupt my interruption, "and they always recovered faster than patients at other hospitals."

Her eyes widened. "Why, Forrest. How did you know all that?" She winked. "You must have been listening to me after all."

"And that's exactly why I want to raise chickens. I mean, I was practically brought up in your henhouse."

She smiled briefly but then turned serious. "Well, I've been listening, too. I think it's a fine idea, but I've got several concerns. How are you going to keep the foxes away? I always closed my birds up at night in the coop. Foxes will kill your chickens as fast as you can put them out there."

"I've thought about that. They've got this great poultry netting now, with step-in posts, and you can move it around very easily. Plus, it carries a shock when you hook it up to an electric fence. The chickens stay where you want them, and you can give them fresh grass each day. It's engineered to keep the foxes out."

She arched her eyebrows. "My word, they certainly didn't have that when I was raising chickens."

"I know. It's . . . kind of a game changer."

She thought for a moment. "But what about cleaning out the coop? Twenty birds is one thing, but a hundred birds make quite a mess. They like to do their business wherever they please, you know. If you want healthy chickens, you've got to keep the *germs* out. When I was in nursing school they taught me—"

"To wash your hands twenty times a day. I remember." I nudged the conversation back to chickens. "But that's the beauty of this kind of system. Where they roost at night, the floor underneath them is made of wire. All the manure just falls right through, onto the grass."

"What do you mean, 'falls right through'?"

"Well, I took an old silage wagon and cut the floor out of it and replaced the bottom with wire. Then I built a roof over it and put a bunch of laying boxes inside. The chickens go in and out whenever they please, laying their eggs, and roosting at night. Since the floor is made of chicken wire, the poop falls straight through. No mess. And the whole thing is on wheels, which means I can just roll them to a fresh spot every day."

Her attention was rapt. "You mean, it's like a coop on wheels? And the manure falls though the bottom, onto the grass?"

"Exactly."

"And . . . you just fertilize as you go."

"Right."

Her eyes drifted far away. "My word," she said. "That's . . . that's clever. Grandson, that's very, very clever. Now that you describe it like that, well, it's a whole lot better than chickens running around getting eaten by foxes."

My heart swelled a little with her praise. In our family, encouraging words were delivered from a cupboard of paucity, as though compliments must be rationed. An endorsement like this from one of my elders was more than just a coup . . . it was a chicken coup.

"So you think it's doable?" I asked.

"Feasible," my grandmother corrected. "My English teacher always told us 'doable' isn't a real word."

I sighed. This was my life in a nutshell, with my grandmother. One step forward, but with edits. "Okay, *feasible*. Do you think it's feasible?"

"I think it's a fine idea. I think it's a very fine idea. I'll look forward to hearing how it goes."

With my first laying hens and mobile coop, 1998.

A month later I drove a pickup load of young chickens through our meadow. I parked the truck next to the mobile coop, where I had placed feed and water as housewarming gifts. Though nervous, I could hardly wait to see the chickens walking around on fresh, clean pasture. Satisfied that I had made every effort to prepare for their arrival, I dropped the tailgate and began shooing birds out the transport crates.

It was like chicken déjà vu. The first five no sooner touched the ground than, confused and panicked, they sprinted wildly into the tall, distant grass. I flashed back to the time when Dad and I inadvertently set the entire coop free and quickly shut the crate before I lost any more. From afar, I could see the grass tops moving haphazardly as the five chickens ran toward a destination I will never know. I later spent hours looking for them, but these birds were never seen again.

In my excitement to get the birds onto the pasture, I had forgotten to set up the poultry netting. Shaking my head, I wanted to kick myself for such an obvious oversight. I unrolled and staked the net, providing an established periphery, a chance for them to gradually acclimate to their surroundings. What I thought would be a flock of one hundred birds turned out to be ninety-five.

Those first five escapees certainly became fox food. And despite my best efforts over the next fifteen years, after hundreds of small improvements made from hard-won experience, they weren't the last. Nature always finds a way to strike a balance.

But a week later, when I gathered my first bucket of brown eggs, it was with an indescribably happy feeling. Cracked into a skillet, the golden yolks glowed like harvested sunshine, rising above a landscape of sumptuous egg white. These yolks were so supple they could be tossed back and forth between my hands like a ball without breaking. Just as my grandmother had taught me, I wiped the inside of the eggshell with my index finger, getting every last drop.

I made myself a big plate of scrambled eggs and toast and was immediately transported back to the days of my childhood, to afternoons at my grandparents' house, where scrambled eggs and fat wedges of homegrown tomatoes were dished onto plates for lunch. These were truly the eggs that my grandmother had raised so long ago, and I knew that once people at the farmers' markets tasted them, they would be amazed.

Still, I tried not to kid myself. A few buckets of free-range eggs and a freezer of grass-fed beef might be commendable, but my marketing was untested, my meat was mislabeled, and ninety-five chickens could lay only so many eggs. As I checked the mail each day, receiving an unending stream of literary magazine rejection letters, I couldn't ignore the invoices and overdue bills that crowded the mailbox. My parents' dining-room table, long ago retired from its intended use, seemed permanently buried beneath a landslide of paperwork. How many dozen free-range eggs would I have to sell before I put a dent in that pile of bills?

After two full years back on the farm, the stack had grown only deeper. Opening day of farmers' market was less than a week away. If we were ever going to turn the farm around, now was our moment.

Chapter Thirteen

It was the night before my first market, and I could hardly sleep. Thinking back on my ventures into firewood and straw, I realized they had been little more than glorified experiments, break-even enterprises as I searched for my proper path. Now that I had finally chosen a direction, I felt an intense pressure to succeed, to make sure that, this time, I got it right. No more mistakes, no more accidents. In many ways, farmers' market was starting to feel like my first last chance.

I lay awake most of the night, tossing restlessly, quizzing myself on prices and inventory, worried whether anyone would even shop with me or appreciate the food that I'd worked so hard to grow. At the same time, I worried that we might be so busy I'd need to serve two lines at once. The uncertainty only fueled my anxiety.

Not knowing what to expect, and frankly just wanting the moral support, I enlisted the help of my dad. He had always been reluctant to squeeze his massive frame into the tight confines of my Toyota pickup truck, punctuating each uncomfortable adjustment—knees against the dashboard, head brushing the ceiling—with a dramatically disapproving grunt. The following morning, however, he was in an especially good mood, and, with only a few muttered curses, he managed to shoehorn himself into the tiny cab. Perhaps the knowledge that one of his discarded dreams was finally coming to fruition brightened his spirits. He had never come out and said it directly, but I sensed a quiet, growing approval for what I was trying to accomplish.

The day was bright and clear, the forecast perfect. Filled with nervous energy, we speculated about what the customers would think of us and reminisced about how far we had already come. I couldn't ignore the butterflies in my stomach.

I had raised and processed another small flock of meat chickens that spring, somehow getting them butchered while simultaneously managing the cattle, starting the flock of laying hens, and making preparations for market. They had been frozen a few days earlier, and I put about a dozen in a cooler. I had no real way of knowing what the demand would be, but a dozen chickens felt like a good, round number. Then, in the middle of the night, wide awake, I reorganized the entire cooler and found space for two more.

The new hens had been laying very well, and I loaded a separate cooler of eggs, about twenty-five dozen total. The shells themselves were gorgeous, rich shades of creamy brown, freckled with dark spots. The cardboard cartons were heavy, each filled with a dozen extra-large eggs. Coupled with my freezer of grass-fed beef, the back of my truck was a veritable cornucopia of free-range food.

The prior evening, as I transferred beef from the chest freezer to the truck, I identified yet another weak link in my strategy: I had never considered what a hundred jumbled packages of meat would look like stacked together in the chest freezer. I realized too late that I was effectively creating an avalanche of frozen beef, with no method to keep the portions separated or make them easily accessible.

Since there were twenty-plus individual cuts, I eventually decided to organize them into "layers of desirability." In other words, I placed what I imagined would be the best sellers on top, and the less popular sellers on the bottom. I drew a little map on an index card as I worked, so I wouldn't forget where things were.

My geologist's trained mind envisioned a cross section of my freezer: the Porterhouse Period, the Eye of Round Epoch, perhaps transected by the London Broil Fault Line. In reality I was fooling no one but myself; I had created little more than a disorganized jumble. After I loaded everything, filling the freezer all the way to the top, my hope was that no one would ask me for a flank steak. Having never heard of this cut before, I placed it flat as a flounder against the bottom, buried beneath five packages of soup bones.

As we drove to market, my dad and I took a rough inventory. After a few calculations, we surmised that there was about two thousand dollars' worth of products on the back of the truck. It was the financial equivalent of fifty loads of firewood, or one thousand bales of straw.

Although the number seemed like an impossible accomplishment, in both the amount of food we had raised as well as its potential value, I had no way of knowing how long it would take to sell it all. One morning? A month of Saturdays? I experienced a moment of panic as I envisioned selling out halfway through my very first market, hordes of disappointed customers howling in anger as I sold my last oxtail, or the final package of chicken livers.

What *would* happen, I wondered, if I sold out of everything? Should I be happy or terrified? I realized I had foolishly loaded every last piece of beef on the truck, with no backup left at home. What would I do the following week, when I would have nothing to sell?

"First things first," Dad replied as I voiced my concerns. "You've got a butchering appointment at Schoen's in two weeks, and it looks like there are a couple of nice steers out on pasture. Besides," he added, "if you sell everything today, it's not the worst problem in the world. You'll just bring more when you can."

He was right, of course. But my inner devil's advocate harped on the fact that growing food this way took a lot of time. Raising a steer from start to finish took more than two years, and even when the animal was finally ready for the butcher, there was another two-week delay for the dry aging. Still, I had a few chickens left in the freezer, and the hens would continue to lay eggs. It would all be okay, I reassured myself.

The Berryville farmers' market was located in the center of town, in a small municipal parking lot adjacent to the town park. Either by foot or by car, it was an easy ten-minute trip from almost anywhere within the city limits.

A few weeks earlier, the manager, a woman named Sarah, had cheerfully answered my telephone inquiry with an immediate acceptance. Not only would she save us a space, but she promised to save us a loaf of her homemade English muffin bread. Both excited and suddenly a little hungry, I circled the date on my calendar as soon as I hung up the phone.

As we pulled into market, the other farmers appeared to be nearly set up. I glanced at my watch, concerned that we were late; I had figured that arriving fifteen minutes before market started would give us plenty of time. A woman in a large, round sunhat approached us briskly, smiling.

"You must be Smith Meadows Farm," she said, extending her hand. I reached through my open window, shaking her hand and introducing myself and my father.

"Oh, I can't *tell* you how happy we are to have you here," she replied effusively. She clasped her hands together, as though about to give an old-fashioned football cheer.

"We're not late, are we?" I asked. "When do people normally get here?"

She waved dismissively. "Most people get here an hour or two before market," she explained kindly, "but you'll know next time."

Oh great, I thought to myself. I had been at market less than thirty seconds and had already managed to screw up. Reading my expression, Sarah did her best to quell my concerns.

"Don't worry. The other farmers will move a little bit, to let you squeeze in. Now, you've brought meat today, yes? I just *know* the customers are going to love you." She was beaming. "I've got a great spot reserved for you, right between a berry farm and the salsa stand. They're both *super* vendors, just wonderful, and have lots and lots of customers."

She gestured to a wide parking space nearby. "It's a ten-foot space, just right for a standard tent." Standing on her tiptoes, she peeked into the back of our truck. "You did bring a tent, right?"

A tent? Were we supposed to bring a tent? I glanced at my father, who shrugged in response. "No, we didn't. Do we need one? I didn't know . . ."

"Oh, it's no problem," she interrupted gaily. "Some people don't." I glanced quickly around the market and noticed that, to the contrary, everyone did. I was feeling like such a newbie. A ripple of uncertainty played over her face, and she glanced again into the back of our truck, searching.

"You probably brought a table, though?"

"Yes ma'am," I answered sheepishly. "We brought a table."

My father leaned across me, toward the open window. "And since we don't have a tent, we brought ten-gallon cowboy hats," he deadpanned. "Wide brims, you know. So the customers will have plenty of shade."

A mixture of confusion and skepticism played across her face. "Hats? But . . . surely, you don't expect customers to, you know, stand under your hats?"

My father began to respond, but I cut the cowboy off at the pass. "He's just joking, ma'am. Pardon his dry sense of humor."

Her confusion slowly melted into relief. A moment later she burst into songlike laughter. "Oh, my! Ha ha! Ten-gallon hats! I *see!*" She winked and shook a finger at my dad as though scolding a naughty child. "Mr. Pritchard! You're too much!"

She glanced at her watch. "Goodness, look at the time. Lots of things to do. Ten-gallon hats," she repeated, shaking her head. "My word, my word. Okay, go ahead and start setting up. It was *so* nice to meet you both! I'll come over later and bring you a loaf of my English muffin bread." With that, she flitted away.

"That's some unique lady," my dad commented after Sarah was out of earshot.

"Yeah, well, she seems very nice. But would you mind toning it down a little with the jokes?"

"Toning it down?" my father replied with mock innocence. "Whatever, sir, do you mean?"

I screwed up my face at him and poked him in the gut. "That's exactly what I mean. And by the way, what were you going to say when I interrupted you about the hats?"

"Just . . . that we also brought ponchos."

"Ponchos," I repeated, almost afraid to ask. "For . . . ?"

"Well, the customers can get under our cowboy hats for shade, and they can get under our ponchos in case it rains."

I shook my head. "You are the weirdest dad. Ever."

"They're very ample ponchos," he deadpanned earnestly, fully committed to his bit. "One size fits five."

Sighing, I parked the truck.

Fortunately, it didn't take us long to set up. We opened our little aluminum folding table, spread a checkered tablecloth over it, and placed the decorative wooden chicken on one end and the scale on the other. On a weekend visit to the farm, Nancy had modified a cast-off artist's easel into a signboard, and we affixed our product list and prices to it with a little Scotch tape. When we were done, we stood in front of the booth, studying our work.

"What do you think?" I moved the chicken a little to the left. Reconsidering, I moved it to the right again.

The other farmers' stands looked so inviting, so professional, that ours felt definitively shabby in comparison. Across the market, fruit overflowed from baskets and bags of spring lettuce cascaded across tabletops. Basil and cilantro sprouted in neatly gathered bouquets, buttressed against parsley and sage. Rows of jarred jams glittered like jewels in the morning sun, and pastries were stacked in geometric patterns. It was a feast for the eyes, as well as the palate.

"I think your stand looks great," my father said, though somewhat distractedly. Why did he use the word "your" instead of "our"? I wondered. He glanced at his watch. "Seems to me like we've got a few minutes. Do you think there's anything to eat around here?"

"Dad, it's a farmers' market. Go get some strawberries."

"Strawberries?" he repeated, incredulous. "Like, in a milk shake?"

"There might be some celery around here, too."

He rolled his eyes, clutching his rotund stomach. "Celery? Am I being punished? Did I do something wrong?"

Almost on cue, Sarah appeared again, this time with a loaf of bread. She paused, taking in our modest display.

"Marvelous. Really. Just *perfect*. And this wooden chicken," she added, lifting it from the table and studying it with admiration. For a brief moment, it looked as though she might even hug it. "Adorable! Oh, I love it!"

She studied our price board, nodding thoughtfully. "Ground beef. Yes. Sirloin steaks. Yum. Filet mignon? Gracious!" She smiled approvingly, and then noticed my father eyeing the loaf of bread.

"And Mr. Pritchard, here's the English muffin bread I promised. Still warm, too."

Dad and me at market in Cascades, Virginia

He received it without hesitation. "We'll put it to good use," he replied by way of thanks. "Is there anyone here that sells jam? Seems a shame to have fresh bread without jam."

"Yes, there's a wonderful jellies and preserves farmer right across the . . ."

No sooner had she gestured than my father was gone.

"My word," Sarah said, watching him go. "He must really like jam."

"He's just always hungry," I replied, straightening the wooden chicken she had coddled. "Good thing the meat I sell is frozen, or he'd most likely eat up any profits."

She smiled, glancing at her watch. "Speaking of which, I think it's time for me to ring the opening bell."

My heart skipped. Market was starting already? It felt like I had barely gotten there. I climbed nervously onto the back of the truck, checking my refrigeration, moving my coolers closer to the tailgate.

Everything was as perfect as I could make it. The opening bell echoed across the parking lot, and I took a deep breath.

In ones and twos, customers arrived at market. The parking lot was fairly buzzing in a matter of a few minutes, with a least two dozen people circulating about. They selected blueberries and salad mixes, munched on fresh croissants, and purchased jars of honey, salsa, and chutney. The sun was out, the market was full, and the people had come to shop.

Customers passed my stand. Many of them smiled in a friendly, noncommittal way, but no one stopped. Don't look desperate, I told myself, try to act natural. I waited attentively, eagerly anticipating my first sale. Minutes passed, then a half hour. I received bushels of benevolent expressions, but no customers. After what seemed like an hour, still without a single transaction, my dad finally reappeared.

"Where have you been?" I asked, annoyed that he had ditched me right from the start.

"I went to find jam," he said, as though it explained everything.

"Yeah, well. That was close to an hour ago."

"You can't rush decisions like that. They had more than thirty flavors."

I shook my head. "How silly of me. What did you end up choosing?"

"Well, there were such interesting choices. Like watermelon-rind marmalade. Have you ever heard of such a thing?"

"Nope. Did you try it?"

"Sounded disgusting. I ended up getting grape."

"Grape? Thirty different flavors, one hour later, and you settled on *grape?*"

"Can't dispute a classic."

While we were talking, a customer approached our stand. "Pardon me," the man said. "What is it that you gentlemen are selling?"

I gestured to the easel where I had posted my prices. "Good morning, sir. We brought . . ."

At that moment I realized the tape had come unstuck. Without my noticing it, the sheet had fallen off and was lying facedown on the asphalt. No wonder no one had stopped.

Clumsily, I made my way to the front of the table and picked up the piece of paper. It had been thoroughly trampled, pocked, and stained by the rough pavement. I made a futile attempt at sticking it back on the board.

"We . . . uh . . . we sell free-range meat, and eggs," I said, flustered, trying to smooth the paper back into shape. "Grass-fed beef, and, um, pasture-raised chicken."

The man studied the marred inventory list. "How do you sell it? Do you take orders?"

"No, we have it right here," I said, gesturing at the back of my truck. "We sell it by the pound."

He appeared confused. "You have what right here? The meat?"

"Yes, in coolers. On the back of the truck."

A light of understanding dawned on his face. "Oh! *That* makes more sense. You know, I walked past three times, trying to figure out what you were selling. From this angle, you can't really see anything but the tailgate and your table."

He was right. The customer's vantage point revealed very little about what we had to offer, especially when our one and only sign was lying facedown on the ground.

He scanned the list a second time. "You know," he said, "it's been a long time since I've had short ribs. How do you sell them?"

My heart leapt into my throat. Oh no, I said to myself. Not the short ribs.

Short ribs had been one of the truly enigmatic cuts I had received from the butcher. They were something I had never personally eaten before, and I honestly hadn't imagined anyone would request them.

Accordingly, I had placed them almost at the bottom, just above the soup bones.

"They come two to a pack," I told him, trying to recall, as I spoke, exactly what they looked like. "I think they're about a pound or two per package."

"Perfect," he replied. "I'll try a pack."

"Yes, sir. It'll just be a moment."

I climbed onto the back of the truck, studying my cheat sheet. Short ribs: six packs, lower left side. I rooted through the steaks and roasts, the hamburger patties and ground beef, piling them to my right as I dug for the ribs. I was about halfway down when the meat pyramid lost its structural integrity and cascaded back into the hole I had just created.

I tried a second time, more carefully, but with the same result. Glancing sidelong at the customer, I noticed him watching my efforts with bemusement. On my third attempt, I stacked the meat everywhere I could, on the cab of the truck, on the cooler tops, along the edges of the bed liner. At last, I found a package of short ribs. All the while, my father munched placidly on a slice of English muffin bread.

"Here you go," I said, puffing a little from the exertion. "Let's see. A pound and three quarters, times two seventy-five a pound. That'll be four dollars and eighty-one cents."

After he was gone, I quickly scrambled back onto the truck and put everything away as quickly as I could. The meat was now a complete jumble, and I gave up any hope of sorting it out at market. As I tried to close the lid, however, I realized in my haste that I hadn't repacked the freezer properly. Meat was now overflowing from the top, making it impossible to shut the lid. I had a lot of rethinking to do.

By the end of the day, we sold five dozen eggs, two packages of ground beef, and the aforementioned short ribs. No one had so much as asked to see a chicken. In fact, Sarah had bought a dozen eggs and a pound of ground beef herself, a last-minute purchase that appeared to be motivated by pity more than anything else. I drove home as my father counted the money. We had made a little less than twenty-two dollars in total sales.

I stared blankly over the steering wheel, this new failure weighing heavily on my mind. We drove past our local supermarket, its parking lot packed with cars, shoppers pushing carts laden with groceries. I couldn't help feeling dejected about the morning.

"What am I going to do, Dad? I didn't even make enough money to pay for our gas today."

For once, he seemed to respect the gravity of the situation. "I'm not sure. But you can't have many more days like this." The twinkle of inspiration that he'd sustained these past few months was suddenly veiled. "I don't want to be the one who said 'I told you so,'" he continued, but his voice carried the slightest note of admonishment. "Look at it this way. You still have time to go back and get your teaching certificate."

He was right, of course. I *could* go back to school. I could spend a few more semesters studying and taking out student loans. It wouldn't be difficult to secure a teaching position, a career with a reliable paycheck, health care benefits, and vacation time. No one could fault me for having tried my hand at farming and coming up short. I certainly wouldn't be the first.

Meanwhile, as I filled out applications and drove to interviews, our family farm would die its silent, inevitable death. As I commuted to work each day, spending my evenings grading pop quizzes and term papers, seven generations of tradition would slip forever through my fingers. I laughed bitterly, thinking about my farming experiences so far. As much as I wanted to believe otherwise, there was no real difference between eighteen dollars of grain and twenty-two dollars of free-range meat. If I lost the farm—but managed to preserve my dignity—would my failure be somehow more honorable?

Everyone in our community was always so sad when a farm was forced to sell. They shook their heads with nostalgic regret, remembering the way things used to be. But a month later, after the land had been sold to pay debts and a new subdivision had armored the earth with asphalt, the old farm would gradually fade from their memories. In a few years' time, it would seem as if it had never existed at all.

We remained silent the rest of the way home, both of us lost in thought. As we pulled into the driveway, my father turned to me. "Hey, try to look on the bright side," he said.

"What bright side would that be?" I asked, in no mood for one of his jokes.

He smiled, but his delivery carried no punch line. "At least you won't have to worry about selling out too quickly."

Chapter Fourteen

That same afternoon, Travis LaFleur appeared at our farm and announced without preamble that he would begin working for us. My parents and I, nonplussed, listened with equal parts confusion and amusement as Travis laid out the details of his employment to us. In crisp order, he informed us of the hours and days he would be working, what skills he brought to the job, and his short but nonnegotiable list of deal breakers. When he was done, apparently satisfied that we had paid attention, he got in his pickup truck and drove away.

We knew Travis, or at least knew of him. He had spent his entire career at a neighboring property, helping manage a cattle and sheep farm. A reliable fixture of the landscape, he was easily spotted from a distance making hay or planting corn. The owner of the farm, a man in his eighties, had abruptly decided to retire and had summarily informed Travis that he no longer had a job. Three decades of Travis's career ended practically overnight.

It was with this same matter-of-fact attitude that he appeared on our doorstep, letting us know that he would be starting that Monday. With a farmer's intuition, knowing when the soil was ready for the seed, Travis seemed to know that he belonged on our farm.

I don't recall that we questioned his decision at all. The reality was, despite being unable to afford it, we truly needed the help. My farmers' market experience had been just short of catastrophic, but I knew I had to keep trying at least a little longer. I still had the cattle and chickens to manage, and now that I would regularly attend farmers' markets, the thought of having Travis's help was an unexpected relief.

In the years leading up to my return, we had endured a spate of especially bad farmhands, culminating with a well-meaning but unequivocally alcoholic man from New Hampshire named Todd Milgrom. After living for a year or so on the farm, Todd began showing up for work less and less, blaming his absences on his splitting headaches. One morning, when the farm well pump stopped working, we entered the basement of the tenant house he lived in, where the breaker box was located. To our amazement, the entire basement was stacked floor-to-ceiling, wall-to-wall with cases of empty beer cans, nearly to the point that we couldn't wedge ourselves inside.

We did the math, and discovered there were over four hundred cases of beer, each containing twenty-four empty cans. He had polished off a case for nearly every day he had been on the farm. Small wonder his productivity was inconsistent.

Our farm manager for several years prior had been a round-faced, snuff-chewing man named Charlie Loudermill. His singular great talent was an uncanny ability to pick the prize-winning Dr Pepper from the nearby country store. It reached the point where he would purchase two bottles, giving me first choice. Reliably, the inside of my cap read: SORRY, TRY AGAIN. Time after time, Charlie's snuff-encrusted smile would betray his results: WINNER! 20 OZ. DR PEPPER!

One afternoon we received two envelopes from the livestock sale, one with our name on it and the other with Charlie's. Since we knew for certain that Charlie didn't own any livestock, we assumed there must be a mix-up. He had delivered twenty-five steers for us the week before, and perhaps the cashier had assumed that some of them were his. Cattle auctions were places where everyone knew one another, and an honest mistake wasn't beyond the realm of possibility.

We opened our check, which showed payment for only twenty steers. Later that day, my parents asked Charlie about his check, which was written to him for the amount of five steers. When they asked how this could be, he insisted he had raised five steers on his own and had taken them along with ours to save fuel. What about our missing steers, they asked, which both records and an afternoon head count clearly showed were no longer on the farm? Charlie shrugged. Maybe they jumped a fence, he suggested. Maybe someone had stolen them.

My parents had a feeling the cattle had been stolen, too. Instead of calling the police, they let Charlie keep his check but informed him that his services were no longer needed. The check was his severance pay.

Travis LaFleur arrived with a reputation for honesty, a strong work ethic, and no lingering anecdotes about his drinking behavior. Relative to the sluggards, crooks, and knuckleheads we had hired in the past, he seemed like an Eagle Scout.

Descended from French and Native American heritage, he was born in 1947 in a two-room house in Rippon, West Virginia. His father had been a peripatetic dairyman, and his mother had raised the children during their father's frequent, unexplained disappearances, which lasted for months at a time. He recalled his grandmother, a native Blackfoot Indian, having ebony and gray hair, which she plaited in two long braids that swayed across her back. When he and his siblings were dismayed to discover that her bare feet weren't actually black, she threw back her ancient head in laughter, but she never bothered to correct their assumption.

My first memory of Travis was from early childhood, watching from a distance as his rusted, baby-blue Volkswagen Beetle navigated a slow progress across the neighboring farm's pasture. It was 1977, he was thirty, and he still didn't have his driver's license. He didn't take the test for another five years, preferring instead to simply drive across the grass and spend his evenings at home.

Even though he stayed off the public road, it still took him an inordinate amount of time to reach my neighbor's farm this way. He could drive only so far before a gateless fence crossed his path, so he parked the car in the same spot each day, hopped a locust post, and walked the final half mile each morning across the dew-drenched pasture. The groundhogs must have breathed a sigh of relief when he finally graduated to paved roads.

Like my grandfather, circumstances had dictated that he quit school early and go to work on the farm. As the eldest child of seven, and with a father who occasionally vanished into the countryside, he didn't need to be told that his family needed his help. He simply found a job and went to work.

Although he could add and subtract, and occasionally multiply and divide when absolutely necessary, his understanding of fractions began and ended with one half.

"My cousin explained it to me once," he later confided, as we collaborated on a carpentry project. "He got out a piece of paper and drew a big pie on it. I mean," he continued, hacking the air demonstratively, "I understand that you can cut a pie up in different ways, fourths and fifths and quarters. I can see it in my mind." Travis had crystal-blue eyes, and he stared at me intently while he spoke.

"But once you take that pie away, it all just goes straight out of my head. You tell me to cut that board five foot and an eighth, and, buddy, I'll tell you where you can shove that board."

To his credit, whenever he told me the chicken feeders were half full, or the hay barn was half empty, I knew I could take him at his word. Fearing splinters, I never asked him to be more specific than that.

Travis LaFleur.

Two days after his announcement, on Monday morning, he showed up promptly at five thirty. I started work at seven, and didn't even get up until six. I found him that morning banging loudly on my front door, rousing me from a deep sleep.

I greeted him, bleary-eyed and tousle-haired, naked except for my boxer shorts. "Hello?"

He took a sharp step backward, eyeing me up and down. "You ain't going to work dressed like that, I imagine."

"Going to work?" I repeated, sleep-addled. I squinted at him in the bright morning light, genuinely confused. "Who are you?"

He placed his hands on his hips, indignant. "I'm Travis." As though feeling the need to clarify, he added, "I'm here to work."

I ran a hand through my hair, and then rubbed the sleep out of my eyes. "Right. I remember now. So, I don't usually get going till around seven . . ."

"Seven? Cows need to be checked before then," he interrupted. "You got a truck?"

"Yeah, but . . ."

"Alright. I'll check the cows, you put on some pants. I'll be back in a half hour."

I still wasn't quite awake. "You'll check the cows . . ."

"Are the keys in the truck?"

"Yeah. Yeah, I think so."

He turned to go and then stopped. "You've got boots, right? You need boots on a farm."

Now it was my turn to feel a little indignant. "Yes," I said, straightening. "I have boots. I've . . . I've got *lots* of boots."

"Mmm-hmm," Travis replied. "See you at six."

Through my window, I saw him driving down the lane in my Toyota, headed toward the herd. Self-consciously, I glanced at my waist, having no recollection as to what I had worn to bed the night before. Pink polka-dot boxer shorts sagged around my hips. It must have been quite a first impression.

A little past six, after Travis was sufficiently impressed with my boot selection, he informed me it was time to check the fences. He made no pretense of relinquishing the steering wheel, so I climbed into the passenger seat beside him.

"You always got to check the fences," he said in a tone that left no room for argument. "Every morning. Trees fall down in the middle of the night. Bulls'll break posts. A farm's got to have good fences."

It was a bright, beautiful morning. Enormous clouds pushed against the blue sky, and for a few moments, I forgot about my colossal failure at the farmers' market. We made a slow circuit around the farm, until we came to a section of fence that straddled the property line where Travis had worked the previous thirty years.

He slowed the truck to a crawl. "I put that fence in right there. Myself." He gestured. "Dug every posthole by hand, stretched the wire and stapled it."

"The whole row?" I asked.

"Yup."

"But . . . there must be three hundred posts in that line."

"Probably."

I considered this in silent awe. I had set perhaps one hundred posts in my entire lifetime, and each of them had been arduous work. If this row was any indication, Travis had probably set thousands of them in his career.

We came to a turn where heavy brace wires were anchored to massive locust posts, tensioned to keep the fence tight.

"Right there," Travis said, pointing, "there, in that corner, was where I first met your granddaddy. Many, many years ago. Twenty-five years or more, I reckon."

"You knew my grandfather?" I replied, surprised. I had barely known him myself, and only when he was a very old man, no longer an able-bodied farmer.

"Oh, yeah," Travis said, coming to a stop and putting the truck in park. "I knew him. Everybody around here knew your granddaddy."

He got out of the cab, and I followed him. He gave the post a firm shove. "Still tight. That was the first corner I ever put in, right there. Holding up pretty good."

I tried to imagine a twenty-year-old Travis meeting my grandfather, who would have been in his early seventies at the time. "What did you think of him?"

Travis looked surprised. "Who? Your granddaddy? Everybody liked your granddaddy. And respected him, sure."

I took vicarious pride in his testimony. "How did you guys meet?"

He thought for a few moments, giving the post another shove for good measure. "Well," he said, "I was putting in this corner brace right here. It's a pretty big post, you can see for yourself. It's probably every bit a hundred-pound locust log."

I studied the large post appreciatively, nodding.

"Anyway, I was out here all by myself, like I said. And it was hot outside. There weren't any trees out here then, not like now, with all these mulberries and sugar nuts that's grown up in the fence line over the years. So it was real hot out, and I was out here working and I'd just gotten done eating my lunch. All of a sudden, I got a big pain in my belly." He groaned in mock pain, clutching his stomach. "I mean, it was one of those kinds that don't give you no warning. Just a hot day, and the sweating. And the beans, I reckon. You know?

"Well, whatever it was, I knew I was in trouble. I mean, it was coming on *quick*. It was too far to make it back to the house, and I knew I was all alone. So I looked around, didn't see anybody, and backed myself up to that post right there."

I had been leaning against this post while I listened, and in spite of myself, I glanced at the ground.

"Oh, don't worry," he said. "It ain't here no more. So there I was with my pants around my ankles, just letting it rip and making all sorts of terrible noise, when this loud voice came up behind me:

"'What are you doing out here?' I heard the voice say. I turned around, and there was your granddaddy standing right behind me. I don't know where he had come from. Maybe he had been out checking the cattle, and I hadn't seen him in the tall grass.

"But anyway, there he was, wanting to know what I was doing. And there I was, my pants around my ankles, hunched up against a post, right in the middle of my business. It was just rolling through me, like water pouring out of a bucket. I probably don't have to tell you, but I didn't need the company right then. So I said the first thing that came to my mind.

"'I'm taking a big shit!' I told him. Those were the first words I ever said to your granddaddy.

"So he said to me, 'I didn't mean *that*. I meant, what are you doing with this fence? Looks like you're putting in a new brace.'

"Well, we were right at the corner of where our two farms met, and he was probably just wondering what was going on, since the man I worked for hadn't told him nothing. But I had misunderstood what he meant, and I got real embarrassed and didn't know what to say.

"So, I told him again, but louder this time, 'I'm taking a big shit!' It was all I could think of to say. And it was true, you know. That's what I was doing. I mean, the whole time, it was just coming in waves. If I had a chance to do it over, I might have said, 'I'm putting in a fence brace.'

"Your granddaddy looks at me, and I look at him, and neither one of us says anything. I was still squatting up against that corner post, and by now my legs were starting to give out, and I kind of wished he'd go away."

"And he just stood there?" I asked. "I mean, I hope you didn't think it was rude, or . . ."

"Oh, no. No, no, no. I think he was just as surprised as I was. He'd probably been walking across the pasture, saw the new brace, and hadn't noticed me there. That's what I always figured. I mean, once he saw what was happening, he turned his back to me. But anyway, after I hollered at him the second time, he walked away."

I was relieved for the both of them. "I bet you guys must have had a good laugh about that!"

Travis appeared confused. "What do you mean?"

"You and my grandfather."

"Oh, I never talked to him about it." He shook his head. "Nope, that was the only time I ever spoke to your granddaddy."

Now it was my turn to be confused. "But . . . I thought you said that you knew him."

"I did know him."

"But that was the only time you two ever talked?"

Travis straightened a little, as though sensing a challenge. "Yeah. So?"

Having known Travis for only about a half hour now, and a significant amount of that time in my boxer shorts, I decided to drop the subject. "No reason," I said.

We climbed back into the truck, continuing our circuit around the fence. The perimeter appeared solid, and we finished our loop at the barnyard, where Travis turned off the engine. Before he got out, he turned in his seat, studying me with those clear blue eyes.

"I've been meaning to ask. You've got indoor plumbing here, right? Toilets that flush, is what I mean."

There was, without doubt, only one correct answer.

"Absolutely," I replied.

He appeared satisfied with my answer. From that moment onward, the rest of the day went more or less flawlessly.

Chapter Fifteen

"The haybine's broke. *Again*." Travis was frustrated, shading his eyes against the bright glare of the sun. He had departed that morning on the tractor with the haybine attached, then had reappeared with the tractor, but now the haybine was nowhere in sight. Somewhere on the farm, I deduced, hay wasn't being made.

"We need more knife guides," he continued. "And remember those hex-head bolts you got? Well, I threw the last handful of them across the pasture, into the trees. I *told* you we need square-seated carriage bolts."

"Right," I replied, feeling appropriately chastised. I remembered him telling me that, now. I had recently returned from the hardware store with a shopping list of about twenty items, and the nuance of bolt types had somehow gotten lost in my haste to get back to the farm. "How many do you need?"

"A truckload. And hardened ones, if they got them. But that's not the main problem. The universal joint's about to go on the PTO shaft. It's flopping around like a fish. I'm not gonna run the machine like that, too damn dangerous.

"My brother Sam got his shirtsleeve caught on a U-joint like that while it was running, and it spun him around four times. Straight between the shaft and the drawbar, then spit him back out." He shook his head. "Four times! And didn't leave a scratch on him. You know how wide that space is?" He held his hands apart. "About a foot. That's just lucky, is all that is. No, sir. Not gonna work with equipment like that. Better safe than sorry."

Something was always broken. Travis had methodically examined our inventory of dilapidated machinery, deciding what still worked and what needed repair. At the end of his survey, he summarized his conclusions into one disapproving grunt.

One of our tractors needed a new water pump, and the other had a leaky radiator. A broken chain on the spreader was buried beneath two tons of manure. The haymaking equipment, starting with the rake and ending with the square baler, required a complete overhaul. This didn't even include the broken-down wagon abandoned near the corner of the barnyard, missing its two rear wheels. Now our haybine had joined the ranks of the infirm.

Equipment repair monopolized our time. Travis taught me how to remove mower blades from a brush hog, replace an alternator on the Ford tractor, and retrofit a new hydraulic pump to a 1950s-era post-hole auger. We had inherited most of the machinery from my grandfather's farm, and, though a few pieces still functioned admirably, none of it was remotely new.

Earlier that summer, when I couldn't disconnect the PTO from the rusty shaft of the tractor, I used a crowbar for leverage. The bar shifted unexpectedly, crushing my thumbnail. Blood squirted at the same rate as my pulse: *beat-squirt, beat-squirt, beat-squirt,* spraying against the tractor tire. I tore a sleeve off my T-shirt, wrapped it tightly, and finally muscled the metal apart. A few weeks later, the nail fell off.

"Have you ever fixed a universal joint before?" I asked Travis.

"Oh, sure. They're no problem to fix, really. Just takes time. The biggest thing is whether you can get to town before the store closes. I've still got half the field to cut, and they're calling for rain by the end of this week."

And so it went. We passed the summer months each year in a three-ring circus of cutting grass, breakdowns, and frantic repairs. It was enough to give a farmer a case of indigestion.

Haymaking was the one agricultural ritual that still brought the entire family together. We tried our best to bale on the weekends, when everyone was home. After the wagons were loaded, my sister and I climbed a wooden ladder into the shadowy barn loft, the rungs worn smooth by nearly two centuries of climbers who had come before us. A long, metal elevator stretched from the barn floor to the loft at a forty-five-degree angle, an oversized conveyor belt delivering the hay to us. Dad stood on the wagon, pitching the bales to my mom, who in turn placed them on the elevator. If things were really rolling, there were always three or four bales moving at a time.

I loved putting up hay. I positioned myself near the top, catching the twin-stringed bales as they crested. Using the momentum of the elevator, I heaved them to my sister, who balanced on bales ten feet above my head. I fell into steady tempo with the work, a human "kicker" at the end of the elevator. My arms were sinewy and taut, streaming with rivulets of sweat and dust. At the end of the day, my biceps twitched and popped with residual electricity, seeming to replay each toss over and over again.

My family was united by the solemn fact that if we didn't harvest enough hay in the summer, our cattle would starve to death come wintertime. Faced with this reality, haying had always been a mandatory activity. My grandfather had kept two years' worth of hay in his barns, safely weathering both winter blizzards and summer droughts. The shadowy recesses of our barn contained bales that had been put up decades earlier; properly cured, hay remains palatable almost indefinitely. I now felt a responsibility to keep my own barn fully stocked.

Still, the longer I considered it, the harder time I had making sense of the math. Labor and repairs topped my list of concerns, and it didn't help that cattle prices had recently fallen again. Our last load of calves had brought only seventy cents per pound at the stock sale, a 10 percent drop from the prior year. As I ran to town on yet another trip for tractor parts, this meager paycheck eroded right before my eyes.

But this was how we'd always done it, I kept telling myself. This was how my grandfather, and all my neighbors, farmed. Haying was simply an unavoidable part of cattle farming, a season of costly aggravation that kept the business afloat. Resigned to my duty, I climbed onto my Ford tractor and headed back into the fields.

One day, by chance, I read about Gordon Hazard, a farmer who grazed cattle on a farm in Mississippi. He was renowned not only because he had raised his animals profitably for fifty straight years (a herculean accomplishment for any business, and doubly so in a commodity-based enterprise) but also for his hard-line stance against owning farm machinery of any kind.

The old farmer owned three pieces of equipment: a pickup truck, a hammer, and a backup hammer. He kept the backup hammer, he said, in case his first hammer broke. I laughed at the wisdom in this. Hazard had long ago terminated his own haymaking operations. Instead, he bought his hay from neighboring farms. If other farms are really good at making hay, he posited, why not allow himself to benefit from their expertise?

By never purchasing hay equipment, he never had to repair it. Extending this logic, he never had to fuel it, change the fluids and filters, pay annual taxes on it, or protect it from bad weather by erecting an equipment shed. After all, he explained, for three hundred and fifty-odd days each year, this equipment sat in storage, unused.

Instead, he put his money into buying hay. He even went so far as to pay someone to place it exactly where he wanted it in each of his fields, eliminating any need for a tractor. Hazard spent the rest of his summer using his hammer to repair and improve his fences. Fences, as Travis had pointed out on day one, were by far the most important piece of infrastructure on any livestock farm.

Cutting summer hay.

This new way of thinking floored me. Here was someone with a farm just like mine, and who adhered to the same grass-fed production model. Yet by using no equipment at all, he had enough profit left over at the end of the year to buy his own hay. Over the course of one afternoon, Hazard's philosophy turned several of my farming beliefs straight on their head.

In our agricultural community, only the wealthiest, most extravagant farms ever bought hay. These farms usually had affluent owners, where no expense was spared as long as their livestock, most often horses, had the best hay available. Each winter I shook my head at the line of pickup trucks idling at the feed store, awaiting their load of premium, retail-priced hay. Invariably, the logo of a horse farm was embossed on the side of their doors.

In contrast, I had always assumed that cattle farms made their own hay all summer long. These farmers spent their time just as we did, running endless circles to get hay into the barn between rainstorms and before the autumn frost. In our part of the world, from May through September, haymaking was the only game in town.

In fact, the most respected farms of all not only made their own hay but also took pride whenever they had excess to sell. These farms set aside their finest cuttings each season, selling it to the very horse and hobby farms they privately derided. For years I had admired these operations from afar, wondering if our farm could ever match their amazing productivity, or ever hope to afford the modern tractors and equipment they owned. Now I regarded them with fresh eyes. Their productivity *had* to come with a high price tag.

Although it was tempting to take Gordon Hazard for his word and simply drop haying entirely, I knew it wouldn't be that easy. First, we had no money to buy hay, even if we wanted to do so. But wait just a second, I told myself. If we really had no money, how did we continue to pay for the machinery repairs? We were tens of thousands of dollars in debt, but we still paid our diesel and tractor bills on time. If we stopped spending this money now, I asked myself, wouldn't it be available to help purchase hay? My head spun with the circular reasoning of the conundrum.

To sort things out, I sat down with a pencil and paper. An average square bale of hay sold for $3.50. Basic math told me that, after maintenance, repairs, fertilizer, insurance, taxes, fuel, depreciation, hauling, and a modest salary of five dollars per hour, the cost for our farm to produce a single bale was nearly ten dollars.

Having made thousands upon thousands of bales myself, I didn't believe this number could be possible, so I double- and triple-checked my math. The figure appeared correct. To top it all off, there was still a missing component, a figure I hadn't been able to quantify: What should I charge for the soil?

The soil. It was the common denominator for every farm. Every backyard gardener understood the importance of rich soil. Fertility was what made a farm a farm instead of a desert, or a parking lot. Dirt, rain, sunshine, and seeds. It didn't get any more basic than that.

There was no confusion in my twenty-four-year-old mind. If my production costs were ten dollars a bale, and hay was made of soil, then the actual cost must be even higher. The *true* price must include re-mineralizing the earth, replacing the dirt sold in the form of hay bales. Sensing I had hit on something fundamentally important, I shared my concerns with older farmers, asking them for a value, in dollars, of the earth beneath their feet. Despite my efforts, not a single farmer was willing to speculate what the price of their soil might actually be worth.

Those farmers I had admired for so many years, the ones who sold their hay, were actually selling their soil as well. They were trading their future fertility to other farms, receiving money that would have to be spent rebuilding the soil they were depleting. On the other hand, that clever old farmer Gordon Hazard was importing nutrients onto his farm, stretching his dollar beyond the economics of diesel and steel. Buying his hay, he improved his fertility year after year. His was an investment of increasing returns.

These revelations exploded like fireworks in my young mind. One path was sustainable, while the other was a road of never-ending labor, machinery, and expense. My thoughts quickly turned to the equipment we had on the farm. What did we truly need? What could we let go? As was becoming my habit, I sat down to make a list.

If I was going to haul my own livestock, I had to have transport. Truck and trailer, column one. Column two filled up quickly: mowers, planters, sprayers, balers and rakes, the disc plow, the corn picker, the forklift, the one-man hydraulic boom, and finally, four (yes, *four*) of our tractors. To save myself from going completely off the deep end, I retained one tractor, a four-wheel-drive, medium-horsepower machine with a large front-end loader. Nearly everything else got the boot.

I was shocked by how much money people offered for our old junk. I ran an ad for each piece of equipment, getting a hundred dollars here, a thousand dollars there. For our larger machines, the tractors especially, I had no trouble making multi-thousand-dollar transactions. By the time I was done, my grandfather's old equipment shed sat nearly vacant.

It was a leap of faith, but so was everything else I had tried thus far. Every dollar went into a special account to buy hay the following year. Our repair and fuel costs now disappeared, and our improving pastures meant that we could graze longer into the winter, further reducing our hay requirements. As near as I could figure, we now had three times as much money as we needed to buy a year's worth of hay.

Skeptical at first, Travis watched the equipment disappear down the road. We retained the broken-down manure spreader and the worn-out feed grinder, modifying them into a mobile chick brooder and a gravity feed bin that required no external power. Travis especially liked helping out on these creative projects, and he slowly grew to appreciate giving old implements a newly imagined purpose.

It wasn't long before I noticed him dreaming out loud. He was mulling over a pile of old tires we had stacked beside the barn, wondering if they could somehow be bolted together and made into a pasture drag. I could almost see the wheels turning in his head.

A few months later, one rainy afternoon, we built it. Made of twenty old tires and pulled behind our one and only tractor, it obliterated fresh cow patties in the field, spreading fertilizer to help the grass to grow. Travis, craving his tractor fix, enthusiastically took to wreaking manure mayhem in the fields. I was happy to oblige. Made of leftover hardware, the drag would never need repairing, and it kept twenty junk tires out of the dump.

No repairs? Fewer bills? Less was truly beginning to feel like more.

Chapter Sixteen

I eventually filled my appointment at Schoen's, and the experience was everything I had hoped. The service was professional, the cutting instructions had been followed precisely, and our label and farm logo looked fantastic. The difference between butchers was as stark as chuck roast and filet mignon.

I arrived at Schoen's with the same small chest freezer I had used at Donny's, expecting that my second steer, which had been of identical weight, would fill it nearly to the same level. I loaded the freezer to the brim but still had several trays of meat left over. That's odd, I said to myself. I studied the inventory, wondering why last time it had fit so well. Convinced that I had simply packed too quickly, I started all over again, trying to free up more space.

Mr. Schoen watched from the loading dock as I emptied and repacked the freezer. "Need any help?" he asked. "Looks like you could use some extra boxes."

"I'll be alright," I said, preoccupied with how best to stack the ground beef packaged in cylindrical white sleeves. "I thought this freezer would be enough, but you guys must have done a better job than my last butcher."

"What do you mean?"

I stacked the ground beef vertically, wedging in three packages at a time. "I think there's just more meat this time. A *lot* more meat."

"Who was your last butcher, if you don't mind me asking?"

I bent over the freezer, nestling New York strips between the sirloin tip roasts. "I'm not exactly sure of the name of his shop," I said from the echoing depths, "but the butcher's name is Donny."

"Oh," Mr. Schoen said, clearing his throat. "*Him*. People have told me a great deal about his place. Actually, he's been good for business."

"I can imagine."

"But as far as the meat goes . . . how should I put this?" He rubbed his chin. "Have you considered the reason that you've got *more* meat now is because you got *less* with him?"

I abruptly stopped my packing. "Wait a minute. Are you suggesting that he stole from me?"

Mr. Schoen innocently raised both hands. "I'm not saying a thing. But other customers have told me stories. Seems as though you had a similar experience."

The likelihood of this scenario slowly sank in. "You know," I said, trying not to sound bitter, "it's funny. By stealing, he's basically putting his own customers out of business."

Mr. Schoen removed his black fedora, smoothed his hair, and then replaced it. "Well, no matter how much we want it otherwise, I suppose we can only mind our own business."

I considered the wisdom in this. "But what if 'minding my own business' means minding someone *else's* business? That's kind of a dilemma, isn't it?"

"I'd agree. And if that's the case," he added, "then you'd better have a pretty good business yourself."

I was beginning to have the same notions.

Sales had slowly picked up at our hometown farmers' market that summer. It was just enough to boost my spirits, tantalizing me with the hope that business might improve the following week. But despite my optimism, our best day that summer barely broached two hundred dollars. I bought a tent, and Nancy helped me make more signs, but these improvements made no appreciable difference. As the weeks passed, I wondered how my expectations could have fallen so utterly short of their mark.

Some customers told me their freezers were filled with meat from their deer-hunting friends, or with beef from relatives who had their own cattle herds. Others said they raised animals themselves and slaughtered a pig or lamb of their own each year.

Still, most people probably *didn't* have a freezer full of meat waiting for them at home. The grocery store deli always had a steady line of customers, and on days when market was sparsely attended, our local supermarket was reliably bustling with activity. Weekend after weekend, I stood beneath our little tent, smiling and nodding to folks who passed by but didn't shop with me. I began to question whether anyone in our community seriously cared about how we were farming, or what we had to offer.

"There's an old saying," Dad said, in an attempt to make me feel better. "'Talent at home goes wasted.'"

"What's that supposed to mean?"

We were seated around the cluttered dining-room table, revisiting the season's numbers. The results were beyond discouraging. Twenty weekends of farmers' market attendance had yielded only three thousand dollars of gross revenue.

"I can't remember who said it. But the idea is, no one appreciates your talent in your own hometown."

I leveled my gaze at him. "I'm not exactly playing the saxophone here, Dad."

"No. But you're trying to stay in business. And if people around here see cows everywhere they go, out grazing along the highway, then maybe they're not going to think what we're doing is special. What's that other phrase? 'Familiarity breeds contempt.'"

Cattle grazing on spring pasture

"So what are you saying? That we pack up the farm and move to Hollywood?"

He shrugged. "Maybe. Or, you could start a little closer. There are a lot of people who live just across the mountain in Loudoun County. There must be farmers' markets there, too. Maybe we'd be just far enough away to seem a little bit different."

The more I thought about it, the more it made sense. Loudoun was the county directly to the east, on the other side of Blue Ridge Mountain. Their population was about twenty times the size of ours, three hundred thousand citizens as opposed to Clarke's modest fifteen thousand. Driving to Dulles Airport, on the far end of Loudoun County from us, there were certain points along the highway where rooftops stretched ad infinitum into the horizon. Surely these communities had some sort of city limits, but whether the houses overlapped into the sprawling communities of Ashburn, or Sterling, or Herndon, I really couldn't tell. The transitions seemed evinced by shiny, high-end shopping malls. Loudoun had one of the highest median household incomes in the entire country. I decided it was at least worth a look.

With a full farmers' market season now behind me, I attended the Loudoun County farmers' market meeting in December 1998. I kept my mind open to all possibilities, anything that might somehow help the farm. Roughly thirty people were in attendance as a woman named Margaret opened the session.

Margaret was a farmer as well, and she sold her goods at the four existing Loudoun County markets. I listened as she spoke at length about the merits of each location, and, as she did, I honed in on two that seemed to make the most sense for us: the markets in the towns of Middleburg on Saturday and Cascades on Sunday. Each was well established, and Margaret spoke about both with great enthusiasm. When she was done, a man in the middle of the room was the first to raise his hand.

He was stocky, careworn, and in his mid-fifties. "Forgive me for being blunt," he began, "but do you have a range of weekly receipts from different vendors at these markets? Just ballpark, you know."

"It depends," Margaret said. She had a slow, deliberate way of speaking. "Some markets are consistently strong, and some go up and down depending on the season. Also, it depends on what you're selling."

"I sell flowers. Cut flowers, for bouquets."

Margaret beamed. "Oh, how wonderful. We've needed cut flowers ever since our previous vendor retired."

"Do you think," the man prompted, "you can recall how much the previous flower vendor made at a market?"

"Hmm," she replied. "Of course, it varied. Varied from market to market, you understand. There are so many factors that contribute to a successful day. Weather, for example, can have a surprising effect. Good or bad weather has a lot to do with customer turnout."

"Sure. I'm familiar with that. I've been growing and selling flowers for more than twenty years. Just a rough estimate is what I'm looking for."

Margaret smiled placidly. "You know, one of the nice things about our market is that we don't require our vendors to report weekly sales. We only take an annual survey, to chart growth."

The man was becoming ever so slightly, but visibly, impatient. "But if you took those annual sales, and divided them by the weeks."

She hesitated. "That's difficult, because sometimes people skip a week, or some personal crisis keeps them from attending market. I've always felt week-to-week numbers are rather misleading."

"Just a guess."

"Well, it's a complicated question . . ." A twitter passed through the crowd as her stalling, whether intentional or not, teetered on the absurd. "But if I *had* to speculate . . ."

"Yes?" he encouraged, rather loudly. Someone across the room muffled a guffaw.

"I would guess, then, that anywhere from two to three hundred dollars would be typical. In fact, I'd say at *least* two hundred dollars, maybe more. And sometimes, naturally, maybe even more than three hundred."

Most of the farmers murmured appreciatively. Next to me, a woman leaned closer to her neighbor. "That beats what I'm getting at my roadside stand. We had a day last week where we only made thirty-seven dollars." Her listener nodded sympathetically.

While I wanted to keep an open mind, I was surprised by this number. Surprised and concerned. Hundreds of thousands of citizens, and markets in every corner of the county, but only three hundred bucks was made on a good day? What were all these people eating, and where were they shopping? These markets were practically on their front lawns. Cows on the horizon or freezers of deer meat clearly wasn't the issue here. I recalled the tractor trailers I had passed on the highway, branded with the names of area supermarkets. Two hundred dollars of farmers' market receipts had to be a pittance compared to revenues of these big-box stores. Something—in fact, a *lot* of somethings—didn't make sense.

Evidently, the flower vendor was thinking along these same lines, as well.

"Two or three hundred dollars," he repeated, polite but incredulous. The satisfied hum in the room came to a halt. "No disrespect, but I don't even *consider* a market unless I can make five hundred dollars. And even that number barely covers my costs."

Margaret was unruffled. "I find it useful to think about markets as an investment of time. No one ever makes a lot of money right off the bat."

The man stood, nodding, and put on his hat. "I respect that. I've been selling flowers for nearly half my life. If I wasn't familiar with investments of time, I never would have made it this far." He saluted from the tip of his cap. "Good luck to you all, and thanks for your time."

He had no sooner exited and closed the door behind him than the whole room, as though holding its collective breath, erupted.

"Can you *imagine* . . ."

"Some people!"

". . . walks in here and has the nerve . . ."

"Too big for his own britches!"

And on it went. A few moments later a large woman in overalls stood and, with hands on hips, performed a loud, whining impersonation of the departed flower vendor.

"I don't *do* markets for less than five hundred. I can't *afford* to." She surveyed the room. "Well I, for one, would *love* to do five hundred dollars at a market." She sat down with a derisive snort, to the laughter and wide applause of the crowd.

I honestly didn't know what to make of any of this. Was this a financial reality or self-imposed defeatism? Based on personal experience, it wasn't uncommon for my own family to spend two hundred dollars a week at the grocery store. We were only one family; there were tens of thousands of families in this county. If only the tiniest fraction of these people shopped each week at farmers' markets, the numbers would simply *have* to be higher. Wouldn't they?

As Margaret tried to get the group under control, I noticed a man seated along the wall who was writing notes on a yellow legal pad. He was shabbily clothed, in stained, brown coveralls worn nearly to rags. The sides of his boots were encrusted with mud, and a faded, frayed ball cap, without logo or insignia, covered his head. A day's worth of grayish-brown stubble shadowed his weathered face.

Most noteworthy of all, he had paid absolutely no attention to the crowd, appearing completely lost in his own frenetic scribbling. He flipped a page back or forth every once in a while, as though referencing a figure or observation.

He raised his hand after the commotion had died down.

"Chip Planck," he began, in a clear voice. "Wheatland Farm. I attended this meeting three years ago, and I've just spent the last few minutes going over my old notes." He squinted at the legal pad. "According to what I've got written down here, the numbers quoted three years ago are roughly identical to those you just mentioned. Am I to infer that these markets have stopped growing in the intervening years, or do you think the markets plateaued sometime before that, and are simply continuing their flat trajectory?"

Now here was someone, I said to myself, who didn't put stock into anecdotal information. In fact, his air of perspicacity left me curious to learn what he *did* put stock in.

"These numbers don't reflect our customers' enthusiasm," she said. "Or, for that matter, the number of new faces we've seen coming through market."

"Mmm-hmm," Chip affirmed, more polite than convinced. "These new faces, though . . . Pardon me," he interrupted himself with a fleeting, sly smile, "these *enthusiastic* new faces—are they buying what we're selling?"

"Oh, absolutely. I think so."

"Even though the revenues are the same as a few years ago."

Margaret stood her ground. "Yes."

"Hmm." Chip clicked his ballpoint pen with the firmness of a judge's gavel. "No further questions."

After the meeting was finished, I made my way over to him and introduced myself. He was a vegetable farmer, he told me, who had been selling his produce at farmers' markets for twenty-plus years.

"So what did you think about the meeting?" I asked.

He folded his arms across his chest and gave me a thoroughly appraising look. "Well," he replied, "as a farmer just starting out, I think the question should probably be, what did *you* think about the meeting?"

"I thought . . ." I began, before pausing. Something about this man made me want to make a good first impression. "Well, it seems to me that a farm needs more than a couple hundred dollars a week to make the effort of going to market worthwhile."

Chip rocked a little on his heels. "Uh-huh," he agreed. "What else?"

I felt like I was back in college, being quizzed by one of my professors. "That . . . the markets should be a little better than they are, considering the population and the high average incomes."

"Astute observation," Chip agreed. He studied me. "But there's something else on your mind, too."

I wasn't exactly sure what I wanted to say, but I knew he was right. I chewed on the inside of my lip. "I've been wondering . . . You know, more than anything, I just want to grow a bunch of really great food and take it some place where people will buy it. Really *want* it, you know what I mean? Someplace where the people are looking for the kind of food we raise. Good, clean food that they can appreciate. I think if I can just find these people, then the rest will take care of itself. I don't know," I concluded sheepishly. "Maybe my expectations are too high."

He chuckled. "If that's the case, then we're *all* in deep trouble." He waved a hand through the air between us, as though erasing a chalkboard. "Look. You've just said out loud what most of us are thinking. That you want to grow food—*great* food—but you have to be able to pay your bills, too. That's not just a reasonable goal. It's mandatory."

I felt relieved. He had summarized exactly what I was feeling. "So, what about these people who are making only a couple hundred dollars?" I asked. "Are they going to survive?"

Chip shrugged. "Don't know. We can only try to answer that question for ourselves, right?"

"How have *you* done it? After twenty years, you must be doing something right."

He closed his eyes for a moment, composing his thoughts. "Let me put it this way. Every two or three years, I come to this meeting, and I ask the same questions. And I always get the same responses. Now, what does that tell you?"

"It tells me . . . that even though you farm in this county, you don't try to sell your stuff here."

"Correct."

"But you have to sell your food somewhere," I reasoned. "So you must take it farther in. To the city."

"You win the prize," Chip said. He glanced at his watch. "Now, if you'll excuse me, it was a pleasure to meet you, but I've got a truckload of acorn squash awaiting my attention." He shook my hand. "I'm sure I'll see you around. Good luck."

The room was now vacant, and I was left alone with my thoughts.

The city, Washington, D.C., had always felt like a million miles from the farm. No, I told myself, dismissing the thought. I would start closer, hedging my bets, trying out these Loudoun County markets for myself. Maybe it would be different for me; maybe I had what they wanted. There was only one way to find out.

Chapter Seventeen

Our next farmers' market was in Middleburg, Virginia. This corner of Loudoun County was famously known as hunt country, with horse farms and stately manor homes sprinkled across the rolling countryside. The drive between our farm and Middleburg was spectacularly scenic, an opportunity for me to explore the back roads of Loudoun. The road stretched from the mountain village of Bluemont to the small town of Upperville, a winding route straight out of Americana. Lovely one-lane bridges, sweeping vistas of stonewalled pastures, and glimpses of rustic barns rose from the misty morning hillsides. Here the resonance of old-time agriculture was still very much a part of the landscape.

We returned to Berryville that season as well, my father shoehorning a couple of coolers into the back of his 1984 Camry sedan and schlepping our offerings to market. To my surprise, he had volunteered to help me each Saturday morning, and I had gratefully accepted. Along with the Cascades farmers' market on Sunday, we planned to cobble these incomes together, in theory tripling our sales. A flawless strategy, I reasoned, as long as we somehow managed to make any money.

I pulled into Middleburg on opening day, a cool morning in late spring. The vegetable and seedling vendors were already in medias res, busily setting up elaborate displays of herbs, spring vegetables, and greenery. I parked my truck, spread a tablecloth over my flimsy aluminum table, and dusted off my wooden chicken. In a matter of moments, the winter off-season was now a memory. Our farm was officially open for its second season.

There were a few other vendors there: a small bakery offering cookies and a modest selection of breads; a jams and jellies seller with a vibrant staircase display of colorful preserves; and two vegetable farms with offerings of herb planters and spring seedlings. I took a few minutes to introduce myself, and then, realizing I still had nearly an hour before market opened, decided to take a short walk around town.

Middleburg was remarkably quiet on a Saturday morning. Main Street was still asleep, with only an occasional vehicle or dog-walking pedestrian breaking an otherwise churchlike silence. None of the scattered shops were open yet, and a circuitous route of seven or eight blocks made for a very peaceful walk but only garnered a handful of citizens on that sparkling May morning. Even Berryville, the sleepiest of sleepy towns, had more bustle by now. I wondered what it meant for the farmers' market.

By nine o'clock, an hour after the opening bell, I had my answer. Only three customers had set foot in market. Even on my slowest Berryville days, I had never experienced anything like it. I exchanged awkward shrugs with my fellow vendors. The market was so vacant, if a tumbleweed had rolled through the parking lot, the baker might have offered it a cookie.

I knew that I remained more or less a newbie to the farmers' market scene, and that my perspective on it was still very limited. But with fewer than a half-dozen vendors, and only one or two shoppers in the entire market, the atmosphere felt palpably uncomfortable. Even the customers could sense something amiss, making shy comments about the low turnout, suggesting that things might pick up later in the day. Doing my best to keep a brave face, I felt like a performer playing to empty seats.

By ten that morning, the traffic slowly picked up, and I had my first sale of the day, a dozen eggs. A few minutes later, I sold a pound of beef stew cubes. Okay, I reassured myself. Maybe it was just a late-starting market. A few folks were now milling around the vegetable stands, and I noticed a young couple buying brownies from the baker. I smiled warmly, thought my most positive thoughts, and waited for the rest of the town to wake up and come shopping.

It never happened. I ended the day selling three dozen eggs and the single pack of stew meat, grossing twelve dollars and fifty cents. It was the single worst market I ever attended.

There was no denying my frustration. I returned home with a personal storm cloud over my head, trying to figure out what I was doing wrong. Was my cowboy hat too corny? Did I come across as desperate? I tried to put myself in the customers' shoes, viewing the business from their perspective. Maybe the world just wasn't ready for a red-bearded, gangly kid jumping from an old pickup with armloads of meat.

Still, in order for people to turn me down, they had to first come to market. Less than fifty people had set foot in the parking lot that morning. The market had felt vapid, neglected, devoid of the optimism that had brought all this amazing food together in the first place.

It occurred to me that without customers, a farmers' market didn't really exist. On the occasions when the Berryville market had been packed with people, it literally hummed. The food itself, artistically displayed, alive with freshness and color and scent, almost carried its own energy. Markets had to be more than just parking lots of food and farmers. When people packed the parking lot and conversation was buzzing, everything felt right, balanced, and I could sense a real future here. By the end of the day, I found myself wishing that Middleburg were more like Berryville.

It wasn't especially helpful when my father returned home with a little less than a hundred dollars himself.

"I guess they weren't excited to see you, either," I remarked, as I helped him unpack his coolers.

"On the contrary. Sarah, the manager, was happy to see me."

"Dad, Sarah's happy to see *everybody*."

"Well, I was happy to see her, too. It was a long, hard winter without that English muffin bread."

"Did you at least save me a piece?"

"Save you a piece? Didn't I make myself clear? I hadn't eaten all winter." He hooked his thumbs behind his belt, tugging it a scant tenth of an inch. "I wouldn't expect you to notice, but I lost two pounds recently."

"Oh yeah?" I said, eyeing his bulging stomach. "Well, it looks like you just found them again."

My parents and I sat around the dining-room table that night, counting the meager pile of money. The results spoke for themselves.

I kept going. Really, I didn't know what else to do. Part of me had fallen in love with the dream of farmers' markets, sensing a potential that I hadn't yet experienced but still believed was there. Each time I pulled into my market space, a quiet, hopeful voice inside of me said, "Today will be the day. Today, the entire town will turn out." Despite my carefully guarded optimism, the markets that season remained modest at best—eighty dollars here, a hundred and fifty dollars there. I scrimped and saved as much as I could, taking home leftover fruit and bread, working nights at my catering jobs, inwardly convinced that some day the markets would hit their stride.

Back at the farm, though, it was a different world entirely. For the first time that I could recall, we were actually getting stuff done at an efficient clip. Now that we had sold nearly all our equipment and finally stopped making hay, Travis and I had more time than ever to spend on farm improvements. We never realized how much machinery repairs and maintenance had sequestered our time. At long last, we replaced broken boards in the corral, mended the infernally potholed driveway, and dropped a dead tree that for years had leaned menacingly over the bridge.

I became better at carpentry and devoted my free time to simple construction projects: bookshelves, barn steps, a porch swing. During my first year, attempts at repairs around the farm had been unmitigated failures, exhibitions of my poor fundamental skills. Few things were as discouraging as spending a day building a new chicken coop only to discover the wind had played havoc with it during the night, or the cattle had easily knocked it down. Standing before my dilapidated projects, I often felt like the First Little Pig, the one who ineptly constructed his home out of straw.

Now, every chance I got, I'd watch professional carpenters at work, noticing how they built a house in town or renovated our public library throughout the course of a year. *This Old House* on PBS became required viewing each evening as I ate my dinner. Slowly I graduated to the rank of Second Pig, stick builder. Better, certainly, but with room to improve.

As Travis and I repaired things around the farm, I came to realize that everything must be engineered with cattle in mind. Cattle *love* to scratch themselves, and they spend a large part of their day seeking impromptu scratching posts. A fifteen-hundred-pound bovine with an itchy rump could take down a poorly built chicken coop in minutes flat. I can honestly credit cow butts for helping me to become the carpenter that I am today.

To this end, I found myself adopting one of Travis's sayings: "tight and good enough." It became our mantra, a verbal signature at the completion of each project. The phrase was simultaneously a goal and a compromise, a standard by which we could declare enough was enough.

Fence needs repair? Cut a patch from a roll of scrap wire. So what if it's still the same fifty-year-old fence from before? Now it's tight and good enough to keep the livestock in.

The cows bent a metal gate as they turned too sharply, briefly stampeding against it? Take it off its hinges, lay it on the ground, and jump on it till it's straight again. It may look a little worse for the wear, but it's tight and good enough.

When I started a new project, I could increasingly tell what was more likely to succeed, and what might be a waste of my efforts. Without exactly knowing it at the time, I was becoming the Third Pig, the power pig, slinging bricks and mortar with practiced nonchalance. When I wasn't at market, I spent my days entirely on the farm, learning to be a jack-of-all-trades. I had yet to make a profit, but I now found myself doing sound, practical work, work that would endure. This, I told myself, was the kind of farming I had always dreamed about.

With our newfound time for projects, Travis and I expanded our laying flock, adding young chickens to our mobile coop. Known as pullets, these hens laid relatively small eggs for the first couple of months. I cartoned these eggs separately, dubbing them "Itty Bitties," and discounted them by a full dollar.

One weekend at Middleburg, a well-dressed young lady passed my stand. She paused, read my sign, and turned to speak with me.

"What in the world is an 'Itty Bitty' egg?" she asked, removing her sunglasses. An hour and a half into market, she was the first person to stop at my table that day.

"Oh, those are our pullet eggs," I said, matter-of-factly.

"Pullet eggs?" She shook her head. "What are pullet eggs?"

"They're eggs from young chickens. The first eggs they lay."

"Huh. Pullet eggs." She let the words linger in the air a few moments, testing their sound. "I've never heard of such a thing."

"You never see them in grocery stores," I told her. "Most people think they're too small."

The day's eggs, gathered, washed, and sorted.

This intrigued her. "What do you think they do with them? I mean, where do they go, if they don't end up at the grocery?"

I wasn't prepared for a conversation about the industrial pullet egg business, but I did my best to ad-lib. "I'm not really sure. Maybe they make them into noodles?"

She raised her eyebrows. "Noodles?" she said, dubiously. "Don't you think that would be a *lot* of noodles?"

"People like noodles," I countered. Why were we talking about noodles, anyway?

"I'd think maybe they'd end up in eggnog," she mused. "You know, around the holidays. Or," she added excitedly, her face lighting up, "maybe in frozen quiches!"

It was a slow day, but this conversation had already become insufferable. "Yeah," I agreed noncommittally. "You're probably right." I snuck a quick glance around the market. Couldn't just one more customer show up and bail me out? "Noodles." I shook my head. "What was I thinking?"

"That's okay," she conceded graciously. "You probably didn't realize how popular frozen quiches are. Can I see the eggs?"

"Sure." I reached into my cooler and retrieved a dozen. Even with the carton closed, the diminutive eggs rattled noticeably in their oversized container. I opened the lid and passed them to her.

"Oh my gosh! They're so tiny! And these are chicken eggs, you say?" She shook her head in wonder. "I've never *seen* such tiny little chicken eggs!"

"Yeah," I nodded sagely. "Most of them end up in frozen quiches."

She called to an acquaintance who was shopping across the way. "Leslie! Come look at this! You have to see these *tiny* little chicken eggs!"

Leslie sidled up to her friend.

"Oh, my word! What are *those?*"

"They're . . . pullet eggs?" the first lady replied, looking to me for endorsement. I nodded, and she repeated herself, this time with more confidence. "They're pullet eggs. Eggs from young chickens. Aren't they just so . . . so interesting?"

"Pullet eggs?" Leslie replied. "I've never heard of that. What's a pullet egg?"

I thought it prudent not to mention the fact that her friend had just told her what a pullet egg was. Instead, I tried explaining it a different way.

"Since the hens are still maturing, the eggs will get bigger as the weeks go by," I said. "Over the weeks you'll notice the gradual change."

The first lady, holding the carton, appeared confused. "What do you mean, they'll 'get bigger'?"

"I mean, they'll eventually get to the size of a normal egg."

Her brow furrowed in disbelief. "You mean, the eggs will actually get bigger?"

"Yes," I replied, uncertain as to the source of her confusion. "They usually go from a pullet egg to a medium, then to a large."

She quickly placed the eggs back onto my table, her face a mixture of disgust and skepticism. "You mean, in my *refrigerator?* Do they have chicks inside? How do they grow?"

All at once I understood. "Not *those* eggs," I explained. "The eggs the chickens will be laying in the *future.*"

"What? You mean . . . ? Oh!" She placed a hand against her chest, breathing a dramatic sigh of relief. "I thought . . . ! I mean, I thought you meant . . . !"

Leslie nodded her support. "I thought the exact same thing. Eggs growing in the refrigerator!"

The two of them enjoyed a long laugh, leaning against each other as they walked away from my stand. They didn't buy anything. I ended up selling about sixty dollars' worth of food that day, including three cartons of Itty Bitties at a dollar apiece. I could have turned more of a profit selling grape slushies at the local convenience store.

Just like a farm, markets had to be tight and good enough, too. Each tent was like a little garden unto itself, with a farmer tending to its needs. Collectively, these gardens created a landscape, a market unto itself. But no matter how excellent the presentation, no matter how fresh the produce, regardless of how well these farmers watered and weeded, tilled, and toiled, the work was all meaningless if there were no customers to buy the food.

If a season's worth of effort meant that the ripe melons languished on the table, then that wasn't "good enough." It couldn't be. Zucchini was planted for people to buy. Peaches were picked to be eaten, not composted. It couldn't be a matter of price or quality if no one was even bothering to show up. At a certain point the farmer could be forgiven for no longer questioning himself, his methods, or his produce, and simply wondering aloud, "Where are all the customers?"

We participated in these markets for the duration of the season, not missing a single day. Each Friday and Saturday evening, I loaded the truck with the very best of what I had to offer, and I woke before dawn the next day to get to market well in advance of the opening bell. That year, between three full-time markets (we attended Cascades on Sundays, with similarly discouraging results), we cumulatively grossed right around ten thousand dollars. Without even bothering to compensate ourselves for our time, our profit barely broke zero.

Still, I believed. My grandfather had farmed through the Great Depression, starting out with only his intellect and his two hands to rely upon, and had emerged solvent on the other side. The work we were doing slowly healed the land, repaired the soil. I was becoming a better farmer with each passing season, more experienced, more productive. We just had to hang on a little longer, and somehow, mysteriously, the correct path would be revealed.

At least, the English major in me consoled, it sounded pretty to think so.

Chapter Eighteen

We offered twenty different cuts of grass-fed beef, free-range chickens, and fresh eggs by the dozen. Despite this selection, our customers wanted one thing above all else: pork sausage. In fact, many took it for granted that we *did* sell sausage. Without so much as a glance at our menu board, customers approached our stand and asked us what varieties of sausage we carried. The word "meat" appeared to be synonymous with "pork sausage" in many people's minds. As the seasons passed, we went from being apologetic to feeling downright negligent in our meat-mongering duties, turning away one disappointed customer after the next.

Perhaps it's the same experience for vegetable growers who don't plant tomatoes, or bakeries without whole wheat bread. Not having sausage was more than simply a missing item on our menu. It was a cultural blunder.

I recalled my first visit to Schoen's butcher shop, and the delicious smells wafting from his smokehouse: hams and chops, sausages and bacon. It was bacon, of course, that when paired with the aforementioned tomatoes, whole wheat bread, and a token leaf of lettuce, made a famously delicious sandwich. Suddenly, the thought of eating my very own BLTs persuaded me as much as anything else: It was time to bring home the bacon.

My own experience with pigs was incredibly limited. I was too young to remember the details, but after my grandfather passed away, our newly hired farm manager somehow convinced the family to construct a confinement hog lot. In short order an enormous slab of concrete, about half the size of a football field, was poured over the old barnyard, elbowed against one of my grandfather's whitewashed barns. Feed bunkers and watering troughs were installed, and several hundred piglets arrived on the back of a large truck. They were turned loose to live the rest of their lives in total confinement, on concrete.

From day one, the farm smelled like a literal pigsty, with reeking mounds of hog excrement pushed into the corners of the lot. I do recall that simply standing near the pigs for more than a minute left a lingering odor in my clothing for the rest of the day. Instead of playing near the pigs, my childhood adventures carried me toward the green, grassy hills, and away from the sun-baked stench of their squalor.

But our industrial pig operation wasn't finished yet. Next our manager built a long, low shed, divided by wooden partitions into shadowy stalls, each roughly ten feet square. This is where the sows were placed, the mother hogs that birthed and weaned the piglets. These females were several times the size of even the largest pigs on the concrete slab. Whereas those pigs were perhaps anywhere from fifty to two hundred pounds, these momma hogs routinely tipped the scale at well above five hundred. It was no exaggeration to compare them to the size of a large black bear.

Pigs are omnivores. Out of legitimate concern that I might be eaten alive, my parents told me I was strictly forbidden from entering a sow's pen. For emphasis, they warned me that I was not to be caught anywhere *near* the pens. This protocol was so imprinted on my young mind that, after knocking over a cinder block and stirring up a nest of stinging hornets, I ran an extra hundred yards around the farrowing sheds to avoid what would have been a shortcut home.

The experiment with confinement hogs didn't last more than a year or two. The farm manager quit, the hogs were sold, and the operation was terminated. We were left with a half acre of barren concrete, a mountain of pig excrement, and thousands of dollars of additional debt. Years later, when the manure had been removed and sunshine and rain had bleached the concrete clean, my sister Betsy and I roller-skated over the undulating surface, our personal rink in the sheltered hills of West Virginia. At least we had found a practical use for it.

Now, at age twenty-five, I was ready to try raising pigs again, but this time on pasture. No other farms near us were currently raising hogs, and books from the library took me only so far. Besides, most available literature was geared toward confinement systems. Since Travis himself had always raised a pig or two each year, in no time at all I had him waxing poetic on the topic of swine.

"We used to raise a little piglet each year, and feed him day-old bread we'd get from the bakery. The first pig we ever got was a fat little butterball we named Piggy."

"Piggy? How did you ever come up with the name?"

"Don't know." He shrugged, devoid of all irony. "That's just what we called him. That's what we named all our pigs. Piggy. You could call them just like a cat. 'Here, piggy piggy piggy. Heeeeere, piggy piggy piggy.' People wouldn't believe it, but it's true." He paused, considering. "You know, maybe that's why we called them Piggy, since we called them 'piggy' all the time."

"Stands to reason," I agreed.

"Anyway, Piggy used to follow us down the road each day to the school bus, and he'd wait there till we got back."

"Really?"

"Yes, sir. Really. He would sit there and wait, and couldn't anything move him. My mom would come along around lunchtime to check on him, and sometimes bring him a peanut butter sandwich. He'd be asleep under a pine tree."

Now I was incredulous. "A peanut butter sandwich?" I folded my arms. "Travis, I don't believe that."

He stared at me with his water-blue eyes. "You don't have to believe it, but that's a fact. She fed that pig peanut butter sandwiches."

"What, he didn't like swiss cheese?"

"Can't say. Never had any swiss cheese in the house. So one day, we got off the school bus, my brothers and I, and Piggy wasn't there. We went home, and he wasn't in any of his normal spots. We asked Mom where Piggy was, and she told us, 'Wait till your father gets home. He'll tell you.'

"Well, you can imagine what happened when my father got home. He came in carrying a great big box."

"Oh no," I said. "He butchered your pig? Did he . . . did he make you *eat* Piggy?"

"Butcher him?" Travis regarded me as though the very suggestion was naive. "No, he was too valuable for that. They sold him, and bought us all new shoes. I was so upset, I ran straight out of the house and hid in the toolshed until dark. My dad whipped my butt for that. In the end, though, I was glad to have the shoes."

I thought this over a few moments. My mind was still stuck on the peanut butter sandwiches. "So, how many pigs have you raised over the years?"

"Hard to say. Twenty? Thirty?"

"Did you keep a sow, too?"

"No, my parents were too afraid we'd climb into the pen and get eaten." Well, I noted, at least I hadn't been the only one. "We'd get ourselves a little piggy from the fair each year."

Waiting for the county fair to roll around each year certainly wasn't the quickest way to start raising hogs. Instead, I answered an ad in our local classifieds. The piglets had just been weaned, and there were five available, each weighing about fifty pounds. Not exactly sure what a fifty-pound pig looked like, I imagined a large sack of flour with a curly tail.

I hooked up the livestock trailer and headed out. It was autumn, and already quite chilly at night, so I scattered a few insulating wafers of straw across the floor. Feeling as prepared as possible, I merged onto Interstate 81. I was finally in pursuit of pork.

The farmer was deeply amused when I pulled into his barnyard with my large trailer.

"You know them piglets is only fifty pounds, right?" he said, after a brief introduction.

"Oh, sure," I said, patting the side of the trailer. "Just wanted to make sure I had plenty of room for them."

He chuckled, his eyes drifting across the length of the trailer. "I'd say you will. They're only fifty pounds, you know. Most people just put them in the bed of their truck."

"Yeah," I agreed, out of politeness more than conviction. "I, uh, do that too, sometimes. Nothing like having them on a trailer, though."

"Nope, can't argue with that. Nice to put them on a trailer. Absolutely." He squinted at me meaningfully. "When they're big, I mean. Once they're *grown*. Not when they're . . ."

"Fifty pounds," I said aloud, as he repeated himself for the third time.

He cleared his throat. "Fifty pounds. Right. Well. I guess we'll just go ahead and get those piglets loaded up, then."

I was happy to change the subject. Give him the benefit of the doubt, I told myself, he probably means well. "Should I give you a hand?"

"No, they're right over here. I can carry them easy enough. They're only fifty pounds."

Had I heard that they were only fifty pounds? Did I realize that bringing my trailer had been unnecessary, and made me look like a laughingstock? Messages received, loud and clear. I followed the farmer into his small barn, half expecting the piglets to be no larger than breakfast sausages, easily carried home in my shirt pocket.

I had to admit, for fifty pounds, there was no denying how small they looked. Compact and stocky, the piglets looked like watermelons with legs. Unlike the human body, a pig's weight is completely centralized, more or less all torso. These piglets in particular were about two feet long, and perhaps a foot tall. They were purebred Hampshires, a breed with the coloration of an Oreo, black on each end with a white belt around their middle.

The farmer picked them up by the hind legs, each piglet grunting and squealing, and placed them in the trailer. Once loaded, they composed less than 5 percent of the floor space. I tried my best not to feel silly, paid the man, and headed home.

I left them on the trailer that evening with a pail of water and a bit of feed, and went to bed. When I woke up the next morning, Travis was up on his tiptoes, peering into the trailer through the upper slats.

"Pretty small, ain't they?" he said by way of greeting.

"Yeah, I know. I probably should have just put them in the back of the truck."

Travis rubbed his chin. "Well, they look happy in there for the time being, but where do you want to put them?"

I had drifted to sleep asking myself the exact same question. Although enthusiastic to start this new enterprise, I was still nervous to actually have my first gaggle of piglets here at the farm. The scant amount of information I had uncovered about pasture-raised hogs suggested success was as easy as keeping them fed, clean, and sheltered. They were like any other animal we raised on the farm, where basic, competent husbandry prevented most problems before they even started. There was one major difference, however, that unequivocally distinguished pigs from any of their other barnyard peers. They had snouts.

A pig's snout is an engineering marvel. In a matter of hours, a half-dozen pigs can flip an entire lawn with the efficiency of a crew of grown men with shovels. In search of roots, earthworms, and whatever other omnivorous treats they might encounter, they eagerly wiggle their snouts beneath the soil surface, flinging it several feet into the air as they happily plow along.

This activity, better known as "rooting," is awe-inspiring and entertaining to behold. Pigs can plow a field with their face. If this doesn't seem especially remarkable, then try it for yourself sometime.

For the piglets' first home, we selected an unused bay in our barn where, decades before, draft horses had been housed. At the bay's entrance, extending into the meadow, Travis and I stapled a temporary perimeter of wire fence, low enough for us to step over but high enough to keep the piglets enclosed. This provided a large apron of grass, a place for them to exercise, sunbathe, and frolic. Since we had no real idea what our ultimate model would look like, this indoor-outdoor lifestyle was as much for our benefit as theirs, giving us a glimpse of two different scenarios at once.

We quickly discovered that, as far as rooting was concerned, being indoors or out didn't really matter. Within a week the piglets had flipped the entire grassy area onto its head, joyfully chewing on juicy root clumps. Soil cascaded from the corners of their mouths as they chomped away. Their little snouts, no bigger than teacups, had pulverized an area of grass thirty feet long by twenty feet wide. When they were going full bore, contentedly flipping, snorting, and munching away, it was impossible not to pause in our work and simply watch the show.

Inside, it was the same story. A hundred years' worth of hay and manure had matted the ground before Travis and I turned the piglets loose. Now, the earthen floor looked as though it had been tossed into a mixing bowl and set on frappé. Ancient hay, fresh straw, and dusty chunks of manure had been blended into an intricate mélange, surpassing the abilities of the finest commercial composting machines. The compacted dirt was now soft and pliable, with a pleasant, earthy aroma reminiscent of forest loam.

The piglets trotted back into their room, collapsing in exhaustion from a morning of rooting, eating, and playing. As the days passed, they continued to work the floor from one end to the other, and did the same for what had once been the grassy plot just outside their door. With each pass they rooted a little deeper, until we could see only their rear haunches above ground, their entire heads and shoulders hidden in the earth.

Precisely what sort of subsoil delicacies they discovered down there remained a mystery. Pigs in France were famous for their abilities to find truffles, and for all I knew, our farm might have been sitting atop the planet's finest underground mushroom trove. A more likely answer, Travis suggested, was that they just liked to dig. I couldn't argue with the evidence.

When the pigs weren't rooting, they were sleeping. Soundly. In the morning, we'd find them stacked on top of each other like flapjacks, eyes closed and snoring. On cold days they wouldn't rouse before noon, not until the sun had thoroughly warmed the bedding of their stall. Groggy with sleep, they'd eventually stand and stretch, making their way outside to the bathroom. This was an area they had self-selected, where they intentionally dropped their manure and urine each day.

It was this unexpected fact—that pigs didn't live in their own filth, but instead kept it separate from their daily routine—that impressed me above all else. Was it possible, I wondered, that most hog operations smelled terrible only because the animals had no choice but to stand in their own excrement?

Several months after they arrived on the farm, there was still no discernible odor coming from their lot. The pervasive stench of the hog lot of my childhood had been replaced with the clean, warm smell of well-kept swine. As I worked near them, giving them a good scratch behind the ears, I noticed that the air around them carried a subtly sweet bouquet, a smell akin to warm maple syrup. Having

Pigs on pasture, with dirt-covered snouts.

never associated the odor of pigs with anything other than something nose-wrinkling, I decided that this was one of the most pleasant surprises of all.

In time, they were ready for their trip to the butcher. By now they were nearly two hundred and fifty pounds apiece, and we had expanded their area several times, utilizing nearly every green inch of barnyard grass to accommodate their appetite for rooting. As bittersweet as it was to see them go, it was satisfying to hear Mr. Schoen say that, for our first try, the hogs were fine-looking stock. From a butcher with generations of bacon coursing through his veins, I took this as glowing praise.

I soon had the first sausages back at the farm, a sweet Italian recipe of herbs and spices that Mr. Schoen's family had been perfecting for decades. I had the kitchen to myself, and as the skillet was heating

I shaped a few patties by hand and began sizzling them. The aroma was equal parts savory and sweet, with the same earthy, maple syrup–like smell permeating the air.

I had kept my vow of selective vegetarianism, only eating meat that I had raised. As such, it had been two years since I had eaten any pork at all. From the first bite, the flavor was unlike anything I had ever tasted. Fennel and caraway seeds added spice to the sweet notes of pork, and a dash of sea salt balanced the recipe. Delicately earthy, the sausage felt surprisingly light against my tongue, completely unlike the heavy, fatty pork I had remembered from my youth. I savored the three patties I had made, barely giving the meat time to cool and licking my fingers when I was done. My stomach still rumbling, I quickly made two more, enjoying the experience all over again.

I took the pork to market, and our small cadre of customers was delighted with the new offerings. Several people remarked at the leanness of the bacon, and at how the sausage cooked up with very little fat. Our pork left their palates feeling clean, so unlike the greasy sausages they were accustomed to from the grocery stores.

Naturally, there's a critic in every crowd, but this one came as a surprise. My father, who had been away on business for several weeks, walked into the kitchen one evening as I was cooking a package of sausage and wrinkled his nose.

"What is that god-awful smell?" he asked, staring into the skillet with disapproval.

"The sausage?" I pressed the spatula against the meat, and it hissed and popped, emitting a large cloud of savory steam. "Since when do you not like the smell of sausage?"

"That's sausage?" he asked, unconvinced. "Smells like you're cooking some kind of spicy curry."

"It's a sweet Italian recipe. Here," I said, breaking off a perfectly browned, crispy end. "Try a bite."

He regarded the offering suspiciously, then tasted it. "Ack!" he said, his face souring as he chewed. "That . . . that tastes even worse than it *smells*." He swallowed with clear reluctance. This, coming from a man known to eat an entire bag of pork rinds at one sitting. "Oh, that's just terrible. What do you call it again?"

"Sweet Italian sausage," I said defensively, flipping the patties. "And I think it's *delicious*."

He frowned. "I don't know why they have to put all that spicy stuff in it. Sausage is supposed to have two ingredients: sage and salt. Whatever I just ate, it wasn't sausage like *I'm* used to."

"Well, our customers love it. We're almost sold out already. And," I added, arranging the patties onto a dinner plate, "it's nice to know you won't be pilfering any of the inventory."

Even so, as soon as the opportunity presented itself, I had Mr. Schoen make a small batch of sage and salt sausage for my dad, and cooked it for him on his fifty-sixth birthday. He performed an identical routine, sniffing the air doubtfully at first. Slowly, his face brightened. As he put it in his mouth and started chewing methodically, a look of pure delight crept across his face. We had found his recipe.

Though I couldn't say for certain, it seemed as though our little farm might finally have something for everyone. My father, at least, was happier than a pig in mud.

Chapter Nineteen

I never set out to sell our food in Washington, D.C., but in the end it didn't really matter. The markets ended up finding us.

Two years had passed since I had vowed to turn the farm around. I had religiously awoken before dawn each Saturday and Sunday morning to drive my truck to the farmers' market, convinced that with enough time, people would eventually begin to support us. My personal habits bordered on the monastic, turning down Friday night parties and college football games each Saturday in order to pack for market the next day. I took no vacations, bought no new clothes, and never ate out. I might have been living a dull existence, but with Nancy still in North Carolina and my friends all working jobs in the city, the only one who might have noticed was Travis.

As much as I loved my life as a farmer, after two full seasons of attending markets in my immediate vicinity, the reality was stark: The bills weren't getting paid. We made the minimum payments on our credit cards each month, and many weeks I still brought home less in sales than it cost me in gasoline to get there. The emotional paychecks I had been living on were inevitably going to bounce.

Any romantic notions I ever entertained about direct marketing were long gone. Though we had a handful of loyal core customers, there weren't enough people in our hometown expressing interest

Southerly view of our brick barn, built in 1822.

in the food we raised. The broader community simply had to start buying our products, and buying them fast, or our farming dream was going to fail. I now made a point of opening and studying the bills as they arrived each day, no longer deferring them to my parents. The people who sent these invoices weren't interested in organic food, nor did they care to hear about my warm and fuzzy free-range philosophies. It didn't matter to them if I had a slow weekend at market, or if my trailer got a flat tire on the way to the butcher. These companies simply wanted their cash.

I happened to learn of a nearby conference that fall, where fellow farmers were speaking about their personal marketing successes and failures. Having run out of new ideas for turning my fortune around, it was exactly the kind of information I needed to hear.

The first speaker, a vegetable farmer named Ellen Polishuk, detailed her experiences with farmers' markets in Washington, D.C., a forty-five-minute drive from her farm near Purcellville, Virginia. The markets were crowded there, she told us, with foot traffic numbering in the thousands. She pointed out that the region had more than two million people in the greater metro area, more hungry people than there were farmers to feed them. Just as Chip Planck had implied about his own farm, Ellen felt strongly that city markets were the way to go as well.

Although she made a compelling argument, I continued to dismiss any notions of driving to the city. Besides seeming impossibly far away, I was completely in the dark about many important issues. For starters, I knew next to nothing about Washington, D.C. Even though I had grown up only little more than an hour away, we rarely visited the city when I was a child. The only exception was every few years when I visited my father in his downtown office, which boiled down to memories of honking horns and somber sandstone buildings. Of course, there would also be additional health department inspections, with unfamiliar rules and procedures, and more applications to fill out and deadlines to meet. On top of it all, I hadn't the foggiest clue how to get in touch with the managers who ran the markets, or even which markets I should pursue.

Besides, most of these markets started at the crack of dawn, which meant leaving the farm several hours before sunrise. With my local markets, I was able to feed the chickens at daybreak and check the cows before I left the farm. Driving to the city, there would be no time in the morning to get any of the chores done.

By the time lunch rolled around, I had made up my mind that, whatever direction we were headed in, Washington, D.C., wasn't the answer. There had to be dozens of other farms already selling meat there, and they would all be vying for the exact same handful of available market spots. No, I told myself. The odds were stacked too high against us.

I found my lunch table and took a seat. Ellen happened to sit right next to me, and we struck up a conversation. I had barely gotten the words "I raise free-range livestock" out of my mouth before she excitedly interrupted me.

"You do?! That's fantastic!" She placed her hand on my shoulder, as though physically prohibiting any chance of escape. "We've *got* to get you into the Arlington market. I was just talking to the market manager, and he was telling me he hasn't found anyone doing what you're doing. What're the odds you'd both be here today?" She scanned the room, momentarily unable to locate him. "I'll track him down for you, and he'll tell you everything you need to know."

She spoke with an unbridled enthusiasm that left me nodding wordlessly in agreement. Truth be told, I couldn't understand what she saw in me. It was as though I had barely finished my first season of Little League, and she was convinced I was ready for the varsity squad.

"I've had *hundreds* of people ask me over the years why there aren't any meat vendors at these markets. Of course, I've always been too busy growing my own stuff to give it much thought, so all I could ever do is shrug. But I've wondered about it myself."

"So there really isn't anyone else doing this?"

"I rotate through five different markets every weekend," she said, "and I've never seen anyone selling meat. This is a huge opportunity. Huge. Not only for you, but for the market as a whole. Win-win, you know? It would help us round out our current offerings."

I munched quietly on my salad, considering. Up to this point, our best market had been the neighborhood called Cascades, a mixture of houses and strip malls about a half-hour drive from our farm. The market was located at the end of a dead-end road, in the parking lot of a community center. Even though it was our most reliable location thus far, sometimes fifteen minutes would pass without a single customer walking by. She was talking about thousands of people at a time, a number that conjured visions of total human chaos in my mind. Trying to make polite conversation, I asked her if anyone else sold eggs.

"Eggs?! You sell eggs, *too?*" She leaned toward me, our faces only inches apart. "Where did you come from? Are you a farmers' market angel?"

She settled back in her chair, laughing merrily at the thought. "Oh, honey. You're going to be such a hit. Free-range eggs? Are you kidding me?" She shook her head, smiling.

"Now look," she continued, suddenly all business. "Here's what you're going to do. You're going to get yourself an application. You're going to fill it out. Then, you're going to make yourself a living wage. Got it?"

I nodded obediently; honestly, I felt like she left me no choice. In response, she struck her hands together—*smack! smack!*—and the matter was concluded.

Near the end of the conference, she shouted over the din of the crowd.

"Hey! Farmer Forrest!" She strode up to me with a man in tow. "This is Dan Douglass, the coordinator of the Arlington farmers' market. He wants what you've got. You two talk." With that, she turned, and was gone.

"From what Ellen's told me, it sounds like your farm might be a perfect fit. Would you be interested in applying?" He opened a folder. "I've got an application here with me."

What could I say? I didn't want to be rude, and a piece of paper wasn't going to bite me. We talked for a few minutes about the market and what I was raising on the farm. In the end, I took the application, thanked him, and told him I'd be in touch.

A week after the conference, Travis and I were in full swing with winter farm work, cutting fallen trees in the wake of a winter storm. I had just come in and was sitting down to my lunch when the phone rang.

"Is this Forrest? Hi, this is Dan Douglass, from the Arlington farmers' market. I was just wondering if you'd had a chance to look at that application yet."

I glanced at the paperwork, sitting half forgotten on my desk. "I haven't yet. You know, I've been thinking about it a lot, but . . ."

"Before you tell me no, I just want to say that I've mentioned your farm to several other producers, and they're really enthusiastic about having you here. Also, I took the liberty of calling the local health department, and from what you've told me about your handling procedures, you should be good to go after some minimal paperwork."

Wow, I thought. I had never imagined anyone being so proactive on my behalf. The excuses I had built up in my mind were falling by the wayside.

"So," he said, "can we expect to see you next April?"

I sighed. I didn't have the courage to tell him what I had privately begun to believe: that our farmers' market business might not be around the following spring. At the rate things were going, there was no sensible way we could stick it out another season. In the end, though, just to keep my options open, I went ahead and filled out the paperwork. A week later, we were accepted into our first big-city market.

"Things back home are . . . unsteady," I told Nancy. We had driven together to North Carolina's eastern shore, several hours from Chapel Hill. I had always promised her we would visit the beach together, and now that she was nearly done with school, I made good on my word.

"What do you mean by 'unsteady'?" she asked. We walked near the water, seagulls floating just above our heads. It was a brilliant afternoon in late fall, and sunlight scalloped the warm sand with light and shadow.

"The markets aren't going well. Mom and Dad haven't said anything yet, but I can tell they've lost confidence. Dad's still helping out at market, but it's mostly because he doesn't want to get stuck with chores now that I'm working weekends." I sighed. "And it's not just the farm. I'm worried about him, too."

"His weight?" she asked, knowingly.

I nodded. "It's gotten worse than the last time you saw him. I cleaned out his car a couple of weeks ago, and there must have been a trash can's worth of junk food wrappers in there. I don't know what to do. The doctor just started him on blood pressure medication. Anyone can see he's not taking care of himself."

"Have you tried talking to him about it?"

"What am I supposed to say? 'Hey, Dad, I might have failed at my own life, but at least I know what's best for *you*.' Yeah, that would go over swimmingly."

She stopped, turning to me. "Hey. You haven't failed yet. And besides," she added, wrapping her arm around my waist, "if you ever *did happen* to fail, it wouldn't be just any run-of-the-mill failure. The farmer I love would figure out a way to fail with *style*."

I laughed. The ocean wind pushed through our hair, billowing our clothes and turning the afternoon decidedly colder. We walked along the edge of the surf. "You're still planning to come back to the farm, right?" I asked. "Even if the business doesn't work out, we can still make a go of it. We'll both get teaching jobs. And there will always be plenty of food, as long as we can keep the taxes paid . . ."

Nancy stopped in her tracks. "Forrest Pritchard! Will you stop it with the eulogy? You haven't failed, and you won't fail. I believe in you. Do you remember how excited you were when you first told me about your plans? 'I'm going to save the family farm,' you told me. 'I'm going to do it all organically, and sustainably, and turn everything around.'" She looked up at me, her eyebrows knitted in concern. "Whatever happened to that guy?"

I frowned. "I still want to be that guy. It's just . . ." I shook my head, at a loss.

"Hey. You still *are* that guy. That farmer." She paused. "*My* farmer." She pressed her face close against my chest. "Just give Arlington a chance before you throw in the towel, will you? Give the markets one last chance. And maybe you should try something new on the farm, to lift your spirits. You know . . . something fun."

It was just the sort of pep talk I needed. She was right; a winter project would be a welcome distraction. I headed back to Virginia as poor as when I had left, but happier than I had been in a long time, and very much in love.

Chapter Twenty

Nancy holding a kid goat, with nanny looking on.

For absolutely no good reason at all, I decided to start raising goats.

Goats are, beyond a doubt, the most frustrating and capricious of all the farm animals I have ever encountered. Don't get me wrong. I like goats. At one point, many years later, we built our flock to more than a hundred head. They're well suited for our farm, hungrily gobbling down nettles, ivies, and thorny bushes that our cattle dismiss without as much as a nibble. Goats are hardy, grow quickly, and have distinctive and charming personalities.

But I soon learned that goats reliably commit the most mind-boggling, annoying, pull-your-hair-out acts of counterproductiveness, and eventually I decided having them on the farm was bad for my nerves. Goats climbed onto the roof of my truck. They squeezed into my workshop at night, knocking my tools across the floor. They wiggled beneath fences and ended up in my neighbor's cornfield. Most noteworthy of all, they managed to poop *everywhere*. By the time I finally stopped raising them, the word "goat" had become a four-letter word to me.

In my defense, this foray into goat ownership wasn't intentional. A friend of a friend called my mother, hoping to find a good home for her animal. The goat, Pedro, had eaten himself out of a job, and his owner had neither the time nor the resources to care for him any longer. Pedro was tame and personable, and had a voracious appetite. Wouldn't we like to come get him the next morning?

Somehow, I agreed. I had no experience at all with goats, but the thought of having an animal that could eat his way through a patch of poison ivy intrigued me. The next day, after morning chores, Travis and I set off in my little Toyota, launching a cloven-hoofed odyssey that we still refer to as "that time I had a bad idea."

The report was accurate: Pedro's meadow, a spacious two-acre lot, was completely defoliated. The ground was eaten down to the dusty soil, the trees stripped clean to nearly six feet high. This, his owner explained, was because Pedro could agilely stand on his hind legs, using his front hooves to pull down succulent branches for an afternoon snack. When he was a kid, she reminisced, he actually climbed into the trees, shimmying onto the branches like a monkey.

Pedro studied us from the shadows of his lean-to, uncertain he wanted to make our acquaintance. A vigorous shake of the feed bucket persuaded him otherwise, and he came toward us at a brisk and jolly trot, his long ears swaying comically back and forth beneath his imposing, spiraling horns.

As seasoned, responsible livestock transporters, we had taken every precaution, considered every scenario, and had come prepared with all the necessary gear to safely move the goat thirty miles back to our farm. In other words, we had brought a solitary rope. This rope, paired with the miraculous discovery of a dog collar behind my back seat, was cobbled into an effective, if minimalist, high-speed goat-restraint system.

After much coaxing, and no small amount of alfalfa-cube bribery, we finally got Pedro to stand still in the middle of the truck bed. We threaded the rope through the dog collar, which he had reluctantly accepted a few moments before. The compact Toyota truck bed, which had seemed perfectly ample on the way there, was immediately dwarfed by the scale of the animal. His head rose above the top of the truck cab. Approaching from head on, his grand horns curlicuing against the blue sky, he must have looked like a bizarre hood ornament affixed to the top of our roof.

We tied the rope tightly to steel grommets in the bed of the truck. There could be no way for Pedro to jump out. Even so, the enterprise carried an air of catastrophe.

"What do you think?" I asked Travis.

"I think it'll work. He shouldn't go nowhere. Muh muh muh."

Oh, no, I said to myself. Here come the muh muhs. Travis's mumming, it should be quickly explained, was an unconscious vocalization he made whenever he felt nervous about something. The first time I had heard him mumming, we had been raising a two-ton barn beam with an untested, rusty floor jack. As the twisted lumber groaned in protest, popping and creaking alarmingly with each pump of the jack handle, Travis had muh-muhed an entire symphony.

This time, only three muhs. Everything was going to be fine, I reassured myself. Sensing our hesitation, the goat's owner tried to boost our confidence.

"Oh, Pedro'll be okay. I've moved him like this before."

"How many times?" Travis asked.

"Lots," she said.

"How far?"

She thumbed over her shoulder. "Mostly just across the road right there, to my neighbor's farm. But that whole time, he's only jumped over the side of the truck twice."

"Mmm . . . muh muh huh!" Travis vocalized, now more nervous than ever. The lady studied him curiously.

"What did you say?" she asked.

"He said we'd better get going," I interjected on his behalf. Once the mumming turned into huhhing, I knew that trouble was right around the corner. We checked the rope one final time, waved our goodbyes, and turned the key in the ignition. We were off.

Driving with a very large goat, tied at the collar but otherwise unrestrained in the back of a pickup truck, was apparently an uncommon sight to the citizens of Martinsburg, West Virginia. Conversations stopped. People did double takes, pointing. We must have looked like a misplaced parade entrant, only needing some festive bunting and the words "Goat Float" painted on the side of our truck.

A police car passed us in the opposite direction, and from my side-view mirror I watched as the officer slowed . . . slowed . . . slowed . . . riding hard on his brakes, looking back at us through the driver's side window. Mercifully, he kept going. We wasted no time getting out of town.

We pulled onto Route 9, headed toward Berryville. At first Pedro tap-danced nervously as tractor trailers zoomed past on the highway. Gradually he began to settle down, perhaps enjoying the feel of the breeze between his horns. The wind carried his ears backwards like pennant flags, flamboyantly flapping in the wind. It was as though Travis and I had stolen the opposing team's mascot, and the mascot ended up enjoying the gag most of all.

One has never truly lived until one has pulled alongside a school bus of bored children with a large goat on the back of one's truck. On our left, two dozen faces leaned out of the tiny rectangular windows, screaming and cheering, a bas-relief of middle school rapture.

Realizing what was happening, Travis smiled and waved to the children, leaning over me with utter disregard for my steering. In the rearview mirror I could see Pedro's lush coat rippling triumphantly, the sun glinting off his lustrous mane. I had a notion he was enjoying the attention every bit as much as Travis. All that was missing was a pair of oversized goat sunglasses, and the picture would have been complete.

Pedro fit in at the farm immediately. He became our daily companion, unquestioningly following us wherever we went. No chore was too mundane or intimidating. He was equally happy following us out to feed the chickens as when we ran two roaring chain saws simultaneously, branches and sawdust flying.

Travis struck up a fast and steady affection for the goat. It wasn't unusual to hear his voice just over the hill, talking to Pedro in an affable monologue whenever he thought no one was around to hear. After years of working by himself on the neighboring farm with no one to talk to, it must have been natural for him to converse with a creature as convivial and attentive as Pedro.

One morning the following week, as I walked up the hill to the barnyard, I discovered a leaky water hydrant spraying a rainbow of mist across the corral. Unable to track down Travis or Pedro, I assumed they were already out doing the morning chores. I pinned a note to the barn door where Travis would see it, hopped in my truck, and headed to town for parts.

A mile from the farm, on the main public road, I spotted at a distance what appeared to be Travis's truck coming toward me. That's odd, I thought. By now, he should have finished feeding the chickens and been back at the barnyard, reading my note. It was probably just a similar-looking truck.

As the approaching vehicle got closer and closer, however, I realized that it was unmistakably Travis's truck. No one else drove a white 1985 F-250 with no front grille and a gray bed cap that leaned precipitously to the driver's side.

As we passed, I got a clear look at Travis, red feed cap and lamb-chop sideburns. He waved curtly through his open window, one arm draped casually over the steering wheel. Seated beside him, serene as an old lady returning from church service, was Pedro. I couldn't be sure, but it looked as though he even had his seat belt on.

I only had a split second to take in the entire scene, but knew my eyes weren't playing tricks on me. I hit my brakes, coming to a stop in the middle of the road. Behind me, Travis's truck maintained its ramshackle course, disappearing around the bend without so much as slowing down. Part of me wanted to double back, but I knew I had to get the hydrant fixed before the corral turned into a mud slide. Shaking my head, I pressed the gas pedal, resolving to get to the bottom of the story after I was finished with my errand in town.

A few hours later, back at the farm, I watched Travis's truck slowly navigate the obstacle course of potholes lining our driveway. He always took an hour for lunch at his house, about five miles from the farm. At long last, he pulled into the parking lot.

I scanned the interior of the cab, which was currently goatless. "Hey, Travis."

"Hey." He shut off his engine, and it rattled to a double hiccup of a stop.

"How's everything going today?"

"Just fine."

I leaned against his fender. His face was inscrutable. "Did I . . . did I pass you on the way to town this morning? Near the four-way stop?"

"Yup."

"That's what I thought." I cleared my throat, giving him ample opportunity to spill the beans. His face remained completely devoid of expression. "So," I tried again, "when I passed you this morning, it looked like you had someone in the truck with you."

Finally, a glimmer of humor appeared in his eyes. "I most certainly did."

"And . . . was it Pedro?"

"It most certainly was."

"In the cab."

"Yes, sir."

"With a seat belt on."

"I had him buckled up. Yes."

"And you had him in the truck because . . ."

"I had him in the truck because he wouldn't ride in the back."

My threshold for diplomacy, judiciously meted, had reached its limit. "Travis!" I blurted. "*Why* did you have Pedro in the truck? What in the world were you doing?"

Travis was unflappable. "I was picking him up. He was eating the flowers off Mrs. Davis's front porch."

"Mrs. Davis?" I said. "But she lives two miles from here."

"I know. And she wasn't happy about finding a goat on her front porch, eating her marigolds."

"But, what was he doing there?"

Travis shrugged. "Beats me. Eating flowers, evidently."

"Okay, okay," I said, raising my hands in surrender. "Look. Just tell me the whole story."

"Well," Travis began, "Mrs. Davis drove in this morning, asking if we have a goat. Yes ma'am, I told her, we do. She asked if our goat has long, curvy horns. Yes ma'am, I told her, he does. She asked if our goat likes eating marigolds off of unsuspecting lady's porches. I told her, well ma'am, I'm not sure about that, but knowing our goat, that certainly sounds possible.

"So, I went looking for Pedro here on the farm, and when I couldn't find him, I had a feeling that it was probably our goat she was talking about. When I got back, she was still standing in the parking lot, waiting for me, so I climbed in the truck and followed her over to her place. And there was Pedro, on her front porch, eating flowers just like she had said. So, I ran him off the porch, and loaded him in the truck."

"Oh, no. Did he do much damage? Does she want us to pay for what he ate?"

Travis shook his head. "He didn't hurt them too much. I mean, don't get me wrong, he was eating flowers all right, but I think she was just more startled than anything. She seemed happy that he belonged to somebody, and that she didn't have to call the dog pound."

"That's a relief. But . . . why did you put him in the cab?"

"I ain't got no tailgate," he said, gesturing with his thumb over his shoulder. "I hit a rut last week and the blooming thing fell off right in the road.

"Anyway, I *tried* to put him in the back. Twice. But without the tailgate, he just jumped right out again. The third time, I told him, 'The hell with you! Your butt's going in the cab!'"

"So you put him in the cab . . ."

"I most certainly did. I shoved him up in there and set him on his butt, and pulled the seatbelt tight across him so he couldn't move."

I blinked, at a loss for words. "And . . . and he just sat there?"

"Yes, sir. Pretty as you please."

Well, I thought to myself, *this* is all rather unexpected. "Where's Pedro now?"

Travis pointed toward the edge of the woods. "I tied him to a sticker briar. He's been eating it for lunch."

So he was. From that day on, his desire to roam apparently assuaged, Pedro reliably stayed put on the farm.

Now that we were out of the hay and equipment business, Travis and I spent many spare hours cleaning up old trash dumps on the farm. To us, "trash" consisted of rusting scrap metal, old bottles, tires, mangled wire, and abandoned, broken-down machinery. For periods in our farm's history, these rusting mounds of junk and garbage were allowed to accumulate instead of being properly disposed. Perhaps the option of "proper disposal" was an assumption on my part; piling up the debris might have been the only available option at the time. Pushed into lopsided pyramids along distant fencerows, or neglected in tangled heaps behind the barn, at least a dozen of these junk piles littered the farm from one end to the other. Travis and I spent countless hours untangling them, loading them as best we could onto the truck, and transporting them to our local dump.

Pedro was there for all of it. He'd clamber to the tops of these piles, exhibiting the grace and balance innate to his species, tightroping along a narrow tractor chassis, or defying gravity at the pinnacle of mounded fence wire.

One trash site stood out as the most egregious and most dangerous: the old spray house. My grandfather, who had otherwise maintained a chemical-free farm, had relied heavily on synthetic pesticides and poisons to keep his orchards humming along. The apple trees he planted had limited natural resistance to pests, and chemical applications existed for nearly every problem. There were antifungals, insecticides, defoliants, and herbicides, many of them appearing in multiple forms, for different times of the year.

Because we lived in an orchard community, and because these spraying practices were so commonplace, our local dump occasionally sponsored days when they would dispose of these chemicals for free. On these occasions, Travis and I carefully loaded bags of toxic powders and bottles of poison onto the truck, covering them with a tarp so they couldn't blow out as we drove down the highway. Little by little, trip by trip, we cleaned out the decrepit old building, until we were nearly done.

We had been working at it steadily one day, and only had a couple of loads left to haul, when we noticed that Pedro wasn't acting like himself. Normally full of energy, with a distinctive twinkle in his eye, he had become lethargic. He wandered away by himself and sat along the shade of an overgrown fencerow.

"Must be feeling bad," Travis commented. "Never seen him act that way before."

The next morning, he was considerably worse. He wouldn't stand for more than a few moments, and was moaning incessantly. In obvious discomfort, he ground his jaw teeth together, emitting the sound of grating rocks. We offered him food and water, but he didn't have an appetite.

"I've never known him to not be hungry. What do you think is wrong with him?" I asked Travis.

"Don't know," he said, his face lined with concern, "but I don't like the look of it. It's just something he's gotta get through, I reckon. Hopefully it'll pass with time."

One final trip to the landfill, and the building would be empty at last. Leaving Pedro in as comfortable a position as we could, we headed back to work, planning to check on him when we returned.

As we entered the back room of the old spray house, my eyes widened.

"Oh no," I said, my heart leaping into my throat. "You don't think . . ."

One of the bags, which had previously been sealed, was freshly torn open. Small green pellets were clearly visible inside, many of them scattered haphazardly across the floor. Like always, Pedro had been with us the day before, but I had never imagined any risk in having him around the old building. The entire house smelled so thickly of chemicals that he rarely stayed inside for long.

Travis crouched, reading the tag that was stapled to the edge of the bag.

"Mouse poison!" he exclaimed. "Oh my God! He's eaten . . ."

I stepped quickly to his side, peering inside the hole that Pedro had torn through the paper.

"A lot. He's eaten a *lot*." A heavy resignation settled over me as I studied the damage. "Travis. He must have eaten a half gallon of the stuff."

By the time we made it back to him, Pedro was nearly gone.

We buried him beneath his favorite sycamore tree, down by the creek, where the ivy he loved clung in twisting spires to the stately, mottled trunk.

It was bitterly ironic, that by trying to clean up our past, we had inadvertently poisoned our present. By waiting so long to clean up the old dump site, I felt as though I had betrayed a friend. From that moment on, we reaffirmed our vow to keep the farm free of toxic chemicals, eliminating the possibility of another terrible accident. It seemed like a small gesture at the time, but it was a promise we were able to keep.

Chapter Twenty-One

The chance meeting with Ellen and Dan at the conference put our farm into motion in ways I never could have envisioned, much less scripted. The farm made it through another long winter, and Dad and I showed up at the Arlington Courthouse Farmers' Market early one Saturday in 2000, at six o'clock in the morning. I was more than a little nervous.

We were assigned a permanent space between a vegetable farmer named Peter Perkins, from Hanover, Virginia, and John Hyde, a baker from Hyattsville, Maryland. As we introduced ourselves, I couldn't help feeling like it was the first day of college all over again, meeting the roommates, getting oriented. I tried not to appear too eager, or uncool.

It now took us a little longer to set up. We had added a ten-by-ten pop-up tent for shade and protection from rain, and felt proud of the improved look it gave to our stand. Somehow, our table seemed more substantial with a tent over it, the ambience more inviting. I had hand-painted a wooden sign that read, in bright green letters, SMITH MEADOWS FREE-RANGE MEAT AND EGGS, which we hung from the front of the tent. Little by little, we had made incremental improvements, minor details that made the business uniquely our own.

A glance at our neighbors suggested we still had a long way to go. Peter, the vegetable farmer, piled bags of micro greens, baby salad mixes, and early spring herbs into an immaculate display. His horseshoe configuration of three long tables overflowed with greenery, the bags almost cascading into the customers' eager hands. John, the baker, brought a van filled to bursting with breads, cookies, scones, buns, and Danishes. His fresh pies—blueberry, apple, lemon, and chocolate—looked irresistible.

Their individual stalls were easily three or four times the size of ours, and they carried the feeling of a storefront unto themselves. Two or three employees helped with sales, restocking, bagging, answering questions. As I watched them make their final preparations, I jokingly wondered aloud if we should do some calisthenics in advance of the apparent customer onslaught.

"Good idea," Dad replied, hungrily eyeing a cherry-and-cheese Danish a few feet away. "You do some toe-touches, get good and limber. I'm going to go meet the baker."

"Don't go far," I said, half in admonishment and half out of nervousness. "I'm going to need your help."

"That's why I'm getting something to eat," he explained without stopping. "To keep my strength up."

He had hardly stepped out of our stand when I felt a touch on my arm.

"You new here?" a woman's voice asked.

I turned, and looked down. A small, disheveled woman with long, gray hair and thick glasses peered up at me. I hadn't seen her enter the tent, and her arrival startled me.

"Yes," I said, trying to hide my surprise. "This is our first day." I extended my hand. "I'm Forrest."

"Glenda," she said, taking my hand. Her grip was warm, but rough from hard work. "I run Bunny's Bakery. We're a couple of stands down. We sell cupcakes, mostly."

"Nice. How long have you been selling here?"

She sighed, her shoulders lifting and sagging beneath her oversized shirt. "Almost since this market started. Next year will be our twentieth year here."

"Wow. So, it must be a good market for you, then?"

"Our best," she stated. "*Has* to be our best. Too hard of work, otherwise."

Without warning, she grasped me firmly by the elbow and pulled me close. "Now, look," she said, lowering her voice to a confidential tone. Our faces were only inches apart, and I could smell coffee and cinnamon buns on her breath. "You look like a nice guy. I can tell that right away. But listen. I've seen a lot of nice people over the years." Her grip on my arm tightened. "I want to tell you something that I wish someone had told me a long time ago."

I was utterly flummoxed by this unexpected intensity. "O-okay . . ." I stuttered.

She pulled me a centimeter closer, holding steady eye contact from behind her smudged, opaque glasses. "What I'm going to tell you, don't ever forget. It's going to make or break your whole career."

"I . . . I don't know what to say. I promise?"

"Good. Now, listen." She glanced furtively from side to side. "Don't ever . . . don't you ever, *ever*, wholesale your stuff. I don't care if you're selling emus or artichokes. *Don't wholesale*. Don't let anyone talk you into it, don't let anyone tell you it's a good idea. Don't let anyone say it's the only way to go, or the only way to grow. Retail, retail, retail. Everything *retail*."

I opened my mouth to speak, but she cut me off with a single syllable.

"Mep!" She raised a gnarled index finger toward my lips. "No talking! Listen!" She cleared her throat with a phlegmy rattle, and swallowed decisively. "The only exception . . . the *only* exception," she repeated, and squeezed my elbow to the point of pain, "is if you've retailed *everything,* every last thing, and you can still produce more." She paused, inhaling for a final sortie. "But before you do that, try to retail it. It's the only way to make it in this business. The *only* way."

With that, she released her grip. Circulation slowly returned to my arm. "Thanks," I managed, thoroughly perplexed. "I'll be sure to remember."

"Remember," she agreed, with a nod. "Do it for yourself. If you're ever going to make it, someday you'll look back and remember this conversation. You'll understand what I just told you." She removed her glasses and gave them a thorough wiping against the tails of her button-down shirt. Behind me, I heard the heavy clomp of my father's boots, and turned.

"I got you a bear claw," he boomed, proffering a sticky baked good wrapped in a piece of tissue paper. "They didn't even charge me anything. The man just said 'Welcome to market' and handed it to me." Dad smiled dreamily, talking around a piece of pastry. "I think I'm going to like it here."

I took the offering distractedly, the woman's voice still haunting my ears. "Dad, this is Glenda. She runs Bunny's . . ."

She was no longer there. I searched for her, but she had disappeared entirely. It was only after several moments that I managed to spot her, somehow already back at her own stand, methodically organizing cupcakes.

"That's her, over there." How had she moved so fast? "Anyway, she just came over a minute ago, and I wanted to introduce you."

My dad, at first disinterested, suddenly noticed the brightly colored cupcakes. "Oh, by all means," he agreed, his face lighting up at the prospect of a second helping of snacks. "But it's probably better if I just introduce myself. You stay here and do some more jumping jacks."

I sighed. When it came to food, somewhere along the way we had reversed father-son roles; more and more I felt like the protective parent, trying my best to influence his eating habits in positive, healthy ways. But I didn't have time to think about that now. As he made his way across the street, I noticed that the market was already filling with customers. Even though the opening bell hadn't yet rung, shoppers were lining up in advance, proverbial early birds intent on getting the tastiest produce. A man ducked into our tent.

"Your sign says you sell eggs?"

"Yes, sir. Free-range eggs, from our farm."

"Sounds good. How much?"

We had decided earlier that season to raise our prices to account for the greater travel distance and fuel—that, and the small fact that we had lost money on chickens ever since we had been raising them. By slightly increasing our prices, we had nothing to lose but our pride at this point.

"Three dollars a dozen," I said, wincing internally, self-conscious that it was the highest price for eggs to ever come out of my mouth.

"Sounds good," the man said, reaching for his wallet without hesitation. "I'll take two dozen."

Two dozen? I said to myself. Why in the world would someone need two dozen eggs? No one had ever bought more than a single dozen before. I repeated this request, just to make sure.

"Yes, two dozen. And your beef is totally free-range? Raised on pasture?"

"Absolutely. All grass. No grain at all. And we don't use any chemical fertilizers, or antibiotics, or . . ."

"Great, I'll take two pounds of ground, as well."

This was uncharted territory. Why, of course, I reasoned, anyone who needs two dozen eggs clearly needs two pounds of ground beef as well. Maybe he just went around buying two of everything.

"And . . ." he added, tapping his chin, studying our list, "a chicken. Say, four pounds?"

I nearly fainted right on the spot. In less than thirty seconds, it was the biggest single order I had ever gotten at a market.

A busy morning market at Arlington.

"Let's see," I said, trying to keep my composure. I climbed onto the back of the truck, retrieved the ground beef and chicken, and weighed the meat on the scales. "That'll be twenty-four dollars and fifty cents."

I made change, thanked him, and placed the money in my pocket. In the distance I heard the opening bell ring. In sixty seconds I had already made more money than at my first market back home. As novel as this experience was, I didn't have time to enjoy it. Two more customers entered the stand, then a third. For the first time in my career, I had a line.

My father bustled in halfway through my fourth sale, a pair of sirloin steaks and a package of sweet Italian sausage.

"Sorry," he whispered loudly as I bent over the freezer on the back of the truck. "I didn't expect you to already be this busy."

I found the steaks and sausage, and pulled my head out of the freezer.

"I didn't expect it either, but I . . . Dad!" I nearly dropped the meat.

"What?"

"You've got pink frosting in your beard!" I shook my head at him. "Come on, man!"

He turned his head away from the line of customers, abashedly licking at the corners of his mouth. "Is it gone now?" he asked, in a small voice.

Exasperated, I made him march to the side-view mirror for self-inspection. When he returned, frostingless, I had already worked my way through the end of the line.

"I should go away more often," he quipped. "As soon as I leave the stand, you get a crowd."

"Don't go away too quickly," I said. "I've got a feeling today's going to be pretty steady."

And it was. Although we came nowhere close to our dream of selling out of everything, we ended the day making more money than we had ever made at a single market before—nearly five hundred dollars. It was enough to pay for our gas and our time, while sparking our optimism that we could make enough in the future to pay some of our bills back at the farm. My father, counting the stack of twenty-dollar bills we had accumulated, was so happy that he bought an entire box of cookies from the baker next door.

"What?" he asked, catching my disapproving look. "I got them to celebrate. Plus, they're your favorite, oatmeal raisin."

"Dad." I sighed. I was happy, too, but my father's eating habits were simply out of control. "You're on medication now. You can't be going around eating boxes of cookies."

Crestfallen, he opened the lid in spite of my chastisement. "Well, here's a cookie for you, anyway," he said sullenly. "Congratulations on your big day."

"*Our* big day," I corrected. "And don't give me that hangdog look. You know I'm just trying to take care of you."

He took no comfort in the brand of care I was offering. By the time I pulled on to Interstate 66, a mile away, I noticed his hand sneaking into the box.

"Oh, for Pete's sake," I blurted. "Just eat a doggone cookie, will you?"

"I thought you'd never offer," he said with transparent glee. He ate half a cookie in one bite. "Another minute or two, and I would have starved to death."

I narrowed my eyes in disapproval. By the time we got home, he had eaten half a dozen.

Over the following weeks, the market got even busier, and our first day turned out to be our slowest by a long shot. As time passed, I got to know my neighboring vendors, talking to them during the rare quiet moments, asking them questions about marketing and production.

I discovered that these farmers were a wealth of information. They had experienced parallel struggles to get their produce and products to market, often overcoming seemingly insurmountable challenges. Some producers made it look easy, their tents staffed with bright-eyed employees, tables overflowing with fruits and vegetables. Others clearly struggled each week, barely bringing enough inventory to make ends meet.

Somewhere between these paucities and cornucopias, our farm staked its own territory. Week by week, we carved an identity from the rows of blue-and-white-topped tents and developed a modest but loyal following.

"Remember what I told you," Glenda coached, frequently appearing out of thin air. "Your best advertising is just showing up. Week after week. Never skip a market."

I was never not startled when she sidled up with these aphoristic pronouncements. "Wait a minute," I replied. "I thought you said 'never wholesale.'"

"Never wholesale?" she repeated, blinking several times. "That's excellent advice. But, no." In her baggy sweatshirt and long skirt, she looked like a gumdrop with glasses. "Never spend a *dollar* on advertising. Just showing up each week is crucial. Better than painting your name on the side of the truck, or some expensive website."

A man's voice spoke up, agreeing. "We don't even *have* a website. Save our money, I always say. Bake more cupcakes."

Glenda's partner, Bert, had appeared like an apparition directly behind me, effectively sandwiching me between the two of them. What was it with these people? I didn't know which way to turn.

"Not a nickel." Glenda nodded, concurring.

"And our station wagon is an Eighty-Two," Bert added with pride. He was very tall and extremely thin, and moved with a willowy air. "Talk about getting our money's worth. We paid that off in . . . what? Nineteen-Ninety?"

"It was a while ago," Glenda agreed, waving a dismissive hand. "But my point, before Bert started in about the station wagon, is that you don't need to spend a lot of money on this. Or at least not on things some people tell you to spend money on. You need to *make* money."

"And you guys have always made money?" I asked.

Glenda nodded emphatically. "Every year. Sometimes not much. Sometimes not very much. But always something."

I nodded appreciatively. "That's remarkable."

She placed her hands on her hips. "It's because we listened to what smart people told us. People who had more experience than us. And we paid attention." She stared at me meaningfully. By now, I knew my cue.

"Right." I checked the points off on my fingers. "Show up each week. Don't worry about painting my name on the side of my truck. Don't spend money on advertising," I recited obediently.

"And . . . ?"

"And?" I repeated, uncertain.

"*And* . . . ?" She leaned in close, poking me sharply in the sternum.

"Ouch! And . . . oh! Always retail! Never wholesale!"

She smiled, slapping me affectionately on the cheek. "Star pupil."

"You know," Bert added, tugging thoughtfully on his ear. I had forgotten that he was still standing behind me. "Come to think of it, I'm pretty sure we had the wagon paid off by Eighty-Nine."

"It was Ninety," Glenda corrected, instantly impatient. "The *van* was Eighty-Nine." She shook her head, grasping him by the wrist and leading him out of my tent. "Come on, Bert."

Summer stretched into fall, and the long season tested my endurance. One cold, drizzly Saturday in November, at 4:00 a.m., exhausted from a week of hard work, I turned off my alarm in my sleep without waking. Somewhere, deep within a dream, Glenda's words echoed through my mind: *Never miss a market! Never miss a market!* I awoke with a start. It was 4:08.

I made myself a pot of coffee, and stumbled bleary-eyed to the truck. It turned out to be my busiest day of the entire season, pulling in almost a thousand dollars in sales.

Later that winter, we wrapped up what was, beyond doubt, our most successful year yet. At last our farm was growing food for a ready audience, people who clearly valued what we offered. Our dreams seemed to be intersecting with economic sustainability. More hopeful than ever, we began to pay down our debt—five hundred dollars here, two hundred and fifty there. It wasn't much, but it slowly added up.

"If things keep going like this, pretty soon you might even get your sister to come back home," Dad said.

"Betsy?" I replied. My sister now enjoyed a successful nursing career and lived with her husband in the suburbs. She had willingly left farm management up to me; not because she was daunted by the hard work, but because she had no reason to believe the land could support us both.

I shook my head. "No way. I could never offer her the salary she's getting. Besides, she's already settled into her new lifestyle. You know, mowing the lawn every Saturday. Cookouts with the neighbors. That sort of thing."

"I wouldn't be so sure about that," Dad said. "From what she's told me, life in the suburbs isn't all that she thought it would be. Besides, with markets getting busier, you're probably going to need her help."

I had never thought about my sister returning to the farm, but the longer I considered it, the more the suggestion grew on me. Still, there was an incident from our childhood that loomed over our adult relationship, a humiliating memory that had forever changed how we felt about each other. She always brought up the story when I least expected it, and it had never failed to devastate me. If we were ever going to work together on the farm, then she would have to promise to never mention it again. I called her up the following day.

Chapter Twenty-Two

When I was four years old, my sister dressed me in a blue satin princess costume and made me perform a fashion show on our front porch. The outfit, complete with shimmering sequins and a puffy chiffon veil, was her bargaining chip; if I agreed to wear it, she would play Star Wars with me later that day. Even though I knew I was getting a raw deal, my desire for her to be a Leia to my Luke outweighed my cross-dressing inhibitions. I put on the silly, frilly outfit and, following the terms of our contract, stepped through the doorway into bright morning sunlight, taking a reluctant turn on the catwalk.

From the front lawn, Betsy studied me up and down and shook her head disapprovingly. "You didn't put on the tiara," she said, snapping a few pictures nevertheless. "No princess tiara, no deal. Sorry."

Perhaps it was this sudden change of terms, a bait-and-switch escalation, that left me feeling betrayed. Perhaps it was her crisp enunciation of the word "princess," a moniker abhorred by little boys the world over. Whatever it was, putting on the tiara was a total deal breaker. I pitched a fit fit for a queen.

"I'm not wearing a tiara! I don't want to be a princess!" I stormed back into the house. Our arrangement was now in

Princess Forrest.

shambles, but I no longer cared. I just wanted to get out of that dress and into something plaid.

Twenty years later, surprisingly little had changed; I found myself once again in negotiations with my sister, trying to enlist her help. She had grown up on the farm much like I had, helping during the summer months, making hay with our male cousins who traveled up from Blacksburg each year. Betsy was six years older than I, and in many ways, watching her work on the farm as a kid had greatly influenced my decision to become a farmer. Like in any sibling rivalry, I spent a good part of my time secretly observing her from a distance, studying her pace, learning how she operated. I patiently awaited the day when I could challenge her skills on the hay wagon, or beat her at picking a sack of corn.

I took the same classes in 4-H as she did and attended the same summer camps each year, trying to win the same awards. Just like her, I received my lifeguarding license when I turned sixteen. When she took an additional part-time job to make extra money, working for a local catering company, I did too. You could more or less plot my entire childhood to a six-year delay behind my sister.

Betsy had never questioned my decision to become a farmer. My first year after college, we shared the old farmhouse together, my parents still living in the house we had grown up in a few miles away. When I was too tired to drop a box of spaghetti into a pot of boiling water, she was the one who made me dinner. She even shopped for me at the local thrift stores, finding the elusive 34 x 36 pants that I had grown into.

It was my sister who, in those initial lean years, wordlessly paid the electricity and phone bills, knowing I couldn't afford anything more than the gasoline I poured into my chain saw. She was always kind to me, without ever asking for a word of thanks. During those first couple of years back at the farm, if my sister hadn't been so generous, I might not have had a place to eat or sleep.

Our nascent success in the big city, however, made me wonder if we could somehow reunite the family farm. I could now envision a time when we would need to grow more food, and perhaps attend more city markets. After all, the Arlington market encompassed only one small neighborhood of Washington, D.C., and this particular market was one of several within the city limits of Arlington itself. It was a big, big world out there. I could certainly use more help.

Our mother had always promised to return to the farm after she retired, and now Dad hinted that he might retire early, coming back home to help as well. If my father was finally buying into things, I told myself, then it must mean the tide was truly turning. Nancy, now my fiancée, was moving to the farm after graduate school, and if I could only get my sister to come home, the entire family would be together. It was little more than a dream, but I took the possibility to heart.

———————

For years now, customers had asked us for lamb. Nearly all the lamb that was available in the grocery stores was shipped halfway around the world, from New Zealand and Australia. Since lambs could be raised on nothing more than grass and water, incorporating sheep onto our farm was an intriguing opportunity to consider.

But I had no experience at all with sheep, and learning the habits of yet another type of farm animal didn't seem like a practical use of my time. When customers made suggestions of this sort, I slid the requests into the "maybe" file, the same place I kept ideas like buffalo, duck eggs, or mythological meats such as turkey bacon. My hands were more than full with cattle, pigs, and chickens. If our farm was to manage a flock of sheep, then someone else would need to be in charge.

Remarkably, when I floated the suggestion past my sister one evening over dinner, she entertained the idea.

"How many sheep do you think we're talking about?" she asked.

"Your guess is as good as mine." I hadn't really expected her to take an interest in the topic, and had no firm pitch prepared. I quickly improvised. "I mean, they usually throw twins, right? So, however many ewes we raise, they should have twice as many lambs. How many lambs do you think we can sell in a year?"

Betsy considered the question. My sister had attended dozens of markets with me over the years, helping out whenever I was away or needed an extra hand. She knew as well as anyone the fluctuations of customer demand. "No idea. Fifty? A hundred?"

"My thoughts exactly. There's no real way of knowing. I was thinking maybe start out on the lower end. Say, around forty?"

"Sounds like a nice round number." She paused. "You don't think coyotes will eat them as soon as they get to the farm, do you?"

I had been concerned about this possibility, too. Coyotes had decimated Virginia sheep populations in the 1960s, and these predators were once again making a comeback. A few years prior, a coyote had picked off a neighbor's lambs one by one each evening. The first casualties left no traces besides a pair of silky, detached ears. The owners soon learned to pen their sheep up at night. At a minimum, we could benefit from their bad luck.

"If it makes you feel any better, I'll keep an extra eye on them, and walk them home at night."

She considered this offer. "So you're saying that I'll be in charge of the sheep, even though we've never raised any before, and I don't know what I'm doing. And I'd be keeping my full-time job in town while managing the flock, and living a half hour away."

"It's like this," I countered. "If we ever want lambs on the farm, this is probably the only way it's going to happen. If you can just keep tabs on them, you know, check on them before and after work, and keep good records, Travis and I can probably pick up the slack in between."

"Deal," she replied at last. "But when it comes time, *you'll* be the one to shear them."

Ah, sheep shearing. That critical first step of turning animal hair into unbearably itchy sweaters. Back in our pioneering past, many livestock breeds had been reared for dual purposes out of practical necessity. For cattle, this meant being first used for milk, then butchered for beef; chickens were kept for eggs before eventually being roasted. Sheep were raised initially for their wool; only after they had served their primary usefulness were they then turned into food themselves. Sheep could produce many lambs, as well as many bags of wool, before they ended up as mutton.

In modern times, however, fewer and fewer people used wool. With the advent of synthetic fabrics such as polyester, demand for wool declined to all-time lows. Raising wool sheep was rapidly becoming a thing of the past, and few farms considered wool to be a profitable enterprise. Shearing had become a sheer waste of their time.

Many farms sidestepped this additional chore by raising "hair sheep" instead. Hair sheep were identical in every way to their woolly brethren, except instead of growing thick fleeces, they maintained a short coat, shedding it off each spring without the help of the farmer and his shears. Since Travis and I already spent so much of our day solving unpredictable problems, preemptively eliminating shearing was an easy decision.

While there were many different breeds of hair sheep, there were only three types that were commonly raised in our area: Katahdins, Dorpers, and Barbados Blackbellies. After thumbing through the classifieds for a few weeks, it became clear that the

Katahdins and Dorpers were by far the most prevalent, but they were also the most expensive.

My sister had volunteered to buy the first flock, using money she saved from her nursing salary. Once the lambs were sold, she would pay herself back from the profits; to that end, we wanted to get the best value we could for the investment. Katahdins and Dorpers commonly traded hands for two hundred dollars apiece. When I came across an ad offering forty-five Barbados Blackbelly ewes for seventy-five dollars each, buyer take all, I was intrigued by the possibility of such a value. Betsy and I drove down to Fredericksburg, Virginia, to have a look.

"These are purebred Blackbellies," the man assured us, leading us to a corral where he had penned the ewes. He spoke very loudly, as though the volume of his voice somehow validated his honesty. "There's a lot of crossbreeding out there right now, and you can't trust what anybody says. People will tell you all sorts of half truths. These are purebred," he emphasized, as we reached the corral. "Good stock."

This was the winter of 2000, and our region still didn't have Internet access. I had no way of knowing what a genuine purebred Barbados Blackbelly looked like, short of going to my local library and hoping it carried a full-color book on hair sheep. My limited knowledge of sheep meant I had to trust a man who had just finished telling me that I couldn't trust anybody.

These animals, bunched closely together in the corral, looked more like diminutive deer than any type of sheep I had ever seen. Their coats were the color of milk chocolate, and their white faces were painted with flamboyant Groucho Marx eyebrows. Just as their name suggested, their stomachs were coated black, as though they had belly flopped in a puddle of tar.

They circled nervously, moving tightly like a school of fish, seeking escape. Even as they turned they kept their eyes focused on us, heads swiveling, ninety glittering eyes studying us intently. Occasionally, a sheep on the edge tried to nose toward the center, as though uncomfortable being exposed along the perimeter.

"They seem kind of wound up, don't they?" I asked. They had a decidedly neurotic energy about them, as though ready to bolt at the first opportunity.

"That's just how sheep are," the man explained. "Squirrellier than a squirrel, that's what I always say. All sheep are like that." A few of the animals now tap-danced in place, like racehorses waiting behind the starting gate. "Wound up tighter than a spring. Squirrelly nut sheep, if you ask me. That's just their way."

All these sayings about nervous, nutty sheep were starting to make *me* nervous. Although I had never personally raised a sheep in my life, I had been around them each year at the county fair, volunteering in the livestock barns. The sheep there had always seemed quite docile, easy to handle. As I studied these Barbados Blackbellies, constantly shifting from one end of the corral to the other, the air almost crackled with electricity.

"These are good sheep," the man said, insisting. "Very productive. Already bred, gonna lamb in five months. Good on grass. I'd keep them myself, but, well. You know how it is." He spread his hands. "Too many irons in the fire. Plus, I'm getting old, and messing around with sheep is a young person's job. Especially with . . ." He inclined his head toward the ewes, but abruptly bit off the end of his sentence. It was as though he had been about to say "especially with *Barbados Blackbellies*" but had caught himself at the last second. Instead, he trailed off in silence.

Betsy wasn't about to give him a free pass. "Especially with . . . ?" she prompted.

The man cleared his throat. "Hmm? Oh, I was just going to say, especially with . . . with, you know, *sheep*. What with having to trim their feet, and everything." He rubbed the back of his neck, avoiding eye contact. "Young person's job. These are nice sheep right here, though," he said, a salesman again. "Good price, too. Fair price. Nice sheep."

I leaned against the fence. There was no denying it: These Blackbellies looked like hell on wheels. Watching them skitter around the dusty lot gave me second thoughts. Still, Travis and I had patched our perimeter fences into fair shape, and our own corral was tight enough to confidently hold them for the first few days back at our farm. Betsy and I talked it over in private, weighing the pros and cons.

Sensing our reluctance, the man said he would knock off five dollars a head if we took them all. In the end, we decided that the price was right. Just like that, less than a month after we had decided to give shepherding a try, we were the new owners of forty-five Barbados Blackbellies.

We loaded them without any trouble, each animal gracefully bounding one by one into the empty trailer. When we arrived back at our farm, however, and opened the trailer door, it was as though we had taken the lid off a jar of grasshoppers. Sensing freedom, the sheep sprang forward all at once, high into the air. Some of them burst through the opening, but many collided and ricocheted off one another, falling with a chaotic clatter to the floor of the trailer. These sheep immediately jumped again, redoubling their efforts to escape. Again, some made it, while others somersaulted, airborne, crashing a second time. They flung themselves about as if the floor of the trailer had suddenly become a trampoline.

This all happened at such a dizzying speed that I was powerless to stop them. Within seconds they were all out, sprinting in a tight flock to every corner of the corral, desperately seeking an escape route. The energy I had sensed back at the other farm was now fully unleashed, and they galloped with the intensity of tiny, black-bellied stallions.

I instantly reconsidered the soundness of our corral. The wooden boards, intended to contain larger livestock, were spaced too widely for this horde of pint-sized whirling dervishes. Just as I identified this flaw, I watched as an ewe slipped her head between two boards, turning her shoulders sideways. Without much trouble at all, she squeezed through to the other side.

The rest of the flock, seeing their sister outside the corral, quickly replicated the maneuver. They poured between the boards like water through a sieve. Within thirty seconds of opening the trailer door, the entire flock had escaped.

I quickly ran to shut the main gate, to keep them in the barnyard, but they easily dashed past me. As they sprinted down our driveway, I could only stand and watch as the cloud of dust and hooves headed for Berryville.

I imagined eventually receiving a postcard in the mail: "Hello from sunny Barbados! You're a baaaad shepherd. —The Sheep." Beside me, my sister stood with her arms crossed, watching them run. *This was all your idea,* her body language said.

It was our pigs that ended up saving us. Earlier that year, Travis and I had rebuilt a lower paddock of the barnyard, an intermediary pasture for the larger hogs before we sent them into the fields. The boards in this area were narrowly spaced and tightly nailed, since hogs could easily escape weak enclosures.

By some miracle, the sheep flocked straight into this area, flooding through the open gate. I raced down the hill behind them, and snapped the latch. Leaning against a fence post, I caught my breath as the sheep turned circles in the paddock. At least I could sleep peacefully that night, knowing they'd still be on the farm when I awoke.

Betsy came down and stood beside me.

"You know," she said, after we had watched them for a few moments, "seeing you run down the hill just then, I couldn't help myself. I imagined you dressed in that baby-blue princess outfit. Remember? The one with the tutu."

I felt my eyes suddenly bulge in their sockets, my blood pressure soaring through the top of my skull.

"You . . . you *promised!*" I blurted. "What's the *matter* with you?"

She shrugged, ignoring my tantrum. "Things could have been a lot different if you'd only worn the tiara."

Fuming, I turned on my heel, and stomped a path back home. Some things, apparently, would simply never change.

Throughout the following season, managing these sheep was akin to working with a herd of wild gazelles. Even calling them "wild" was an understatement. They were so reliably jittery, ready to flee at the first sign of human interaction, that I suspected they pounded double shots of espresso each morning behind the barn.

In the end, though, the farmer had been at least somewhat honest. After five months of chasing them back onto our property, through holes in our fences we had never known existed, each of the ewes ended up having a robust, healthy lamb or twin. We gradually developed a feel for their temperament, learning how to approach them in ways that were more conducive to farmer-sheep diplomacy.

A year passed, and we brought our first cuts to market. Succulent lamb chops, rosemary garlic sausages, and plump legs of lamb now graced our market board. We sold out of our cuts faster than we ever anticipated.

Nevertheless, at our earliest opportunity, we sold these ewes to a Barbados Blackbelly breeder, who was delighted to have them. As their new owner drove them away, Betsy and I looked at each other askance, silently lauding our good luck. We used the money to buy a smaller but vastly more manageable flock of Katahdin ewes. With our Blackbelly experiences officially behind us, from that point forward, raising sheep was a genuine pleasure.

Of course, nothing ever goes exactly according to plan. It wasn't long after this that my sister announced she and her husband were expecting their first child, and she would no longer be able to help with the sheep. Suddenly I was going to be an uncle, and a full-time shepherd as well. Our family farm was growing in ways I had never imagined.

Chapter Twenty-Three

B y now we had been raising pigs for nearly a year and had moved them out of the barn and entirely onto pasture. We placed them in our old apple orchard, where the gentle hills, abundant clover, and cool shade provided an idyllic setting for porcine habitat. Our first load of piglets arrived early one spring morning. They sniffed the wildflowers, grunted quizzically at the apple trees, then rushed across the pasture with a frolicking abandon usually reserved for kindergartners turned loose at recess.

From day one, the pigs appeared to be in hog heaven. They set straight away to rooting in the grass, flipping it six inches deep in search of tender roots, grubs, and mice. As omnivores, they taste-tested everything that appeared edible to them, including our boots and blue jeans as they congregated around us each morning. Being careful not to turn the pasture into a sty, we gave them fifteen acres to explore, a big enough space to add more hogs if the experiment went well, but not so large that we had difficulty finding them each day during our livestock checks.

A few modest A-frame sheds provided necessary shelter from the elements, and we kept the floors deeply bedded with bales of clean, bright straw. Gravity feeders of corn and barley allowed the piglets to eat whenever they liked, and fresh water was piped from our well.

The philosophy was simple, and the hogs were easily managed. We began stocking a few additional pigs every month, until eventually we had about sixty hogs of varying sizes trotting across the field at any given time.

After several months, they had rooted up *everything*. In fact, they had pulverized the field so thoroughly that what had once been a lush pasture now looked like a moonscape. Due to their nonstop rooting, no vegetation was able to grow, and without grass to supplement their diet, they now relied completely on pig feed for their sustenance. They had, in effect, manufactured their own enormous feedlot. Inadvertently, they had created the exact same environment I had been trying so hard to avoid.

Thinking about this new problem, I considered the behavior of our cows. After many years of observation, we were finally beginning to understand our cattle's grazing habits. They spent a few hours eating fresh grass each day before moving on, loafing the rest of the afternoon beneath the shade trees. The next morning, even if they still had plenty to eat, they always desired fresh, unspoiled pasture, craving the greener grass on the other side of the hill.

When I was growing up, neighboring farmers told me that when their cows bellowed for fresh pasture, the animals were simply "spoiled." Cattle, they said, had to be controlled by the farmer, forced to eat everything in the field before they were moved. Those fussy cows were just like children: they should eat everything on their plate before they could be excused from the dinner table.

It dawned on me one day that perhaps cows weren't like children at all; perhaps cows were like cows. By mooing, maybe they were trying to communicate with me, letting me know that they were finished with the field, ready to move. Was it possible that cows could know more about being cows than I did?

When at last I listened, doing my best to "speak cow," magical things began to happen. We moved the cattle to a new pasture each day, keeping fresh, thick grass in front of them at all times. Because the grass was no longer grazed to the ground, the pastures now grew more quickly than ever. Plant roots became stronger, reaching deeper into the soil for nutrients. When rain fell, the trampled grass allowed time for water to soak into the soil, and when the hot sun reappeared, the same grass shaded the earth, keeping the ground cool. In our previously overgrazed pastures, water evaporated right out of the exposed topsoil, which caused it to bake hard as a brick beneath the withering sun. Somehow, the cows knew exactly when it was time to eat and when it was time to move. We, as farmers, just needed to be better listeners.

What if, I asked myself, the pigs were trying to talk to us as well? These were once wild creatures that had been domesticated. They still retained many of their ancient biorhythms, their own unique piggish habits. If I took the time to learn their language, could they teach me things as well?

In nature, hogs would probably root over a meadow or woodlot, eat whatever was available, and move on. It wasn't in their best interest to create a barren feedlot environment. If they did, they would eventually starve to death. Travis and I stood with hands in pockets, looking over a field that was as barren as an army bombing range. What would the pigs do? we asked ourselves. Much like the cattle, we reasoned, they would pack up the herd and move.

We rotated the pigs into a new field, and left the original pasture completely alone. No tractor work, no seeding, no animals other than the birds and the bees. If we were going to raise hogs on grass, and make a career out of it, I wanted to understand the cause and effects, the benefits and consequences. In nature, there had never been a farmer coming along behind them to tidy up what they had done. Maybe nature could take care of herself.

When the hogs exited the field, all that was left of the once pristine pasture was desiccated root balls, softball-sized chunks of clayey soil, and muddy, sloppy hog wallows. Now, for a year, it rested. Rain fell and the sun shone. In an adjacent field, the pigs did their very best to create a sequel, flipping and rooting and chewing, working the earth from one corner of the pasture to the next.

In the bustle of raising cattle, chickens, goats, pigs, and sheep, as well as attending farmers' markets each weekend, the prior year's pig field gradually drifted from my consciousness. I had intended to observe its progress and make notes. Instead, a busy year passed without much notice of what transpired just across the other side of the fence.

The following season, we started our spring graze as always, rotating the cattle on a daily basis, keeping pace with the frenetic flush of April pasture. Eventually the herd arrived at the decimated field. This time, instead of bypassing it as we had done the previous year, Travis and I opened the gate, expecting to find the field overgrown with thistles and rosebushes. We hoped there would be enough grass between the nasty briars for the cattle to find a few mouthfuls of nourishment before moving on.

We were dumbfounded by what we discovered. Across the fifteen acres, lush clovers, grasses, and succulent forbs were flourishing. Red-top clover heads, normally ankle-height, reached above our knees, and white clover, perhaps two inches tall in most of my fields, was three times its normal height. As we walked we left deep footprint impressions in our wake. Orchard grass, timothy, and fescue swayed above our belts. It almost felt as if we were wading through the pasture, instead of walking.

At ground level, although the soil was still uneven and lumpy from the rooting, nearly all the exposed dirt had filled in with vegetation. To be sure, there were a few nasty weeds here and there, and a handful of open patches of dirt, but there were fewer in this field than there were in many of my finest pastures.

As we opened the gate and called to the cattle, they too seemed startled. Typically, a "lead cow," elected by her fellow cattle, is the first to investigate a new pasture, making sure it's safe for the rest of the herd to follow. Today this cow ran to the gate, crossed into the pasture, and came to a halt. She stood awestruck, staring at the sea of forage before her. It was as though she was disbelieving her own eyes.

Her moment of hesitation quickly passed. The other cattle crowded behind her, pushing. She plunged into the pasture as if diving into a swimming pool, leading the way through the neck-deep sward. Inspired, bounding and bucking like rodeo broncs, the others raced past her as she settled into her graze. Soon all we could see were their shining backs, tails swishing, as they went about the serious business of chowing down. Their heads were lost below a canopy of food.

We chalked up the amazing pasture rebound to several factors. One, the pigs were obviously responsible for a lot of fertilizing; that many hogs, during the course of the year, put a tremendous amount of manure onto the ground. But more important, they had lightly plowed the soil, decompacting the earth and making the dirt more fissile. Just like tilling a garden, it made a gentler environment for plants to take root, as well as created more crevices for rain to soak in and linger. From that point forward, we regularly rotated the pigs onto fresh pasture. They provided the perfect recipe of tillage, fertilizer, and a good, long rest.

———————

Not everything with the pigs went so serendipitously. Every other Monday, Travis and I loaded hogs for a trip to the butcher. We had a reliable method of getting them onto the trailer, herding them down a fenced alley that bottlenecked into a sorting pen. We then selected the hogs we wanted, opened a gate, and they more or less walked onto the trailer. It was a system we developed through several seasons of trial and error, and eventually we had the process down to a routine.

Then came Blackie.

We were loading the hogs just like on any other day, and had picked out a nice group that was the correct weight and size. As we started to load them, however, one completely black-haired hog grunted and squealed, lowered his head, and charged past Travis and me.

It was the first time anything like that had ever happened. We considered trying to round him up a second time, but we were already late for our appointment. Instead we simply loaded the remaining hogs, and headed up the highway. What a mistake.

Two weeks later, he broke from the herd before we had even approached the loading chute, barking and snorting in alarm, hauling pig butt through the tall grass. We tried once more to round him up, but after another failed attempt, I stood with hands on hips, watching him gallop away.

"I think he's on to us," I said. The black tips of his ears navigated the distant seed tops like the periscope of a submarine.

"I think he's *been* on to us," Travis edited. "Next time, we better make sure he goes on the trailer."

"Isn't that what we said last time?"

Travis glanced at his watch. "Well, let's just take what we got, and try harder next time."

Two weeks later we stood, sweating and out of breath, watching Blackie run away from us yet again. We had spent the previous hour trying every trick we knew, tightening the loading area and herding the hogs in an entirely different direction.

Each time, Blackie had dashed from the otherwise sedate group. Travis and I had run ourselves ragged trying to keep him with the others, until finally, our lungs burning from exertion, we conceded defeat.

"What . . . " I managed between breaths, "what . . . do you think?"

Travis's blue eyes blinked several times. "Muh muh muh," he muttered. "Huh huh huh."

Uh oh, I said to myself. The pig was getting to him.

Our failed attempts turned into weeks, then months. We created "funnels," gated alleyways where Blackie would have to walk in order to get water or feed. We took turns watching as every pig in the flock happily trotted down this path, enjoying a drink or a bite of food. But not Blackie. Never Blackie. Not eating the feed was understandable, because the pastures were a forage paradise for the hogs. But no water? We wondered if we had stumbled across some kind of pig-camel hybrid.

Perhaps, Travis speculated, he was drinking only after dark. We closed off water access during the night, opening it each morning to a passel of thirsty hogs. All of them but Blackie. He'd watch us from the shadows of the apple trees, or from the safety of a distant hilltop. He was always somewhere in the distance, studying us.

As the months passed, he grew bigger. Much, much bigger. Typically, a perfectly raised pasture pig is two hundred and fifty pounds. That was how big Blackie was the first time we tried to load him. Now, he was easily five hundred pounds and growing. Compared to the other hogs, he looked like a horse standing next to a pony.

Nothing we tried worked. Word got around, and Blackie became a bit of a local legend. An old farmer who had raised hogs for many years suggested that we simply "wear him out." In other words, we should walk behind him until he became tired enough to make a mistake and blunder into an alley. "Just keep walking him, even if it takes a couple hours. A hog that big only wants to do two things: eat and sleep."

It was worth a try. Travis and I waited for an especially warm day, hoping the extra exertion, combined with the glaring sun, would encourage Blackie to stop for a drink. When he did, we would simply close the gate behind him. To stack the deck in our favor, we set up several more alleys in the tall grass, a gate at one end and a water trough at the other. We felt certain that this time we'd get our pig.

He wasn't hard to find. In fact, as we approached the group of pigs, sixty pink, dappled hogs dozing in the pasture, Blackie rose from among them like a shadow in broad daylight. With a flourish of dust, he vanished over the hill.

The chase, or at least the walk, was on. We followed him through the field for an hour, then two. Each time he approached one of our new alleys, he stopped for a moment, studied the terrain, then sprinted off in the opposite direction. So much for stacking the deck, I thought.

After three hours, I was getting tired. Travis had already stopped for a break, leaning against a fence post in the shade. By now it was quite hot out, and Blackie was panting visibly, lying down to rest at every opportunity. Each time, as I walked toward the massive animal, he leaped to his feet and took off running.

As we approached the water trough for the twentieth time, I watched in amazement as this time he walked straight into the alley, headed toward a cool, refreshing drink. At last, I said to myself. After all these months, I've finally got you. The old farmer had been right!

I cautiously made my way to the gate, not wanting to spook him. He was well down the chute, almost to the water, when he looked over his shoulder, spotted me, and charged back down the alley. If I had stood in his way, he would have certainly knocked me over.

One more round, I told myself. One more trip around the field, and I was sure to have him. We crossed the hot pasture. My shirt was drenched with sweat, my lips parched. "Come on, pig," I said out loud. "Let's get this over with."

He must have heard me. He turned without warning, charging at me with the ferocity of a mother bear protecting her cubs. A roar rumbled from deep within his chest, a terrifying, primal sound. Foam flecked the corners of his mouth.

I screamed.

The old farmer had been wrong! I stood fully exposed in the open pasture, with no escape. The trees. The trees were my only hope. He thundered toward me. I sprinted into the apple orchard.

I raced through the trees, the limbs slapping my body, crisscrossing my face with welts and cuts. A panicked glance told me all I needed to know: in another second, he would have me. I leaped into the nearest tree, flinging myself across the limbs, hoping they were strong enough to bear my weight without breaking.

Blackie snarled, snapping at the air. He placed his forefeet against the trunk, trying to climb the tree after me. With all my strength I held onto the upper branches, scrambling into the uppermost limbs.

I looked down. The hog now stood on his hind legs like a human, his front hooves in the lower branches where I had just been. Tree bark flew into the air as he sought traction against the trunk. I saw his white teeth flashing, the black depths of his open maw. The hog was altogether furious for a piece of me. At the top of the tree, the thin limbs swaying, I was trapped.

I thought of yelling to Travis for help, unsure if he had seen what had happened, but didn't want him to get hurt. I didn't know what to do. Now that I was just beyond Blackie's reach, we were at a stalemate. With diminished growling and slavering, he finally dropped to his four feet. Grudgingly, he hulked away, snarling at me several times over his shoulder.

At last, he was far enough away from me to make a run for it. The safety of the truck was through a nearby gate, and the timing was just right to make a mad dash. Blackie was still huffing angrily, but was now at a reasonable distance on the edge of the orchard. I jumped from the tree, keeping my eyes fixed on the hog in case he turned and charged again. I intended to hit the ground running. Perhaps I should have mentioned this plan to my feet.

Dropping ten feet vertically, I landed with my full weight on an exposed tree root and snapped my right ankle. My vision flooded with white light as I blacked out.

When I next opened my eyes, I was lying prostrate on the ground, disoriented, unable to walk. With every ounce of strength and adrenaline I possessed, I crawled to the tree and pulled myself back into the limbs, arm over arm.

My ankle needed emergency attention, but I didn't dare move. When I had lost consciousness, I had also lost track of the hog, and couldn't risk exposing myself. Beyond the pain, I now felt a budding shame that I had pushed an animal so far that it had attacked me. I fought back tears, not just from the agony, but from my own guilt, and the hopelessness of the situation.

First I heard the snap and slap of tree branches, then the low hum of a motor. Travis guided the farm truck through the orchard, searching for me.

"Forrest! Forrest! Did he get you?! Are you hurt?" Travis yelled from an open window, unable to see me.

"Here! I'm up here! In the tree!"

He pulled the truck as near as he could to the apple tree. "I heard you scream, and I thought he had gotten you! Jesus Criminy! I thought you might be dead!"

Travis helped me down and drove me to the Winchester emergency room, thirty minutes away. By then my ankle had swollen to the size and color of an eggplant.

A few weeks later, one of the men who worked at Schoen's drove down to the farm and shot Blackie cleanly through the head. The hog weighed nearly seven hundred pounds. I donated the carcass to the butcher's family, only requesting twenty pounds

A butcher from Schoen's, with Blackie.

of sausage. This I divided among the friends who came to visit while I recuperated.

As for me, I never ate a bite. It felt particularly karmic that if this special pig couldn't eat me, then I shouldn't eat him, either.

Chapter Twenty-Four

Now that I was selling meat on a street corner in our nation's capital from the back of my pickup truck, I knew that fame and celebrity couldn't be far behind.

As I leaped from my tailgate cradling armfuls of frozen meat, I received no shortage of attention at farmers' markets. Passersby examined me from a safe distance, like spectators watching an exhibit at the zoo. Who was this crazy-looking man, they seemed to wonder, and what was he doing on the back of his truck? The way we marketed our products ran deeply counter to most displays at market, where sumptuous offerings of fruits, vegetables, and baked goods provided feasts for the eye. Bent over inside my cooler, my rear end thrust in the air and wearing a bandanna and sleeveless T-shirt as a uniform, it was a wonder I ever attracted any customers at all.

The fact was, the more farmers' markets we attended, the more I realized we *weren't* normal. In a landscape of peaches, potatoes, and pastries, our products were every bit as fresh and local, but they had to remain frozen, shrink-wrapped, and tucked out of sight. Peers regarded us with well-intended skepticism, shaking their heads as we unloaded our coolers in a few moments, while they spent an hour and a half carefully stacking multicolored peppers and pyramids of heirloom tomatoes. Our unusual market stall was a source of particular amusement for several older farmers, and they gave me a thorough ribbing each week, wondering aloud if I'd ever do some actual work at market.

One morning in Arlington, one of these farmers, a wizened vegetable grower from Virginia's eastern shore, noticed the name of our hometown.

"Y'all are from Berryville?" he asked. He sported Chester A. Arthur sideburns, navigator sunglasses, suspenders, and brown knee socks pulled up to the bottom of his stained khaki shorts. My father and I had previously made note of his eccentric wardrobe, marveling as much at his absence of fashion sense as his commitment to wearing the exact same outfit each week.

"Berryville," he repeated, his heavy Southern accent changing "berry" into a word that most closely resembled "burry." He paused, reflecting. "Y'all know Harry Berry?"

"Harry Berry?" my father repeated. "Can't say that I've heard of him."

The old farmer appeared incredulous behind his reflective black sunglasses. "Y'all say you're from Berryville?"

My father nodded. "Yup."

"Berryville," the man intoned. "*Virginia.*"

"Correct. Berryville, Arkansas, exceeds the producer-only radius."

"And y'all don't know Harry Berry?" The old farmer tugged at his suspenders, in clear disbelief that we were true Berryvillians.

My father glanced at me. "Harry Berry?" he asked. I shrugged, stumped. Not that I knew everyone in the phonebook, but Harry Berry certainly didn't ring a bell.

"Never heard of him," I replied.

The old man seemed exasperated. "Never heard of Harry Berry? And y'all are from Berryville?" He shook his head. "That's something. That's really something."

A light went off in my head. "Wait. Do you mean Harry *Byrd?* The senator?"

"Yes!" he blurted, so loudly that customers in the market stopped and turned. "Harry Byrd! From Berryville!" He rocked back a full step, apparently unprepared for the explosiveness of his own outburst.

Suddenly self-conscious, he lowered his voice. "You know," he said confidentially, "I voted for him, back in Nineteen-Sixty. Against Kennedy." He paused, waiting for some form of acknowledgment. My father and I studied him, utterly at a loss for words.

"Yup," he continued, after it was clear we had nothing more to add. "Harry Byrd. From Berryville. Yup, yup." He straightened his glasses. "Well," he concluded, "better get back to work. Y'all have a good day."

We watched him pace away, shuffling in his Reebok sneakers, his discolored shorts pulled high on his waist by the tension of his suspenders. Spontaneously, uncontrollably, the moment he was out of earshot, we burst into laughter. From that moment on, "Harry Berry" became our inside joke, a punch line anytime we couldn't remember someone's name.

A few months later, we learned that this same farmer became involved in a livestock dispute with his neighbor, an attorney, back at home. The argument started when the farmer's bull crossed over property lines, impregnating a herd of heifers owned by the lawyer. The disagreement escalated in intensity, and ended when the lawyer shot the old farmer dead in his own front yard. The news was both sad and surreal, and made national headlines.

The same summer, Nancy, now living with me on the farm, staffed our new farmers' market in Del Ray, a neighborhood in Alexandria, Virginia. Since we still had only one truck, we purchased a small trailer, loading it with an identical setup to our existing model: a freezer, a tent, a table, and a couple coolers to hold eggs. We also purchased a large magnet with our name and logo, and the words FREE RANGE MEAT & EGGS, on it, and placed it on the freezer. Although I knew this defied Glenda's fiscal advice, it doubled as our farm sign at Del Ray. People could easily read the bold lettering from across a crowded market, or as we drove down the highway.

It was five o'clock in the morning, and Nancy and I were headed to Alexandria. As we passed an exit ramp, a police car merged behind us, started to pass, then slowed and got behind us again.

"Uh-oh," I said, nodding into the side-view mirror. "Cop."

"How fast are you going?" Nancy asked.

"Fifty-five, like normal."

"Just take it easy," she replied. "You're not doing anything wrong."

The police car rode right behind us for another mile. As we approached the exit for Leesburg, he turned on his lights and hit the siren.

"Damn it," I muttered. "Must have a taillight out. And I checked everything before we left."

We pulled onto the shoulder, cars slowing to rubberneck as they passed. The police officer was a tall man in his early forties, with a large black mustache and a bow-legged gait.

"What's the problem, officer?" I asked politely. "I didn't lose a cooler lid back there, did I?"

"No," he said, smiling. "No cooler lids. No problem at all, actually. It's just . . . I noticed your sign back there, on your freezers. Do you guys *really* sell free-range meat?"

I assumed I had misunderstood him. Were we being pulled over for being farmers? I asked myself. I looked sidelong at Nancy before responding. Her expression appeared equally nonplussed.

"Umm . . . ," I said cautiously, half suspecting some sort of setup. "Yes?"

"No kidding," he replied, and casually leaned against the side of our truck. "Wow, you're never going to believe this. Just yesterday, I was at my doctor's, and he thinks I've got an ulcer. A stomach ulcer," he clarified, pointing to his midsection. "He told me I had to stop eating regular meat and find a farm that sells free-range meat. And here I am, driving to work, and I see you guys right in front of me. I mean," he added, tipping back his cap and beaming, "what are the chances of *that?*"

I was still unsure if this was some kind of charade. "Uh . . . yeah," I answered neutrally. "That's some coincidence."

"So you guys raise all this stuff? On your farm?"

"That's right."

"And how do you sell it? I mean, do you take orders, or can I just get some right now?"

Get some right now? Had he really just said that? "Well, we mostly sell at farmers' markets. In fact," I added, glancing meaningfully at my watch, "that's where we're headed right now. We're actually running a little late."

He smiled. "Farmers' markets. Yeah, that makes sense. Now tell me," he continued, easing deeper into his lean. "Is there really that big a difference in the way you guys raise meat? Compared to the other way, I mean."

The blue lights flashed in my side-view mirror, and I squinted against the glare. "I mean, yeah. Definitely. Grass-fed animals are raised totally differently."

"Isn't that something," he mused. "Cows . . . just out there." He gestured willy-nilly with his hands. "Eating grass. Doing the nature thing. I mean, who would have figured *that?*"

I wasn't especially concerned about cows and their mind-blowing grass-eating habits at that moment. Instead, I held up my watch and tapped against the glass face.

"Like I mentioned, we're on our way to a farmers' market. We've got to be there by a certain time or . . ."

Our first year at the Takoma Park Farmers Market.

The officer completely ignored me, peering instead into the back of our truck. He produced a slim black flashlight, clicked it on, and shined the beam across our freezers.

"So you guys've got the meat right here, in the freezers. Isn't that something. I don't suppose . . . nah." He shook his head dismissively, and then appeared to reconsider. "I mean . . . I don't suppose . . . You wouldn't mind if I bought something right now, would you?"

Abuse of power was one thing. Getting hit by a passing car for a pound of ground beef was another matter entirely.

"No!" I said, perhaps a little more forcefully than I would have liked. "No," I repeated, more softly. "You can buy some at our farm store, if you want. Here," I added, fishing into my jeans pocket. "Here's our card. Now, seriously, I've got to get to the farmers' market. I mean, if there's nothing else . . ."

He snapped out of his reverie, clearly disappointed. "Oh. No, nothing else. Don't want to keep you guys." He glanced wistfully at the freezers, as though holding out hope I might change my mind. I stared at him, unblinking.

"Right," he added, and studied the card. "Smith Meadows, huh?" He straightened his hat. "Okay, then. Hey, I'm going to be a customer of yours, you'll see! You guys have a great day now. Drive safe."

With that, we were released. Nancy and I shook our heads, not quite believing what had just transpired. We placed odds on the chances that we would ever see him again. The following Monday, however, the officer proved himself a man of his word when he showed up at the farm in street clothes.

"Told you I'd be a good customer," he crowed, holding up two large bags of meat as he emerged from the store. "You're going to help me fix my ulcer!"

Great, I said to myself, smiling my most gracious smile. Making ulcers disappear was a noble pursuit. I just needed to make sure that *I* didn't get one.

The vagaries of fame kept coming. A month later, my sister and I made the front page of the *Washington Post's* Weekend section, a full-color photo of us posed in front of our Arlington stand, holding a dozen eggs. The photo, titled "The Producers," overlayed a backdrop of tomatoes from Toigo Orchards, peers of ours from Shippensburg, Pennsylvania. All day long, customers at the farmers' market brought us copies, congratulating us for our newfound celebrity. Naturally, our fellow farmers chided us the hardest. Toward the end of the day, an old man who worked for Toigo ducked his head under our tent.

"Did you see the front page of the Weekend section?" he asked.

He was probably the one hundredth person that morning to ask me the question. "Yes," I said, already slightly numb to the fame. "It's really something, isn't it?"

"Sure is," he replied proudly, holding up a copy for me to see. "Those are *our* tomatoes on the cover."

"Huh?" I replied, momentarily taken aback. I had expected him to say that he recognized us, just like everyone else had done all morning, but he pointed at the backdrop of tomatoes instead. I attempted a diplomatic recovery. "Yeah . . . uh . . . it's been great press for us, too."

He looked confused. "Why is that?"

"Because . . . that's our picture."

"No," he disagreed. "Those are *our* tomatoes. Says so right there, at the bottom." He pointed a grimy finger at the fine print, where, next to my sister's and my name, it read, "Tomatoes from Toigo Orchards."

I suddenly realized that he hadn't even noticed our photograph; he couldn't see the Forrest for the tomatoes. I had spent the morning viewing the vegetables as nothing more than an attractive backdrop to our photo, and he had probably spent the morning annoyed that two random people were covering up the splendor of his harvest. He walked away, muttering to himself. To this day, I don't believe he ever made the connection.

My final brush with celebrity that season was a case of mistaken identity. Nancy and I were in Tysons Corner, Virginia, at a posh martini bar for the birthday of a friend. We didn't know many of the people there, and I ended up talking to a stocky, muscular, middle-aged man in a suit, an individual who was introduced to me as "the second wealthiest man in Northern Virginia." I was clearly out of my league, but I did my best to make conversation.

"The second wealthiest man in Northern Virginia," I repeated, a sobriquet he made no attempt at refuting. "That's quite a title. You know, I made my way up to seventh wealthiest at one point, but when the wheels come off . . . yikes." I made a nosedive motion with my hand, accompanied by a low, sliding whistle. "Well. I certainly don't have to tell *you*."

He raised his eyebrows. "Oh, really? What happened?"

"Sorry," I said, realizing that he was taking me seriously. I quickly backtracked. "That's my sense of humor for you. I'm just a farmer."

"A farmer?" he asked, regarding me anew, disbelievingly. "Are there still farms in Tysons Corner? What do you grow?"

I had mentioned to Nancy earlier that evening that I had never seen so much asphalt in one place in my life. Even the landscaping appeared to be made of imported soil. "My farm's about an hour away, to the west. I raise cows. Cows and chickens. And pigs." I cleared my throat awkwardly. I had never talked with the second wealthiest man in Northern Virginia before, and I was a little nervous. "Cows and chickens and pigs. Yes. Oh, and also some sheep. Boy, these lights are sure warm, aren't they?"

He snapped his fingers, his face brightening. "I read about you! Yeah! You're that dot-com guy who bought the farm in Little Washington!" He wagged his finger at me shrewdly, adopting a conspiratorial tone. "Brilliant move, bro," he whispered loudly.

"Organic farming is super trendy. Big momentum. Build it and flip it while it's hot. Killer ROI."

"Well, you might have read about me, but . . ."

"No, no, I totally did. It was just last month in, what . . . the *New York Times? Newsweek?*"

I was equal parts amused and terrified by the direction of this conversation. He was so excited to tell me about myself, I was almost disappointed to let him down.

"I mean, there was a photo in the *Washington Post* a couple of months ago . . ."

"No, no. This was in *TIME,* or . . . or *U.S. News.* You're raising those special cattle. You know, the ones they massage. Ahh, don't tell me." He pressed his fingertips to his temples, and squeezed his eyes shut. "Wiggy . . . wiggy . . ."

"Wagyu?" I suggested, just trying to be helpful.

"Yes!" He clapped his hands together, thunderously. "Wagyu! See, I *knew* it was you!" He studied me again, this time with a new appreciation.

"Japanese. Niche. *Smart.*" He slapped me solidly on the shoulder. "Good stuff, man."

"But I . . ."

Before I could finish my sentence, or any of my sentences, for that matter, someone loudly called his name from across the room. He raised his fist in response, smiling broadly at his friend. Then he grasped my hand, and pumped vigorously on my arm.

"Nice, bro. *Niiice.*" He nodded, looking intently into my eyes. "Great meeting you. Hey! Dan! Danny Boy!" he roared, still locking me in his handshake, but now making eye contact with his friend. The second wealthiest man in Northern Virginia continued to squeeze my hand while shouting banter above the din of the crowd, apparently forgetting that we were still attached. All at once, like a ship breaking free of its moorings, he released me without a word, the crowd parting in his wake as he muscled through the room.

It was enough notoriety for one year.

Fame couldn't make my grass grow any faster, or make the rain fall when the fields were dry. It couldn't make me a better farmer any more than a fancy logo could make my ground beef taste better.

Still, I enjoyed it more than being chased up a tree by a man-eating pig. One rarely had to look far for a little perspective, living on a farm.

Chapter Twenty-Five

There are certain moments of the year when the farm is breathtakingly beautiful. Mornings in early September, when mist lingers over the emerald-green pastures, droplets of dew caught in the gossamer web of a yellow-and-black garden spider, sparkling opalescent in the first light of dawn. Or midsummer, the sacred calm before the storm: sycamore trees effervescent with fireflies and the air thick with kinetic energy, not so much as a leaf stirring; the sky an indigo bruise before suddenly stitched with jagged white lightning.

Today was one of those amazing days. It was February, and a light snow had fallen during the night. A winter's worth of mud and dreck had been transformed into whiteness resplendent. Sunlight glittered against the sweeping snow, reflecting golden light from the highest tree branches. I stepped out of my door that morning into a pristine world, the farm sublimely peaceful.

The previous afternoon, Travis and I had worked in the stalls of the barn, repairing a worn-out hay bunker. We stood in the semi-thawed manure from several decades of livestock, imploring our frozen fingers to hold a nail steady enough to strike it with an equally frozen hammer. Later that evening, warming my ashen knuckles in front of the fire, my bones ached from the dramatic shifts in temperature.

Winter view of Smith Meadows, looking west.

As the saying goes, "A bad day of fishing beats a good day in the office." I felt the same way about farming. Even on frigid mornings, standing in mud and occasionally hitting my thumb with a hammer, I now had no doubts about my career choice, no regrets. The work was honest, and meaningful. On this particular morning, after a good night's sleep and waking up to a Bing Crosby–esque winter wonderland, my good spirits were only further reinforced.

It was the middle of the week, and now that our schedule at Schoen's was clearly established, every other Wednesday meant loading and hauling cattle to the butcher shop. Travis and I had developed a nice two-person technique for loading the cows, each of us learning how the other operated, modifying the flow and pace until we had established a consistent rhythm. There was no hollering, no running, no cattle prods. For us, getting the cattle onto the trailer simply involved working in tandem, being in the right place at precisely the right moment.

That morning, even in the snow, we had several cattle loaded in no time. It was an hour's drive to the butcher, and as I drove the truck through the drifting snowflakes, Travis told jokes, laughing louder than I did at his own punch lines. We arrived at Schoen's on schedule, dropped off the cattle, and headed home.

At the time I was knee-deep writing my own version of The Great American Novel. I had carefully structured the story to include a setting, a protagonist, and a central conflict. I knew in my heart it would eventually be a bestseller.

That morning, I had been mulling over some dialogue ideas in my head, and in between Travis's jokes, I conceived a few paragraphs that I wanted to get down on paper. I suggested to Travis that he drive the truck home so I could write, and he affably agreed.

This was the same Travis, of course, who hadn't gotten his driver's license until he was thirty-five. The same Travis who had learned to drive with a VW Beetle in a pasture, and who had never in his life driven a full-size truck with a trailer in tow. Or, for that matter, driven on a major interstate. Through six inches of snow.

Looking back on it now, although it wasn't my finest decision, I should be happy that we made it thirty miles without incident. I had wedged myself cocoonlike into the warm burgundy Naugahyde of the passenger seat, my notebook pressed against the worn fabric of my blue jeans. Recalling his modest driving résumé, I initially glanced at the road every few minutes, reassuring myself that our trajectory was true, if not especially graceful.

Travis was doing just fine. A little jerky on the turns, a tad firm on the brakes, but these criticisms were more a matter of style than safety. We exited the interstate and made our way along Route 9, the two-lane highway that led toward home. Snow continued to fall, but most of it had already been plowed into piles along the shoulder. As the miles passed, I became more absorbed in my writing and less concerned with my surroundings. Beside me, Travis drove wordlessly through the bright February morning.

I recall some sort of internal alarm sounding, alerting me that something was amiss. I blinked several times, my eyes adjusting from the dull whiteness of the paper to the blinding brilliance of the sparkling snow. As my vision gradually cleared, I couldn't believe what I was seeing.

Hands on the wheel, Travis was no longer looking at the road ahead. Instead he was staring out of the driver's side window, utterly absorbed in the passing scenery. It was as though he had reverted to being a passenger, completely indifferent to the fact that we were traveling sixty miles an hour down the highway. I waited a second longer, thinking perhaps I had caught him looking away for just a moment. But his head remained fully turned, mesmerized by whatever had caught his attention.

I glanced at the white warning line marking the edge of the asphalt, clearly visible beneath a dusting of fresh snow. In the few seconds I had been watching, we had gone from straddling the line to fully crossing it. Now, we were less than a foot from the snowbank, and heading straight for it. I hastily tossed my notebook onto the dashboard and turned toward Travis. As I did, the right front tire grazed the edge of the snowbank.

"Travis!" I yelled. "Watch where you're going!"

Three crisply distinctive—though almost simultaneous—events ensued. First, Travis snapped out of his reverie, faced the highway, and screamed the word "*ghahgch!*" (This is pronounced like "gock," but with a desperate, throaty gravitas. It was undoubtedly a *ghahgch!* kind of moment.)

Second, after perfectly vocalizing our mutual concern, he spun the steering wheel like a stunt driver, so vastly, *vastly,* overcorrecting his mistake that the truck and trailer immediately jackknifed.

Third, we entered a hopelessly out-of-control sixty-mile-an-hour perpendicular skid down the center of the two-lane highway. Travis frantically muscled the steering wheel in the opposite direction, but it was no use. Physics had taken over. We monopolized the entire road, our truck in the oncoming traffic lane, the trailer in the other. The jackknifed hitch pointed like an arrow along the double yellow lines.

In front of us, white oblivion. I had no time to think, but I'm sure I must have braced for impact.

The only thing that saved us from catastrophe was a snowplow approaching from the opposite direction. The snowplow had tied up the oncoming traffic; behind it, dozens of cars crept slowly along. This lucky timing allowed us to glide down the road like kids sledding on an icy hill, unimpeded but completely out of control. We slid at least a hundred yards before the truck forcefully lodged itself into a deep snowbank. As the snowplow crept past us, followed by the slow trickle of cars, I had the surreal experience of looking into the faces of people that we had almost killed.

In the driver's seat, Travis was turning the ignition, grinding in vain against a motor that was already running.

"The motor's cut out!" he shouted. "Motor's cut out! Damn it! The damn motor's cut out!"

My own heart was pounding loudly in my ears. Was it possible he couldn't hear the motor running over the noise of his own heartbeat?

"Travis. Travis! Settle down, man. The motor's still running. It never stopped."

His hand trembled as he released the key. "I can't hear it. I can't hear the motor!"

I managed a few deep breaths. "Nice and easy, man. Just put it in four-wheel drive, and let's get out of this snow."

With the help of the extra traction, we managed to free ourselves from the snowbank and slowly eased back onto the highway.

Travis didn't appear to be taking it well. His attention was now rapt on the highway, but his face had metamorphosed. I watched him from the corner of my eye, trying not to make him more uncomfortable than he already was, but concerned for my own safety as well. His normally genial expression had been replaced with saturnine concentration. Clutching the steering wheel, his fists were white-knuckled from the intensity of his grip.

Perhaps most troubling of all, he was mumming incessantly under his breath, a noise that resembled a motor boat with a tank of bad gas.

"Mum mum. Huh huh hum. Muh. Muh."

His nervous vocalizations continued as we sped down the highway. In fact, as I glanced at the speedometer, I realized that we were literally speeding. He was going nearly seventy miles per hour.

"Travis."

"Mum mum."

"Travis . . ." Seventy-five, now.

"Hum mum . . . mum."

The engine roared. "Travis, slow down."

"Mrr . . . mum mum."

"Travis! You're going eighty-five miles per hour!"

"Mmm huh huh huh! Mmm . . . huh huh huh!"

The needle on the speedometer inched higher. "Travis! Slow the hell down! You're going to kill us! We're going to die!"

Well, *that* worked. His mumming and humming slowed, as did our truck. Gradually, cautiously, he pulled off the road and onto a safe patch of cleared asphalt. Slapping the transmission violently into park, he remained silent for several moments before erupting.

"Damn it! God damn, damn it! I don't want to drive! I don't want to drive!" He snatched the key from the ignition and flung it recklessly across the dashboard; it landed, clattering, against the windshield. "I don't want to drive, and I'm not gonna do it! Mumm mumm! Hrrr . . . muh muh muh!"

I was no clinical expert, but this new, highly agitated mixture of humming, mumming, and cursing couldn't be a good sign. We wordlessly traded seats, and after several minutes I managed to fish the truck key from the defrost vent on the dashboard. We were soon on our way again, this time at a safe forty-five miles per hour.

The rest of the trip passed uneventfully, save for a few forceful "mrrh hums!" that were unmistakably fired in my direction. We arrived back at the farm and agreed to take the rest of the day off. It had been a long morning.

Later that afternoon, I decided to drive to the Shenandoah University library, about twenty miles away, to work some more on my novel. I was still physically wound up from the near catastrophe and thought it would be a good idea to do something to take my mind away from the turbulence of the morning. I always did my best work in the quiet alcoves of academia.

Pulling into the parking lot, I had hardly stopped the truck when a wave of nausea soured my stomach. I pushed through the doors of the library bathroom, barely clearing the stall before vomiting into the toilet.

It took about fifteen minutes, but eventually the bathroom stopped spinning. I washed up as best I could in the tiny sink, blotting my face with the horrible brown paper towels of public restrooms. My notebook had been abandoned outside the door, and as I stooped to pick it up, I felt another surge of vertigo trying to topple me. Time to call it a day, I told myself. Go home. Go to bed.

In the parking lot, I discovered that I had locked my keys in the truck. Emotionally exhausted and utterly forlorn, I took a small measure of comfort in the fact that I had enough pocket change to make a call from the pay phone.

"Hello? Dad?"

"Yeah?"

"You're in D.C. today, right?"

"Well, that's the phone I'm answering, so it stands to reason."

I rubbed my temples. "Right. Sorry. Look, I've just had a pretty bad day. A *really* bad day. And now I've locked myself out of the car, and it's starting to snow again. Do you think . . ."

"Where are you?"

"In Winchester. In the university parking lot."

"You got someplace warm you can hole up?"

"Yeah. The library's open."

"I'll be there in two hours."

"Thanks, Dad."

A couple of hours later, almost to the minute it takes to drive midday from Washington, D.C., to Winchester, Dad met me in the parking lot with the extra key he kept on his keychain. I had never been so happy to see him. I caught him up on the day's adventures.

"So, he started in with the 'mum mums'?" he asked, after we had unlocked the pickup.

"Yeah," I said. "Wait a minute. How do you know about the 'mum mums'?"

"Remember last summer, when you were a counselor at 4-H camp?"

"Yeah?"

"Well, that week, Travis and I were fixing the radiator on the tractor, and as we were lifting it out, I kind of dropped it on his foot."

I winced. "Ouch! Was he alright? He must have gotten pretty mad."

"Actually, he took it pretty well. The radiator didn't have any antifreeze, so it wasn't as heavy as it looked. It was when I dropped the car battery on his other foot that the 'mum mums' started."

"A car battery! What were you doing with a car battery?"

"That's just it," he replied. "I wasn't doing *any*thing with it. After I dropped the radiator on his foot, I lifted it onto the workbench to get it out of the way, and I accidentally knocked off a car battery that was sitting along the edge."

"But that must be three feet off the ground . . ."

"At least."

"It's a wonder you didn't break his foot!"

"It's a wonder he didn't break my face."

I considered this a few moments. "And that's when the 'mum mums' started."

"That's when the 'mum mums' started. Although, as I recall, there might have been a few 'mrrh hums' bandied about, as well."

I laughed, and I noticed my stomach felt better already. There was something about being together, even if it was in a vacant, frozen parking lot, that felt comforting. It had begun to snow again, but neither of us seemed to care.

"Do you think he's going to come back to work tomorrow?" I asked, only half joking. "He seemed pretty ticked off when he left."

Dad shrugged. "Guys like Travis, they're born to farm. It's just how he's made. Remember, he was the one who hired himself. It's not like we had a choice in the matter."

"That's true," I acknowledged. I looked into my father's eyes. "It's not just me, right, Dad? Travis is kind of weird. Like, maybe *really* weird."

He nodded. "I feel comfortable with 'really weird.' But, you know, we're all a little weird to someone." He cleared his throat, and then performed a perfect impersonation.

"Huh huh. Muh muh muh."
Only in this family, I told myself, smiling.
"Huh huh huh," I replied without hesitation. "Mrr . . . huh huh!"

Chapter Twenty-Six

It was the spring of 2002, five years since we set out to turn the farm around. I had read somewhere that year five is a magic number for businesses; statistically, most ventures fail within that period, and the ones that survive have greater success going forward. As winter thawed into spring, and the pastures began their annual greening, I had an unflagging sense that it would be a year to remember.

Several amazing things had already happened that winter. Nancy and I were now married, and although she had a full-time job as a public school art teacher, she came to me one evening with the idea of starting her own pasta business. After all, she pointed out, no one else at the markets we attended made pasta, and it would provide a missing vegetarian offering in our lineup. She could even create an entire line of sauces and pestos. What did I think?

My stomach and brain had a quick meeting, and decided that this was a superb idea. For years she had made fresh, handcrafted pasta in our home kitchen, using eggs from our chickens and herbs from the farmers' market. The doughs she devised were inspired creations, flavored with rosemary and sage, basil and thyme, cilantro and chive. They were a complete departure from the wan, brittle noodles of my childhood. The quality of her homemade dishes, garnished with fresh tomatoes and crushed garlic, leapt off the plate.

We spent several hours with a pencil and calculator, trying our best to figure out expenses. Our excitement buoyed our spirits, and it wasn't long before we devoted all of our spare time to starting a pasta business.

Her parents, on the other hand, both native Italians, needed additional convincing.

We sat across the dinner table from her parents like generals engaging in wartime diplomacy. My father-in-law, of the magical meat truck fame, had worked most of his career in the US Senate dining hall. He was a firm believer in an ironclad paycheck, health benefits, and a retirement pension.

He had fought under Mussolini during World War II, and was captured as a prisoner by the Americans in 1942. He once placed his hand on my shoulder, looking straight through my eyes. "I walked on top of the dead, Forrest. Oh, yes. I've seen terrible things in this life."

He prided himself on his talent for quickly debunking specious logic. When he caught wind that Nancy was considering quitting her steady teaching job for an uncertain noodle business, he considered the idea tantamount to selling the family cow for a handful of magic beans.

"You know," my father-in-law began, wagging a finger from across the table, speaking in his heavy Italian accent, "I watch you for many years now. I keep a sharp eye on you, when you don't think I do."

He took delight in my expression. "Oh, yes! I watch you close. I see you every weekend at the market. Drive the truck, make new customers. Slowly, slowly . . ." He tumbled his hands like the paddle of a steamboat. "Very slowly, you build the business. The *family* business. I think is good."

He winked at me. "I'm sharp, like a fox. I watch you grow, and I tell you true, I like what I see you do."

He took a long drink of water, swallowing noisily. The grandfather clock ticked in the hallway.

"Make no mistake," he continued at last. "When you first tell me these ideas, selling meat, I don't think you gonna succeed. I say to myself, 'He too nice.' Oh, yeah. You a nice boy, I congratulate you. And that's good. But in business," he said, lowering his voice to a deep rumble, "you gotta be tough!"

Without warning, he slammed his fist on the table, making the glasses jump. Involuntarily, Nancy and I both jumped, too.

He leaned back in his chair, nodding. "But I give you credit. You tougher than I thought. Nice and tough both?" He shrugged. "Maybe you prove me wrong. We see, we see." He placed his elbows on the table, and his chair creaked as he leaned closer. "But tell me, Mr. Pritchard. Is one thing for you, raising the animals. Drive to butcher, drive to market. But Nancy . . ." The old man shook his head. "Nancy has a good job, good salary. Pension. How she's going to make any money, selling this pasta? Who bought those shoes you're wearing?"

Wait, what? Who bought the *shoes* I was wearing? I tried to recover from this surprise angle of attack. He already knew that Nancy had given them to me that year for Christmas; he had been there when I opened the gift.

"I don't really understand why you're asking, but . . . Nancy did."

He snapped his fingers, pointing. Apparently, I had just fallen into his trap. "Ah!" he shouted. "Correct! Nancy give! Is nice shoes, Mr. Pritchard. Very nice shoes. Tell me something." His eyes narrowed. "How come you cannot afford to buy for yourself?"

"Can't afford . . . ? They were a Christmas gift!"

He folded his arms over his chest, unmoved. "A man who cannot afford to buy his shoes got *no* business telling his wife to quit a good job. You buy your own shoes, *then* maybe we talk."

I felt my face flush to the tips of my ears, utterly flabbergasted by this line of reasoning.

"But . . . but . . . " I stammered.

His smile broadened as I fumbled for words. An inability to quickly refute his claims, in his mind, was additional proof of my guilt.

Finally, I blurted, "But I bought her sapphire earrings for Christmas! I saved up for them all year . . . and they were, like, five hundred dollars!"

My father-in-law remained stone-faced in spite of this counterevidence. Slowly, he inclined toward my mother-in-law, keeping his eyes locked with mine the entire time.

"Is this true what he say? That he buy her expensive earrings?"

"Yes," she confirmed. "And they were *lovely.*"

I didn't dare speak. I might be nice, and I might be tough, but I didn't want to be stupid. Several moments passed before he spoke.

"This . . . was something I didn't know."

"I may not be rich," I replied, more than a little hot under the collar, "but I can buy shoes if I need them." Even so, I subtly tucked my feet beneath my chair, keeping them well out of sight.

For the first time in my life, the old man appeared remorseful. "Is just . . . how do I say? Forrest, you must understand. Once she go, once she quit, is no guarantee she get her job back. A lot of risk in this," he said, heavily shaking his head. "A lot of risk."

"I know," I said, straightening in my seat. "I know it's a big risk. But I *believe* in what we're doing. It's like you've always said. This is a family business. A *real* family business. Plus, you've tasted her pasta. You know what a good cook she is."

"Ah, is true," he agreed. His eyes went distant at the thought of a big plate of pappardelle and Bolognese sauce. "She's a good cook. And the family business," he added with the smallest trace of a smile, "is nothing more beautiful. I dream this dream for you."

"So," I said, "we've got your blessing?" I looked at them both in turn.

"Is good," he replied at last, nodding. "But still, I worry for you. I wish you luck."

"I think it's wonderful," Nancy's mom added, in her softer Italian accent. "I'm just so proud of you both. I think it takes a lot of courage."

And so, a few months later, Smith Meadows Kitchen began. Like any new venture, it started very slowly. But after selling ten thousand boxes of pasta, ravioli, and sauce on her own, Nancy hired her first employee, then another. Customers eagerly responded to her creativity, and the business eventually took on a life of its own. The rewards were beyond delicious.

———————

At the same time all of this was happening, the city of Washington, D.C., had come completely unglued. The Pentagon, a five-minute drive from the Arlington farmers' market, remained in ruins from the 9/11 attacks. Deadly anthrax circulated through the mail, sent to office buildings throughout the capital. Meanwhile, a sniper killed innocent people as he fired bullets from the trunk of his car, terrorizing the entire metropolitan area. People were murdered while pumping gas, walking down the street, mowing the lawn.

The cumulative effect of these events was utterly unnerving. Attendance at farmers' markets fell sharply, as people were afraid to so much as leave their homes.

Dad had been at work in downtown Washington during the 9/11 attacks. I hastily phoned his office that morning, only getting through after several attempts because the circuits were jammed.

"Dad! Have you heard what's happening? Are you okay?"

"I'm fine. But it's absolutely crazy out there. It's gonna take me a while to get back home tonight."

I exhaled a sigh of relief, comforted to hear his voice on the other end of the line. "I understand. Look, you be careful out there, okay?"

"I will. I'll stop by the farm on the way home to say hello."

Later that night, waiting for him to arrive, I stood on a hilltop above the farm, studying the night sky. Ordinarily, dozens of airplanes twinkled among the stars, their red and blue lights competing for attention with the greater cosmos. On that night, not a single plane flew. The sky, illuminated by a billion distant suns, felt impossibly dark and empty.

At last my father's headlights crested the hill, brightening the gravel road. I hurried to the parking lot to meet him.

"You alright? I was worried about you," I said.

"Who, me?" he replied. "You should know better than that." He raised his fists and took a boxer's stance. "I might be big, but I'm shifty. I'll always find a way to get through."

I wanted to take him at his word, that he was larger than life, invincible. The truth was, his health had been steadily deteriorating. He was only in his late fifties, but decades of bad eating habits and a sedentary office job had accelerated the aging process.

For years I had begged him to eat the food that we raised on the farm, and to take advantage of the amazing fruits and vegetables that were bartered each week at the farmers' market. He greeted these opportunities with indifference. A visit to his refrigerator revealed half-eaten packages of hot dogs and bologna, products he bought at the supermarket, packed with chemical preservatives and salt. Processed cheese, mayonnaise, and white bread occupied the space where spinach and lettuce, literally handed to him for free at the market, could have been. The vegetables he was given at market were left to rot, slimy and wilted in the recesses of the crisper.

His life had become a trail of crumbs and wrappers. The floor of his truck was ankle deep with empty soda cans, and discarded bags of chips littered the dashboard. Occasionally I'd get so frustrated by his behavior that I'd take a garbage bag to his car and clean it out from top to bottom. Within a matter of weeks, whatever progress I had made was methodically replaced with new trash.

Insisting that he would soon retire from his office job and help me at the farmers' market, he dreamed aloud of new locations. A few more months, he promised, and he'd come home to work with me

Me as boy, with Dad and a farm kitten

full-time. He smiled, spreading his arms, breathing deeply. "Fresh air and exercise," he said. "Just what I need."

The irony was he was surrounded by some of the most nutritious, abundant food to be found anywhere on the planet, yet chose not to eat any of it. It was as though something was missing from his life, something he couldn't communicate, and he was filling the void with garbage. Nothing I said persuaded him.

"Dad, your first grandchild is on the way. Don't you want to be healthy when he arrives?"

"Dad, we raise such good food. Why are you eating that junk?"

"Dad, have you looked at yourself in the mirror lately? You don't even look like yourself."

After accompanying him on a trip to the doctor's office, I discovered that his weight had ballooned to more than three hundred and fifty pounds. He had never been so heavy in his life. A few weeks later, he told me he had the onset of diabetes, a disease that no one in our family had ever had before. Something was very, very wrong.

For as long as I had known him, my father had never been sick. Whenever my sister and I brought home colds as children, our mother became ill a few days later, but our father never caught the bug. Now he was taking daily medications for hypertension, joint pain, and blood sugar. He had scheduled a surgery to have his knees replaced later that fall. Watching him slowly hobble in and out of his truck, his thick beard now long and white, I suddenly saw an old man.

One night in early May, he called me, waking me from a dead sleep. My mother was away on business. It was nearly midnight.

"Hello? Dad?"

"I need you to bring me those flavored waters I bought." His voice sounded strange, vacant of emotion, distant. "I left them in the trunk of the car."

My father always had an eccentric sense of humor, but this was simply odd. "Dad, it's midnight. Is this a joke?"

"I'm thirsty. I bought a pack of flavored waters and left them in your parking lot. I want you to bring them to me."

I rubbed my eyes. What in the world were "flavored waters," anyway? Some kind of medicine? I asked him as much.

"It's water with low-calorie sweetener," he said, as though this explained everything. "It's healthier for me, now that I have diabetes."

"What?" I was incredulous. "Dude, just drink some regular water!"

"If I wanted to drink regular water, I wouldn't have bought the flavored waters," he said, his tone becoming angry. "Now, when can I expect you?"

Travis and I had built a new line of fence that day, and I had worked until dark, falling asleep in my clothes. My shoulders ached as I bent over the phone.

"You're telling me you want me to get out of bed at midnight, and drive five miles so you can have a chemical spritzer? You're out of your mind!"

His voice became an angry hiss. "So you're not coming, then? After all I've done for you! All these years!"

What was the matter with him? Was he going crazy? "Dad! Just get a drink of water!"

"You'd better be on your way. I'm *thirsty*. I need those waters!"

"Dad, I'm hanging up."

"Don't you . . . !"

I placed the receiver back in the cradle, too tired to even think. A moment later, I was sound asleep again.

Around four in the morning, the phone rang again. I roused myself from black, dreamless depths, fumbling for the phone.

"Mr. Pritchard?"

"Yes?"

"Are you Edward Pritchard's son?"

"Yes."

"I'm an EMT with the Jefferson County Fire and Rescue, Mr. Pritchard. We got a 911 call from your dad." The voice paused. "Sir, he's not doing well."

I sat upright in bed, my heart pounding.

"What? What?" I tried to shake the cobwebs from my mind. "Is he . . . is he okay?"

"No, sir," the voice said firmly, this time without hesitation. "No, sir. He is *not* okay. Not at all. I think you need to get down to the hospital as soon as possible."

I leaped out of bed, stumbling through the dark, struggling to put on a clean pair of pants, find a fresh T-shirt. I rushed to the hospital as fast as I could, doing my best to shake the sleep from my head. Above me, as I drove, an enormous electrical storm wreaked mayhem across the night sky, illuminating the darkness with violent bursts of cloud-to-cloud lightning.

By the time I made it to the hospital, my father lay alone on a stainless-steel table, a hospital sheet draped over his body. After his call to me, he had gone into cardiac arrest. Though he had managed to dial 911, they were unable to resuscitate him.

As I walked toward him, I entered a space of sacred stillness. His spirit was still in the room. I could feel him there, nearby, but leaving. Already leaving.

I patted him gently on the shoulder, lovingly.

"Oh, Dad," I said. I shook my head, looking down at my father. "It'll be okay."

I leaned over his body, giving him the best hug I could. He was still so real to me. Tears overfilled my eyes.

"It's all going to be okay, now. I'll take care of everything."

I stepped back, looking for the final time at the man I had loved so dearly. The man who had carried me on his shoulders when I was a child, and who had wanted to stand beside me as a grown man.

"I love you, Dad. Good-bye."

I don't remember walking out of the hospital, or driving back home. I don't remember the rest of that day. But the following week, as I delivered his eulogy, speaking of his generosity, his kindheartedness, and his ever-present sense of humor, rain lashed the windows, a torrent pouring from black clouds hovering above the church.

Then, just as the service ended, sunlight illuminated the rain-streaked glass. The thunder and lightning passed, rumbling into the distance, and the final drops of heavy rain splashed against the church steps. As we opened the broad wooden doors to the world, we were greeted with the most vivid, magnificent rainbow I'd ever seen.

We paused as one—Nancy, my mother, and my visibly pregnant sister. The vision was breathtaking.

Nancy was the first to find her voice. "It's beautiful, isn't it?"

We stood together as the congregation filed slowly out of the church, admiring the colors of the rain-washed sky. I couldn't speak; my heart was breaking from anguished beauty. We made our way across the puddled parking lot and headed back to the farm. As I drove, I occasionally looked over my shoulder, checking. The rainbow stayed with us the whole way home.

Chapter Twenty-Seven

My father died on a Thursday. Two days later, on Saturday, I loaded the truck with meat and eggs and went to the farmers' market. I had no choice; there were too many bills that had to be paid. I didn't, couldn't, tell anyone at the market what had happened. The pain was too raw. Somehow, my silence allowed me to get through that weekend.

We buried my father on a magnificent hilltop, rising above the West Virginia valley where he had spent his childhood summers. Here the grass grew so tall that the seed heads bowed in the wind, nearly touching the ground before straightening again. Below, expansive views of hay fields and forests stretched to the horizon, mountains rising on all sides.

I sat for a long time on that hilltop, surrounded by grass. There was so much I would miss. Besides the laughter, besides the companionship, I felt overwhelmed that, despite all of his misgivings, he had ultimately chosen to support me. What greater honor than for a father to stand behind his child? He had found something in me that had changed his mind about the farm.

I see now, I could hear him say. *I see where you're headed, what you're trying to accomplish. You're really going to make it. I'm proud of you.*

At the Pritchard grave plot, in Pocahontas County, West Virginia.

The wind moved, and the grass swayed around me. I had finally learned to manage the land with only the barest of inputs. Now I needed to buy the farm a little more time, time enough to navigate the drastic changes that life had just dealt.

Sunshine and rain, carbon and nitrogen. These things were available for free as long as the land was properly managed. I dreamed of a farm that was self-fertilizing, drought-resistant, sustainable both economically and environmentally. As I looked out over the fertile valley, I knew there was nothing stopping us from making our farm one gigantic, living solar panel.

I recalled standing on the front porch with my mother all those years before, seeing the concern on Albert's face as he revealed, bill by bill, how our plans had failed. A few years later I learned that he was out of farming entirely, taking a job as a mechanic for a national courier service. Albert had been a hardworking, honest, intelligent farmer. The conventional agricultural system had simply set him up for almost unavoidable failure.

In the five years since working with Albert, we had more than doubled our amount of pasture using nothing more than natural, organic methods. Rotational grazing, buying our hay from other farms, and dedicated patience had made this happen. Each year, we retained a few extra cattle and added a few more sheep, and had now almost tripled our flocks and herds.

There were no concrete feedlots, no antibiotics, no supplements laced with hormones. This was the very definition of "slow food." As I entered my late twenties, I found myself moving at a more tranquil pace as well, finding a rhythm with the subtle change of the seasons. My definition of success began to fall out of step with the anxious hustle of modern life.

This wasn't New Age thinking. It wasn't fringe or alternative. It wasn't left wing or right, and it certainly wasn't a temporary fad. It was the way we were, on our terms, successfully growing food. Lots of food.

I sometimes lay on my back in the soft, clean pasture, staring up at the blue sky, relaxing while the animals placidly grazed around me. The air was fresh, and the pastures thick and green. The cattle sniffed curiously at my boots, my hat, my outstretched fingertips.

This version of productivity ran contrary to every business book I had ever read. Instead of taking, we were leaving. Green space was restored to the landscape, and airborne carbon was recycled into the earth, building new topsoil for future fertility. We were literally gaining ground. It was an equation of increasing returns.

Each year, the soil responded with more abundance. Almost by accident, I felt as though we had tapped into something much bigger than ourselves, a natural equilibrium that transcended culture and politics. I only wished my father could have been there to enjoy the journey.

Perhaps more than anything else, my dad had been a dreamer at heart. He had attended those direct marketing conferences years before because, despite the legions of naysayers, he wanted to believe we could make it in farming. In his own way, he had encouraged me to explore these dreams for myself, wrestling with the specters of his own self-doubts, but hopeful about what his son could accomplish.

All farms require a resident dreamer, someone to thumb through seed catalogs in the cold days of late January, imagining summer fields of squash and cucumbers, tomatoes and sunflowers. Fall harvests are the reward of winter dreams. Someone must decide where the next fence should be placed, or conceive of a clever new way to organize the market stand. On a farm, there's no shortage of little dreams needing to be dreamed.

"Have you ever thought about the word 'hayseeds'?" a writer friend asked me one day, as we walked through waist-high pastures. "What an amazing metaphor. Out of the entire English language, someone chose that word as an insult, but it has a poetic double meaning. What are the odds?"

I had never considered it before. As a child, being called a hayseed meant that I was worthless, small, simpleminded. It was a word city kids used to taunt us on the playground or at summer camp, implying they were more intelligent, more sophisticated. It always hurt.

But my friend was right. The word suggested that we were dreamers. Innovators. Producers. Go ahead, I wanted to tell those city kids, and all those patronizing voices who had later told me to grow up, to get a real job. Call me a hayseed if you want. I'll thank you for the compliment.

What a tiny dream a hayseed is! What an outrageous assertion, that a seed could ever amount to anything more than just a single blade of grass. And yet, raveled into that tiny husk is everything our farm has ever needed, or will ever need in the future. Coaxed awake by rain and sunshine is not just one, but an infinity of future seeds. It is beyond the control of industry.

These little seeds, broadcast by the wind, blanketed our farm with life. A hayseed is such an ordinary miracle, people could be forgiven for never noticing. But this magic happens all around us. The leaf of grass must only be allowed to grow.

My father gave me permission to dream. I couldn't have asked for a greater gift. Over the years, following his lead, I watched as one seed landed next to another, then another. After a while, a verdant pasture emerged right before my eyes, almost as though it had been dreamed into existence.

————————

Travis showed up on Monday morning, ready for work. The cows needed to be checked, the pastures rotated. From the front porch of the farmhouse, I yawned and stretched and breathed the cool morning air, dawn a brightening glow above the Blue Ridge Mountains. Music played softly on the radio as Travis waited for me in the truck. Life went on.

Later that morning, we loaded three cattle and hauled them up the road to Hagerstown. This time, I drove. Pulling into Schoen's, we backed up to the unloading ramp and opened the sliding door of the trailer. The cattle were supposed to walk up a short incline, cross a large floor scale, and proceed into a clean receiving pen.

I had already made dozens of deliveries by this point, and everything had always gone smoothly. Today would be different. I hadn't noticed that a large gate near the top of the ramp, normally latched with a thick chain, was not only unhooked, but also wide open. The first two steers walked up the ramp, across the scale, and into the pen. The third, however, noticed the open gate. The animal studied the situation, quickly considered his options, and leaped from the ledge, toward freedom. He landed neatly as a cat, hooves clattering on the pavement four feet below the dock.

From here there were no fences or gates, only a wide-open barnyard with cornfields in the distance. Travis and I were unable to do anything at all. I momentarily felt my heart stop.

At that moment, Mr. Schoen stepped from around the corner, his small black hat perched primly atop his head. He froze in his tracks.

"That . . . " he said, trying to make sense of what he was seeing. "That is incorrect."

The steer looked right, then left, and promptly took off at a trot toward the distant hills

"What do we do?" Travis asked, a note of panic in his voice.

Mr. Schoen hastily shut the gate across the scale, making sure we didn't have the same problem in triplicate.

"We need to get him back toward the barnyard," the butcher said. "You guys go round him up and bring him around the north side of the barn. I'll put up some gates while you're gone."

"After him!" I said, and took off running in my heavy work boots. The steer hadn't paused for a moment. A terrain of tender corn shoots pushed through the May soil, and last winter's husks crackled and crunched loudly under each step, prompting him to move at a brisk canter. Ahead, on the far edge of the field, was a newly built subdivision of houses. At his current pace, he would be there in less than a minute.

"Travis!" I shouted, becoming an impromptu field commander. "Break left! I'll run wide and get in front of him!"

Travis, a lifelong smoker, might have moved faster if he had been driving a steamroller. Twenty yards later I saw him doubled over and wheezing, hands on his knees. It was just me and the steer now, mano a hoofo.

My only chance was to run a wide circuit, somehow racing ahead and intercepting his trajectory. As though sensing my thoughts, as soon as I made my cut, the steer stretched into a full gallop. I didn't stand a chance. Reaching the edge of the housing development, he pushed his head into a thick row of green border hedges, and plunged into suburbia.

Now it was my turn to double over, bent on one knee. My lungs burned from exertion. Travis slowly made his way toward me, huffing and wheezing as he walked.

"What do you think?" he asked, gasping between breaths.

I stared at the tall row of bushes where the steer had vanished. "I was about to ask you the same question," I replied.

We made our way to the hedge. On the other side was a vinyl-sided one-story house, a swing set and a pink plastic sandbox adorning the manicured backyard. The steer was nowhere to be seen.

"I think . . . we're probably in big trouble." I turned, headed back toward Schoen's. "I hate to say it, but we'd better call the police."

By the time we got back to the butcher shop, the police were already well aware of the situation. The citizens of suburban Hagerstown knew something was amiss when an eleven-hundred-pound black steer trotted past their bay windows. Thanks to an abundance of calls from concerned homeowners, several squad cars now flooded the small neighborhood, blue lights flashing.

By some stroke of good luck, the animal ended up in the fenced backyard of a retired dairy farmer, where, after taking a cursory lap, it had settled down and begun grazing the lawn. After a bit of explaining, and a few gates trucked over from Schoen's, the old farmer graciously helped us transform his yard into a makeshift loading chute. In short order, without any damage, we had the animal back on the trailer.

The police seemed to take it all in stride. I assumed there would at least be a ticket, something to the tune of "failure to operate a steer without a steering wheel." After a few good chuckles, though, and a round of handshakes, the officers drove away in their cruisers. I exhaled a sigh of relief.

The old dairy farmer, who had moved from Minnesota to Maryland to be closer to his children, couldn't help but shake his head.

"You know," he said, "I thought that if I quit the cattle business and moved a thousand miles away, that would be the end of it. And there I was this morning, sitting in my recliner with a cup of coffee, when a steer walks through my backyard." He laughed. "I'm not ashamed to say, I thought I might be seeing things."

"Well, I sure appreciate your help," I said. "That could have been a real disaster."

"That?" the old man replied. "Oh, that wasn't too bad. Let me tell you, I had my whole herd get onto the interstate once, grazing in the median. Shut down six lanes of Minneapolis traffic for hours, and had to get the local chapter of the National Guard out there. Three hundred Holsteins. Now that," he said, gesturing to his head, "will give you white hair."

I agreed, laughing. "You've definitely got a few years on me."

"Well, don't rush yourself. You'll have plenty of cattle stories by the time you're done farming."

Without preamble, Travis spoke up. "Sometimes I dream about cows." A faraway look came over his face. "I'm in the middle of a field. There's cows all around me, and I can't see a way out. I go to leave, and a cow steps right in front of me. I turn around, and there's a cow right behind me. No matter which way I try to go, I'm trapped."

I glanced sidelong at the old farmer, who studied Travis with silent wonder. I didn't know what to say. An awkward silence hung in the air.

Suddenly Travis looked at his watch. "Well, time to gather the eggs," he said, snapping out of his reverie. "Let's get going."

The old man regarded him quizzically, and when Travis headed toward the truck, he spoke to me from behind his hand.

"When's the last time that man had a vacation?" he asked.

I shrugged. "I don't think Travis takes vacations."

"If I was you," he confided in a low voice, "I'd make him take a few days off."

"I've tried. But he just keeps showing back up."

The old man sighed, and gave a knowing nod. "You know, I hate to admit it, but farming will sometimes do that to a person."

I wanted to better understand what he meant: whether farming engendered tireless dedication, or eventually drove you mad. I didn't get a chance to ask. Travis blew the horn, impatient to get going. The chickens, after all, were waiting.

Chapter Twenty-Eight

Friends at home often told me they wanted to support local organic farms, but in their opinion the food was just "too expensive." Without telling me so outright, I knew that this included my products, too. Even though the price of our ground beef was very comparable to what was currently in the local supermarkets, perception seemed to trump this reality, and the meat in their refrigerators never had our label on it. That the food they purchased had traveled thousands of miles to get to their kitchen didn't seem to make an impression on them.

As a farmer, and as their friend, I did my best not to let any of this bother me. But I can't say I didn't notice, or didn't spend time thinking about it. If they bought their food locally, I reasoned, they'd be supporting the country life that they seemed to value so much, the fresh air, the sweeping vistas. They always lamented when a nearby farm went out of business and was forced to sell. If only a few of them had changed their buying habits, perhaps even persuading their neighbors to do the same, some of these farms undoubtedly could have been saved.

In certain aspects of our society, price and value go hand in hand. No one questions the sticker price on an Italian sports car or is shocked that a luxury hotel could command five hundred dollars a night. In these instances, people have made the connection between high quality and higher prices. Although a Rolex keeps time just as well as a five-dollar wristwatch, the difference in value is unquestioned.

For some reason, even to this day, food has largely escaped this price-quality association. Dom Perignon aside, food is more or less food. Although none of my friends said it out loud, I could tell what was on their minds: Food was supposed to be *cheap*. Society had conditioned them to expect bargains when they entered the supermarket, placing price above freshness and quality. My sausages might cost only a dollar more per pound, but for many people, it might as well have been a million. When it came to food, the price tag was where the story both began and ended.

Part of me wanted to challenge my friends. Spend a year of your life growing acres of vegetables, twelve months of physical toil and sweat. At the end of the season, sell it all for twenty-five cents a pound. Then, let's have a conversation about what's cheap and what's expensive.

Not surprisingly, nobody likes hanging out with a supercilious jerk. My friends were all overworked and underpaid; implying that my life was somehow more difficult than theirs would have been a great way to have my text messages go unanswered. So instead of defending my prices, I tried a different tack. When they asked me why organic food was so expensive, I came up with a new response. "First, shouldn't we figure out why the other food is so *cheap?*"

On our farm, the food we raised reflected our true cost of production. When we set our prices, we did exactly what every other business in America did. We factored in our expenses and established a modest profit margin. That way, we'd still be around to farm the following year. It was Economics 101.

"Well, Mr. Smarty Pants Farmer," my friends retorted, sensing that, despite my best efforts, I was still being a little patronizing. "Tell us, if you've got the numbers all figured out, then why aren't these other farms asking for their true cost of production, too? Why *does* the food in the supermarket cost less?"

Much of this food was already discounted, I explained, paid for in advance by government subsidies. Tax dollars, the same taxes that were taken out of my friends' paychecks before they received them, were used to partially pay for this food before it ever arrived at the supermarket. This "cheap" food was expensive, too. Unbeknownst to them, my friends were simply purchasing it on an installment plan.

"But if it's already being taken out of our paychecks," they argued, "doesn't it make sense to keep buying food at the supermarket?" Sure, I said. If you think a hamburger is just a hamburger, or that all apples are the same, then absolutely. But if you believe there's a difference between a burger made from a single cow versus a burger made from a thousand cows, or apple juice squeezed from a local farm versus barrels of concentrate shipped from China . . . then the conversation becomes more complex.

Government policies hand out advantages to big farms that small farms can only dream of. The more corn and soybeans these big operations plant, the more tax money they can receive. Even crop insurance, money paid out in case of catastrophe, is subsidized. This reliable flow of cash gives owners confidence to build the infrastructure they need to support their operations, making these large farms hum with the highest modern efficiencies.

In the end, the owners of large farms are secure in the knowledge that huge sums of money are electronically transferring into their bank accounts while they sleep. They become the preferred partners of billion-dollar food companies, each with their own massive, nationwide processing and distribution centers. It's all an economy of scale, and the scale is often gigantic.

Small farms like mine never have the economic firepower to match our larger counterparts. Our acreage is too small to adopt the efficiencies of big agriculture, and though we are entitled to subsidies as well, these payments are a pittance compared to what larger operations receive. As one secretary of agriculture famously proclaimed in the middle of the twentieth century, American farmers either needed to "get big, or get out."

Over the years, instead of following this advice, many small farms turned to organic production instead. By forfeiting government handouts, however, the production costs of smaller operations automatically became higher. Banks studied the balance sheets of these nonsubsidized farms, viewing them as shaky lending partners and denying them loans. As they turned to organics as an economic alternative, farmers were forced to rely on human labor as their number one input instead of subsidized oil, machinery, and petroleum fertilizers. Prices for organic food simply *had* to be higher, because an unleveled playing field rewarded those who raised food on the largest scale.

For me these discussions were never intended to be a battle of big farm versus small. Farmers everywhere shared an unspoken passion that united us all, defined our core values. Although I might not agree with many of their practices, I've never considered industrial-size farms to be my enemy. The world was entitled to make its own food choices, and these farms simply provided a very different product than what we offered on our farm. But whether my friends realized it or not, every dollar they spent on this kind of food was an endorsement of these practices, a vote for more cheap abundance, continued industrial output, and subsidies quietly siphoned from their salaries.

This was never the response my friends wanted to hear. Reliably, about three sentences in, I could see their eyes glaze over. "There goes Forrest, giving his stump speech again." They politely allowed me to finish, but after a while, I could tell they were no longer listening.

The subject was too didactic, too scholarly. Part of me wanted to jump up and down, shouting "Hey, we're only talking about an extra dollar or two! How can you fawn over a Ferrari but not appreciate the beauty of a herd of free-ranging cattle?" Instead I let the topic go, steering the conversation toward the new Wilco album, or college football. If I couldn't even get my own father to eat the food we grew, I asked myself, what chance did I have with them?

After a while I finally understood. It wasn't anything against our farm, or organic food, or buying local. Their shopping habits were simply the result of a life filled with children, mortgages, commutes, student loans, and credit card debt. Making the effort to buy locally was just that: an extra effort. Despite their best intentions, it was easier to make one simple stop, where food was discounted in bulk, along with their toilet paper, fabric softener, and deodorant.

I took this as a lesson. I stopped trying to persuade my friends to shop with us, and put my energy into establishing a self-serve farm store instead. Now if anyone in the community wanted to shop with us, they could persuade themselves. The store, unstaffed, operated on an honesty policy. People drove in, took what they wanted out of the fully stocked displays, and either left cash, a check, or swiped their credit card. It was pretty much the exact opposite of every other store I had ever been in.

Located in the center of the farm, our store allowed customers to be fully engaged with their shopping experience. As they drove down the lane, they passed cows and sheep grazing in the pastures. A map inside the store pointed to where they could walk to see our flocks of free-range chickens, or where the pigs were rooting. People were pleasantly startled when they realized that, completely unsupervised, they were trusted to pay for their food. Gradually, year after year, our store found its way into people's routines. If they really wanted to shop locally, we were always open.

Our products began to grow in popularity. As demand rose, however, it became increasingly clear to me that our farm could supply only so much. This wasn't to say that our farm was incapable of producing tremendous amounts of food; to the contrary, our reinvigorated pastures hinted that we had only begun to glimpse the land's true potential. No, I told myself, supply had to be a function of what our land could sustainably provide, not a response to how vociferously people demanded our products. As hard as it was to do, I restrained myself from quickly ramping up production and tried instead to better understand how the soil and the seasons functioned together.

Despite its humble origins, grass-farming eventually became enormously trendy. As new farmers rushed in to start their own grass-based operations, I shook my head as far too many focused on satisfying customer demand instead of placing emphasis on long-term sustainability. The allure of grass-fed animals quickly wore off as overgrazed, stressed pastures couldn't support the enormous public appetite these farmers had courted. Grass-farming might be founded upon simple principles, but inexperienced growers quickly learned that sustainable production is exquisitely complicated. Expansion was more challenging than simply ordering another box of lambs the following year, or planting another row of piglets.

As much as I wanted to make all of our customers happy, our farm inevitably began to sell out of certain items each week. Eggs were normally the first casualty, but it wasn't long before we occasionally ran out of sausage, or steaks, or lamb chops. I did my best to sensibly increase supply, trying to anticipate how much pasture the farm could produce the following year. When we ran short, there was no warehouse I could call to order more, no international calls to a factory in Hong Kong. When things were sold out, they were sold out.

Still, I wrestled with my cultural economic upbringing. I had been taught that businesses should constantly grow and expand.

Cattle grazing thick fall pasture.

Owners should demand annual productivity increases, and resources were to be tapped for their maximum potential. Like most things in our melting-pot society, the message was a uniquely American blend— equal parts Manifest Destiny, Yankee ingenuity, and Protestant work ethic. A dash of Horatio Alger seemed to be thrown in for good luck.

Throughout my life, the message had been constantly thrust in my face.

Be more! Live more!

Drink this for more energy! Eat this to lose weight!

Consume! Produce! Be the extreme!

It was, in a generalized sense, the advertising campaign of every product anyone had ever tried to sell me.

Sitting in my field one day, my back propped against an old walnut tree, I wondered what a major international company would think if an advertising firm, hired to come up with the next big slogan, suggested the following: *Please try our food. But . . . there's only so much of it, so don't be angry or frustrated when it runs out. We promise to grow more, eventually. In the meantime, you can always buy it from a different farmer, or even try growing it yourself. That way, everyone wins!*

In my mind's eye, I saw corporate executives clutching their chests and falling sideways out of their leather armchairs. What would the shareholders think? The board of directors would have a conniption. Not even a clever jingle could salvage such transparent capitalistic sabotage.

But this was exactly how I felt. For nearly twenty years, from when my grandfather passed away until I returned to the farm, we had tried to be something that we weren't, listening to voices that propelled us to the brink of failure. I would no longer trade tractor trailer loads of food to commodity traders in Chicago who offered me eighteen dollars for my efforts.

What if, at the end of the day, just growing what we could grow was good enough? And what if we genuinely wanted other family farms to succeed as well? These were the ideas that I valued most, and the questions I wanted to answer. Everything else began to feel like noise.

Chapter Twenty-Nine

I never really expected it to all come together. On the last day of the season at Arlington, the baker who set up beside me, John Hyde, called me over to his stand.

"You know, I bet you'd do really well in Takoma Park," he mused. "Have you ever considered it?"

Had I considered it? I had never even heard of it. After two seasons in the big city, I still wasn't completely comfortable navigating the heavy traffic. Most days, I was relieved to get home each afternoon without getting lost.

"What's the market like?" I asked politely, though I doubted I would take the suggestion seriously. "Is it the kind of neighborhood where people like to cook out, have barbecues?"

John brayed a short laugh. "Quite the opposite. In fact, it's probably the most vegetarian neighborhood in all of Washington, D.C."

"Right," I replied, with good-natured sarcasm. "So, you're saying we would be a big hit, what with meat being ninety percent of what we sell."

"That's just it," he countered. "You'd be the first people selling meat there in at least a decade, and certainly the first to offer a free-range option. I have a feeling folks in Takoma would genuinely appreciate what you guys are doing. At least they probably wouldn't despise you."

The thought of not being despised wasn't exactly a ringing endorsement, but I figured it was at least worth investigating. The Takoma Park market was open on Sundays, so the next day I made a return trip into town and checked out the scene.

I was greeted by a bustling open-air market, one that carried the vibrant energy of a street festival. Customers moved from stand to stand, filling their bags with vegetables and bread, sacks of autumn apples or potatoes slung over one shoulder. Music drifted through the air as an old man played his banjo, and a juggler entertained children while their parents shopped. A young girl waddled by in flip-flops, cradling a large pumpkin in her arms. The market was packed with people.

I sat on a bench in the center, anonymous, imagining myself as a shopper. I allowed the hum and flow of conversations to wash over me, listening, observing. Customers chatted with farmers, asking questions and advice, searching for just the right produce, double-checking their shopping lists. Sunlight sifted through the canopies, dappling tables laden with the last of the fall tomatoes. I witnessed the delight of two friends bumping into each other unexpectedly.

To me, seated in the middle of it all, the sounds and smells and vibrations felt simultaneously new and ancient. This was a cultural phenomenon that stretched back into antiquity. Crowded with food and people and golden autumn light, the Takoma market felt alive, and vital. It was something I immediately wanted to be a part of.

I drove back to the farm, my thoughts swirling. Why weren't the markets at home more like these? Like my own family, these growers had found their way to the city markets because they couldn't support themselves in their own hometowns. Here the farmers created a food bonanza, pooling their time and resources one morning each week to provide the freshest seasonal produce in the entire mid-Atlantic region. The community seemed to recognize what the farmers had to offer, and responded with unflagging support. This was a market that had truly found its place in the world.

Back at home, our own farm remained at a crossroads. Of course, I had long worried about my father's health, but I had never imagined he was anywhere close to death. His retirement had been only a few months away, and I had already taken it for granted that he would return home to help, collaborating with me on new farm projects, spearheading an additional market or two. Now, the responsibility of balancing both farm and markets felt heavier than ever before. Despite the enormous progress we had made, the farm had only recently begun to turn a profit. Still, we remained tens of thousands of dollars in debt, and without my father's salary to help chip away at the number, I knew that these profits were really only an illusion. It had taken my parents fifteen years to accumulate all that debt. At the rate things were going, it would be another ten before we could hope to pay it all off.

The family sat down for an emergency meeting. Surprising us all, my mother announced that she was retiring from her job as a realtor in the city and coming home to help. What was more, she had decided to cash out her retirement savings and eliminate our old debts. Relinquishing her only safety net, she was going all in.

No, we protested, it was too risky; with Dad gone, she needed that money more than ever. But she wouldn't be dissuaded. If we were going to make a go of it, she insisted, we needed a fresh start, and now was the time. Besides, she said, retirement would be meaningless if she couldn't live on the farm that she loved.

Betsy had also made new plans: She had decided to move back to the farm later that year, bringing her husband and young son with her. She could pitch in on weekends, helping with chores and doing her share to keep the markets going. I couldn't quite believe what I was hearing. Our family was more united than ever.

We came up with a plan. As before, I would be in charge of daily farm operations, and Nancy would manage her growing pasta business. Mom was put in charge of bookkeeping, and she would pursue her dream of starting a bed-and-breakfast on the farm. My sister volunteered to once again manage our flock of sheep, and she hinted that she could handle a market or two of her own. And Travis would . . . well . . . We could all agree on one thing: Travis would simply remain Travis. He was, undoubtedly, the finest Travis we had ever met.

There was one big sticking point. As much as we loved farmers' markets, we needed to take a hard look at our sales strategy. Our flocks and herds continued to expand, and we were now producing meat year-round. With the heavy demands of daily farming, could traveling each weekend to market really be the best use of our time?

Each day, unsolicited, we now received requests from online customers, asking us to ship our products all over the country. This was without any promotion on our part; merely having a website with a product list seemed to spark this interest. We were currently turning away easy money, money that came without the headaches and logistical challenges of driving into Washington each weekend.

Wouldn't it be easier, we wondered, if we simply created an online store and shipped products at our convenience? Advances in refrigeration and overnight deliveries made the prospect seem relatively effortless. After all, our attention should be focused where it was most needed, right here on the farm. We could put away our market tents and wooden chickens once and for all, transforming our farm into a global company overnight. This was simply a natural business evolution, wasn't it?

The more we thought about it, the more absurd the idea became. Raising local food was an integral part of our identity. Our farm was easily accessible for our customers, and any time they wanted to see how their food was grown, they could take a quick field trip.

Internet sales would only distance us from the people who bought our food. While online videos and lengthy farming descriptions might substitute as a virtual tour, there was simply no replacing the real experience.

Most important, we found ourselves inextricably connected to the people who shopped with us. At markets, we communicated with our patrons face to face, shared in their weekly joys and occasional sorrows, watched as their children grew up on the food we provided. When new customers learned that I was the farmer who grew their food, their expressions ranged from startled to doubtful to delighted. Farmers seemed to be more myth than reality to many people, and shifting our business to online sales would only perpetuate this disconnect. I loved that by simply showing up to market each week, I could help bridge the divide.

As the seasons passed, our connections became even stronger. One weekend we lost power at the farm and were forced to miss a full weekend of sales in the city. At eight o'clock in the morning, just as opening bells were ringing across market, our cell phones lit up with dozens of calls from concerned customers. They wondered whether we were okay, and if there was anything they could do to help. Thinking back on it, I wonder whether there was another business on the planet whose customers cared about its welfare as much as ours did.

—An older farmer at market explained it to me this way: "You know, there's nothing stopping these people from shopping at the supermarket. They've got organic food in all the stores now, things you can't even get at a farmers' market. Organic shampoo. Organic beer. I mean, if this was just about *food,* most of these people wouldn't bother to shop here."

He nodded toward his helpers, busily restocking green beans and squash, barely keeping ahead of the customers as they filled their shopping bags. "No," he continued. "People come here looking for something. They're *searching*. It might be for information, or a greater understanding of how this all fits together. But whatever it is, they find it here." He pointed at the ground beneath our feet. "Here, and nowhere else. We give them something the other places can't."

I knew that he was right. Grocery stores still dominated food sales, but farmers' markets thrived because of authentic human connections. Relationships like these transcended the simple pursuit of money, and the dedication of my customers inspired me in ways that an online business never could. Farming might have started out as something deeply personal, but I now found myself wanting to farm for these customers as well.

I thought back to the time I met Ellen at the conference, and how she described the markets as a "win-win." Something about that phrase struck a lasting chord in me, and over time I began to measure our farm's successes in wins. Heal our depleted soils? Win. Produce more food? Win-win. Grow food for people who believe in our practices? Another win. For the first time in a generation, we paid our bills on time. More important, we awoke each morning to a job we actually loved. The wins kept mounting.

Now when people called or e-mailed, asking if we shipped our food, I offered a new response: "Thanks for asking, but we don't ship. We encourage you to find someone in your community who's farming like us, and support them."

Internet customers were amazed when we'd turn down their business, and surprised that we'd recommend buying from a farmer we didn't even know. One person suggested that the idea struck at the very heart of capitalistic principles. "It's still capitalism," I replied. "Just not the way we're used to hearing about."

Still, others resisted our no-shipping philosophy. "But we've looked," they sometimes said. "There's no one else around growing the kind of food you guys raise. Please ship to us."

"Have you been to your local farmers' market?"

"Yes. No one there is growing free-range meat or pasture-raised eggs. Please, please ship to us?"

"Have you asked your neighbors and friends where they're getting their food?"

"Yes. They can't find anybody either. We all want your food. Will you please, please, pretty please ship? We'll buy in bulk, to make it worth your while."

I stuck to my guns. "One last suggestion. Have you and your friends tried going directly to a local farmer and saying, 'Will you please grow this food for me?'"

On the other end of the phone, silence. Then, "You mean, we can *do* that?"

"Why not?"

More silence. "I've never heard of that. So, you mean, just drive up to a farm, and ask them to raise a cow for us, or a pig?"

"It's worth a shot. I would have loved it if someone had asked me to do that. It would have saved a year's worth of marketing headaches."

"But it seems like a pushy thing to do, doesn't it?"

"Then try this. Get your friends together, and invite your local farmers out for coffee, or throw them a barbecue. Call it Farmer Appreciation Day. I was invited to one, and I *loved* it. Anyway, tell them you want to discuss buying their food, and talk about it over lunch. Then tell them that, by next year, you want the sandwich you're eating to have *their* ham on it, or *their* tomatoes. Above all else, farmers are businesspeople. If you give them a financial opportunity, they'll listen."

"So, what you're saying is, we need to recruit our own farmers, tell them what we'd like them to grow for us, then buy it directly from them."

"Exactly. You're supporting another farm, promoting the type of food you'd like to see being grown, and staying local. Win, win, win."

A long, long pause. "Oh my gosh. I'm *totally* going to do this."

Win, I'd think to myself.

Occasionally I'd get a request from someone who said there were no farms at all near them, places that were frozen most of the year, or locations with extremely arid climates where farming was nearly impossible. These folks made the point that since the food in their area was already being trucked in from far away, we might as well ship to them as well.

To these customers, we recommended seeking farms with locations that were much more isolated than ours, and helping these farmers stay in business through online sales and shipping. I understood that not every farm had access to a major urban customer base like ours did. It was our hope that by deferring our sales to these "off the beaten path" farms, more farmers could stay in business, strengthening the agricultural community at large.

As for our own farm, the city markets continued to resonate with us. We applied for and were accepted into Takoma Park. Each weekend, Nancy, Betsy, and I spread ourselves from one end of the Washington, D.C., metro area to the other, working hours I can now scarcely believe. Eighty-hour weeks were the norm. We met new customers, became familiar with the region, and showed up for market regardless of rain, wind, or even occasional snow. We might not have been the US Postal Service, but we were something close.

One year blended into the next. I sold my little Toyota and bought a sturdy box truck. We joined several other city markets—Dupont Circle, Falls Church, and Chevy Chase. As one farmer put it, "When it comes to these city markets, I had to kiss a lot of frogs before I found a prince." We ended up kissing our fair share of frogs as well, but eventually found the right mix. To our surprise, customers sometimes asked if they could staff these new locations for us. Absolutely, we said. Over time, each of these markets adopted a year-round schedule, remaining open fifty-two weeks a year.

We started an apprenticeship, mentoring young people who wanted to farm like we did but had nowhere else to learn. By the time we paused to breathe, five more years had passed. Our farm was finally on solid ground. It was the most satisfying win of all.

––––––––––

Of course, there never came a point where we turned to one another and said, "Hey, we did it. We saved the family farm." There was no balloon drop, or confetti canon, or party we threw in self-congratulation. No one showed up at our door with an oversized key to the city, or nominated us for the first annual Grant Wood trophy. I'm sure most people drive past our farm without so much as a second glance. After all, it takes a special kind of personality to enjoy watching the grass grow.

One afternoon, in the middle of teaching my nine-year-old nephew how to change the fan belt on our market truck, an avuncular sort of question popped into my head.

"If anyone ever asks you what we do on this farm, you know what to tell them, right?"

"I'll tell them we raise livestock," he replied without hesitation.

Anticipating this response, I shook my head. "Nope."

"No?" He appeared surprised. "Hmm. Tell them we sell stuff at farmers' markets?"

I pried against the tensioner pulley as I ratcheted the bolt. "Not even close," I said, smiling. "Care to try again?"

He furrowed his brow, considering. "Well, if it's not livestock, and it's not farmers' markets . . . then I guess I'm not really sure."

I placed my tools aside and leaned toward him meaningfully. In a loud whisper I said, "If anyone ever asks what we do on the farm, don't tell them we raise cattle, or chickens, or sell meat. Just say this: 'We fix things.'"

"We fix things?" he repeated, perplexed. All at once, his face brightened considerably. "Oh!" he said, nodding enthusiastically. "Yeah! We *do* fix things. I get it."

I had a feeling he would. The desire to fix things—to try our best, at least—seemed to run in our family's blood. I gave him a wink, and made him carry my toolbox back to the workshop.

We rarely got it right the first time. We often didn't get it right the second or third time, either. But we never stopped trying, never gave up on living the life we had always dreamed. We grew simple food, and honest work nourished our spirits. Ours would be a story of never-ending labor, unexpected setbacks, and daily revisions and corrections. I always loved a challenge.

Chapter Thirty

February 16, more or less the dead of winter. If there was ever a predictable stretch of doldrums on a livestock farm, February is the month. Oh, sure, the days are getting longer, but who are we kidding? Little, if anything, even thinks about growing in February, unless you happen to be watercress. The farm is dormant, bleak, half frozen, half muddy. Spring, tacitly beyond the horizon, is a reward for the faithful.

I was poking around the barnyard at dusk, waiting for the chickens to return to their coop. A coyote had recently discovered the flock, watching camouflaged from the tall grass until no one was around, and then brazenly picking off a hen or two in broad daylight.

During this time of year, wild food is extremely scarce, and it isn't hard to imagine how a thousand free-ranging hens might look like manna to a hungry canine. Still, my job as a farmer was clear, and one dead chicken was one dead chicken too many. Few things on the farm are as depressing as finding a half-eaten, feathered carcass lying cold and stiff in the frozen gray mud.

While I waited, a mangled scrap of fence wire, hidden by tall grass all summer but now revealed, caught my eye. It was precisely the right size to puncture a truck tire in the coming spring, or entangle an uncoordinated young lamb.

Disposing of old wire is always tricky. Grass and roots grow through the mesh, firmly weaving it into the matrix of the earth. The springiness of the metal makes every encounter unique, and it's just as likely to remain stubbornly affixed to the ground as it is to suddenly break free, sending me stumbling with a rusty, razor-edged waltzing partner.

I laced my fingers through the cold metal, and pulled. On this occasion, it released with surprising ease. Woven between the wires were strands of brittle, taupe-colored grass, as well as a few green blades of overlooked timothy. I set the tangled mess aside and lowered myself to my knees, studying the freshly exposed ground.

A small swath of earth was now revealed. The soil, protected beneath the mangled wire and last fall's matted vegetation, was soft and dark. I slid my fingers into the dirt, cupping a handful of earth to my nose. The aroma of the broken ground was profoundly rich, at once mysterious and inviting.

In the depths of winter—with the pastures grazed low, the sycamores stark and leafless, the creek banks rimmed with ice, and the sky a gray blanket spread from mountaintop to mountaintop— here the earth abided. The soft warmth spoke to me, saying, *I'm waiting now, but I will be ready. We are mutual participants, you and I, intertwined.*

The language was as clear as if spoken aloud. It was no accident that I found myself on my knees, held there, transfixed. My ancestors knew this communication. It tapped into who they were, and who I was. We flowed together.

Potential. Respect. The sweet simplicity of toil, the satisfaction of working in harmony with the land. Bounty, and the grateful reward of harvest. These phenomena are both timeless and contemporary, deeply and constantly present. Over the course of a lifetime, farmers grow straight out of the soil, wizening into abstractions of their former selves.

The earth sends out its pulse. Balance. Simplicity. The land provides our nourishment, the common denominator of our human experience. It allowed our ancestors to cultivate our trajectory.

In a few weeks, the tiny heralds of the vernal equinox, the spring peepers, will begin their annual chorus. Roughly the size of the tip of my thumb, these stalwart frogs brave the final frosts of winter, reliably prognosticating the daffodils, the crocuses, the first wispy tendrils of wild oats beneath the dormant apple trees. It's not unusual to hear their first tentative chirps while snow still blankets the pastures. The sound bends the human heart toward thoughts of miniature, frog-size long johns and tiny, knitted stocking caps.

The first batch of chicks will be hatching soon. The March lambs will follow, then the spring calves. Buds of emerald clover will hesitate beneath the residue of last fall's orchard grass, before spreading their leaves horizontally across the ground. The cold will melt into shadows, and soft rain will fall. The arc of the seasons is a shared global experience.

Farmers are a spiritual lot, and I frequently knock on wood. But we control the earth with sleight of hand, illusions of a street magician. Ego drives us to false expectations. Predictability. Perfection. On this farm, I count only on entropy and renewal.

My son now is in second grade. Nothing breaks the heart with love so cleanly as hearing that he wants to be a farmer, like his father. Our farm must have turned out okay after all.

Like my family was for me, I will be there for him. When the summer sun bakes the ground and no rains fall, I will be there. When the snow is unexpected and water must be hauled, I will be there. And when I am gone, I will be there, like my father is for me, and my grandfather. This is the contract I signed, the dotted line where I volunteered my commitment.

The family farm will continue as long as its existence is valued. There is strength in a family, and balance. The earth appears to respond to these things. And who is to say what defines a family? Certainly not I. My best attempt would suggest a congregation of like-minded hearts.

Saving the family farm will forever be a process, not a goal or a destination. Like any necessary chore, the work never ends. It only waits for us the following morning, or the following season. So I wake, and enter the day.

Somewhere, another farm awaits its farmer.

ACKNOWLEDGMENTS

First, to the team at Lyons Press, *thank you* for your enthusiasm and talent, and for making this process more rewarding than I ever imagined it could be. At each turn throughout the revisions, my wonderful editor, Anna Bliss, helped me to better understand the people and relationships in my own life and express my feelings onto the page. Thank you, Anna; it was a remarkable gift to give a writer. Special thanks also goes to my outstanding agent, Stephany Evans, who confidently insisted that our family's story was one worth sharing with a broader audience, and quickly found a perfect fit with Lyons.

I'm deeply grateful to my family for their courage, and their belief in something greater than themselves. To Ruth, Betsy, Nancy, and Liliana, who gave me support and love when the odds seemed utterly impossible, this book is for you. For Linus, Benson, and Michelle, I look forward to a life filled with new stories.

The following people gave me invaluable advice as I temporarily set aside my hammer and turned my attention to writing: David Pratt, Corey Mead, Shannon Hayes, Lyric Winnik, Rachel Kahan, Nina Planck, and Jennifer Unter. Thank you to Nell Newman, Rochelle Bellin, Tanya Denckla Cobb, Barton Seaver, and Sally Fallon Morell for enthusiastically reading an early version of the manuscript, and to Lindy Swimm and Lee Taylor for digging up old photographs of the farm.

A big thank you to Joel Salatin for graciously agreeing to write the foreword. His work has inspired an entire generation of new farmers. And in lieu of thanking each of my farming peers individually, allow me to thank Chip and Susan Planck and Hui Newcomb on behalf of all of us. Their vision of sustainable agriculture has nurtured dozens of farms into existence.

Steve and Adri Vargo, thank you for your help and generosity. Old friendships have deep roots.

To W. Perry Epes, Fraser Hubbard, and Bill Hannum, thank you for your passion for teaching. I might not have been your brightest student, but I loved your classes.

Thanks to my talented photographer friend, Molly Peterson, for rearranging her schedule on a moment's notice to come to the farm and shoot the cover. It was a morning filled with cows, coffee, and stunt chickens.

I couldn't have written this book without the help of Robert Albright, Steffany Yamada, and Aaron Johnson, who skillfully managed the farm while I wrote. Of course, thanks especially to Travis LaFleur, who has already begun suggesting stories for the next book.

Finally, to my farmers' market customers: If you hadn't been so dedicated—waking early each weekend to shop at your local market—not only would this story never have been written but our farm might not be here today. I hope you now realize what a difference your food choices make; I can't say thank you enough. You're the ones who saved our family farm.

31901052087477